CHICAGO PUBLIC LIBRARY

R03011 75411

```
NK        Kuntzsch, Ingrid.
7306
.K7713  A history of jewels
1981      and jewelry
```

cop-1   27·50

DATE			

© THE BAKER & TAYLOR CO.

D1223990

INGRID KUNTZSCH

A History of Jewels
and Jewellery

INGRID KUNTZSCH

A History of Jewels and Jewellery

ST. MARTIN'S PRESS / NEW YORK

NK
7306
K7713
1981
cop.1

R03011 75411

Translated from the German
by Sheila Marnie

Copyright © 1981
by Edition Leipzig
For information, write:
St. Martin's Press,
175 Fifth Avenue,
New York, N. Y. 10010
Manufactured in the
German Democratic Republic
Library of Congress Catalog
Card Number 80-51939
ISBN 0-312-38088-7
Design by Gert Wunderlich
First Edition

Contents

Introduction

One is almost tempted to classify the history of jewellery as the history of human vanity of baubles, bangles, and beads, for has not jewellery, and indeed, all forms of ornaments always been the epitome of what is useless, superfluous, even wasteful? One would think that history has given us more important things to think about, that life would go on without bracelets, necklaces, and rings. And yet, jewellery has accompanied man from the beginning of his cultural development, up to the present. Archaeological finds have proved that jewellery was even being produced when man was still battling against nature, when all his energies were required to fight for his very survival. What made him even in this early stage of his development devote his mental and physical energies to the production of such obviously superfluous objects? Or were they not superfluous?

The ethnographer, Bronislav Malinovski, has described the numerous customs connected with the jewellery of the inhabitants of Melanesia, who up to the 20th century retained their ancient social customs. One of the most interesting examples is the custom of the *kula*: the inhabitants of the island groups south of Papua, the Trobriand and D'Entrecasteaux Islands, the Louisiade Archipelago still used to observe the ceremonial ritual of exchanging specially made pieces of jewellery. More than 1,000 people belonged to the *kula* ring, and each of them had, according to his social rank, four, five, or even 100 and more *kula* partners. The pieces of jewellery, long necklaces of pinky spondylus shells or bracelets of white shells, were kept by a *kula* partner for only a few weeks or months, before being passed on with great ceremony to the next partner: the giver of a necklace then received a bracelet in return. Thus the bracelets progressed in the opposite direction to the necklaces. The most important aspect of this custom, the rites of which were considered sacred, and were passed on from father to son, was the close personal relationship, even friendship, which existed between the partners of various tribes, often from very distant parts. In an apparently foreign and alien place the seafarer would find a friend in his *kula* partner, who would guarantee him protection, hospitality, and security. In this case jewellery was a precious material symbol used to preserve and extend man's social cohesion. It did in fact play a vital role in his life.

The jewellery customs of the non-European peoples living in a matriarchal society were researched and reported mainly during the last century and the first decades of this century. They help us to draw some conclusions about the many aspects of the social function of jewellery and its connection with that particular stage in technical and economical development, with social life, with the way of life, and spiritual world of primitive society.

Ethnographic research has been able to fill in much of the fragmentary picture of the period from the European Stone Age to the Bronze Age which has been put together by archaeologists. It has done this by supplying us with living examples to illustrate the effect which jewellery had as a whole, the particular occasions when jewellery was worn, the persons who wore it, its production, the deeply rooted traditions in which it played a role. In those early stages of cultural development jewellery's functions were, of course, closely bound up with all areas of life, and here its origins become clear. For birth, engagement, marriage, death, celebrations and ceremonies as a mark of rank and status—jewellery was especially made and worn for all these and many more occasions.

When the Aztecs saw the Spanish conquistador, Hernándo Cortés, approaching the coast of Veracruz in 1519, their mystical religious beliefs led them to assume that this was the long awaited homecoming of their Gods. The chief of the Aztecs, Moctezuma, sent representatives to meet the Spaniards and to give them a suitable welcome. One of the presents he sent was the "Treasure of Quetzalcoatl"—the robes and jewels of four Gods. The messengers honoured Cortés as a God; his ceremonial welcome is described as follows in the *Codex Florentino*: "With great care they fastened the snake mask over his face, the turquoise mask with the cross ribbons from quetzal feathers, and they hung the golden snake earplugs onto it ... They laid the woven petatillo collar round him, the chest jewellery made from green precious stones, with the gold disc in the middle ... Then they attached the cross mirror to his hips, covered him with the Tzitzilli robe, the "ringing bell". They laid huoxtec straps round his legs, painted with precious chalchihaites, and with golden bells ... They spread the other holy robes out carefully in front of him, so that he could see them."

In the early class societies precious jewellery was owned only by the gods and their chosen rulers on earth. Rare materials which usually required much knowledge, skill, and workmanship became symbols of rank and importance, and to presume to wear them without having attained such rank was a strictly punishable offence. It was from this stage in man's cultural development that a high value began to be attached to precious metals: not only were gold and silver rare in comparison to iron or bronze, they were also too soft to be used directly as work materials. "... their aesthetic qualities made them the natural material to use for shows of pomp, jewellery, splendour, Sunday needs, in short, to a positive form of superfluousness and wealth".

"In all the ancient peoples collecting gold and silver was originally the privilege of kings and priests ... only they were entitled to possess wealth as such." (Marx). Precious metals and stones were treated more and more as a display of excessive wealth and in the slave owner society and the feudal society they finally became a means of showing one's social position.

In the mid-15th century Philip of Burgundy, known as "the Good", gave his niece Anne of Cleves, a dowry consisting of 28 stately dresses covered with jewels, six golden necklaces with pearls and precious stones, one large gold chain, a paternoster with beads of gold enamel, four brooches, and six gold rings with precious stones. There are also reports that Elisabeth, daughter of the German Emperor Sigismund and the wife of King Albrecht II, pawned her jewels in 1440 for 2500 gold gulden, after she had been widowed in 1439. These jewels included not only necklaces, bracelets, but also her crown.

Since the Late Middle Ages jewels have been amassed in the treasure chests of kings, princes, and other members of the ruling nobility. There are numerous descriptions of the princes' obsession with such treasures. But jewellery had another function—in times of good fortune it was a kind of luxury product used to enhance one's life as a whole, but it was also a kind of security set aside for times of need and misfortune. Alongside the reports of unimaginable pomp and splendour, there is also abundant evidence that jewellery was pawned and redeemed or sometimes remained unredeemed. The dowry of a wife from the upper class usually took the form of small precious objects or jewels, which she received from her parents or relatives; it was a form of capital which was supposed to guarantee that her lifestyle could continue in the manner to which she had been accustomed, even in times of need.

Only in recent times has jewellery become a general means of expression of an individual's personality. Access to material and artistic training are decisive factors in determining whether jewellery is looked upon as an investment, or a miniature work of art which is worth collecting. Jewellery also has a high value as a way of reinforcing one's individual charm. The Swedish jeweller Sigurd Persson formulated this concept: "My starting point is that jewellery is a game. Jewellery helps to emphasize beauty and is a way of protecting oneself. Jewellery is a means of making one's individuality visible".

This function is generally accepted today. From the point of view of its functions, the history of adorning oneself with jewellery is closely tied up with the history of man. This relationship dates back to the development of man as a social being, i.e. with the start of human civilization. Jewellery became one of the most important examples of man's growing productive abilities. It reflects philosophical and aesthetic values and its thousands of years of history sheds light on the constantly changing, increasingly complicated relationship of man to nature, to society, to his own individuality. However, only part of this book is concerned with the social functions of jewellery, its communicative spiritual and cultural qualities. The book also looks at the producer, the creator of jewellery, who gives it its various shapes and sizes, and looks at his position in society. To do justice to technical and artistic achievements in the field of jewellery, one must also consider the relations to production in the society concerned. The social status of the wearer of jewellery also varies according to the structure of society. (Jewellery has served not least as an indication of the social status of a man or woman).

As far as was possible within the confines of this book, an attempt has been made to relate the history of jewellery with other aspects of man's cultural development, such as economy, technology, art styles, all of which have always been interrelated with the production of jewellery. Many customs and traditions as well as the influence of the fashion and taste of any given cultural era also spring to light when looking at the history of jewellery.

I would like here to mention all those who helped in the production of this book and who gave me advice and support. In particular, I would like to thank Winfried Herrmann, Edith Hoffmann, Renate Krauspe, Rolf Krusche, Heinz Kucharski, Wolfgang Liedtke, Eva Mahn, and Peter Schuppan.

Ancient Forms of Jewellery

PALEOLITHIC

It is impossible to establish with any degree of accuracy exactly when man began to wear jewellery; the oldest archaeological finds stem in fact from the early stages of the Paleolithic Age (*c.* 50,000–10,000 B.C.). This coincides with the first phase of primitive society. Objects made from inorganic material, such as stone, fossils, jet, or clay have managed to survive for thousands of years. Organic material which was undoubtedly used as well for jewellery-making—bones, horns, mollusc shells, fish bones, and amber—have also been found as the remaining parts of chains or amulets.

The beginnings of a death cult can be traced back about 100,000 years. It has been shown from finds dating from the Ice Age (in Bohemia, Italy, and the Crimea) that since this time man has, in many areas, ceremonially buried his dead in caves and has provided them with more and more funerary gifts such as tools, victuals, and jewellery to equip them for the after-life. Jewellery was thus part of the personal belongings of the deceased.

In the Grimaldi Graves in Monaco gifts were found including some 35,000-year-old chains made from Mediterranean sea shells and snail shells, as well as necklaces made from deer's teeth and fish bones. In other graves pendants and bracelets made from carved ivory and antlers were found. These were decorated with geometrical linear engravings or with embossed, true-to-life animal shapes. The Paleolithic man of this period could also drill decorative discs made from the same materials and do stipple work. Their fine work and precision lead one to suppose that the production of these objects was already the prerogative of a small particularly skilled group of society, who were engaged in this kind of work as well as carrying out their main task of providing food.

Rock drawings by the past Ice-Age hunters and gatherers in Europe, such as those found on exposed rock faces along the Spanish Mediterranean coast-line, depict human figures in exaggerated poses; scenes which are clearly taken from primitive dances and which also shed light on the jewellery customs of this time. The necks, arms and legs of the people in the drawings are covered in colourful ornaments, their garments are decorated, and their heads are covered with sophisticated ornaments. Earrings were sometimes worn, and on some drawings there are nose and lip ornaments. Decorations of this kind, the details of which are not distinguishable, were undoubtedly made from vegetable and animal materials, such as birds' feathers, flowers, pieces of wood, grass, bast, i.e. inner bark, shells, fruit or seeds. These materials, although perishable, must have been extraordinarily colourful and effective. This can be clearly seen by looking at the present jewellery traditions of some African, Brazilian, and Oceanic peoples.

NEOLITHIC

At the end of the Ice Age, in the transition period between the Paleolithic and Neolithic Ages, agricultural economies based on land cultivation and cattle breeding began to replace hunting and gathering as the basis for survival. This process took several thousands of years and began in the Near East in the 10th millennium B.C. due to the particularly favourable conditions in this area. During this process primitive society flourished for the first time. In 5000 B.C. land cultivation and cattle breeding spread to Central Europe and became the basis of the European

Neolithic Age. The increased security guaranteed by the improved living conditions led to increases in population, and man improved and developed his work tools and work methods. There was soon a constant surplus; an important prerequisite for the exchange and purchase of goods made from raw materials which are not indigenous, such as spondylous shells, amber, marble, copper, and gold.

Thus a sense of the aesthetic began to be developed and materials with a direct use value became of secondary importance. The value placed on precious metals was to stem from this new attitude towards jewellery.

The jewellery of this period bears witness to growing craft specialization, stonework in the real sense of the word was mastered for the first time, partly due to the development of new techniques. The Neolithic man could cut, drill, and polish minerals such as carnelian, jasper, and chalcedony. Bracelets made from marble, spondylous shells, pearls, and magical figures of stone and semi-precious stones were carefully cut, shaped, and polished. Chain links were bored and made into collars and necklaces. At the same time other materials which were easier to work, such as bones, horns, animal's teeth were still used for jewellery-making. Copper and gold jewellery dating back to the end of the Neolithic Age has been found. The metal was initially heated only slightly and then hammered into shape, but later it was possible to melt metal from ore and shape it in moulds.

Trade was carried out over extraordinary distances—this can be traced from an analysis of style and materials. Amber from the Baltic Coast (in Jutland thousands of beads and pendants were discovered, and amber carving had been developed on the Kurland Gulf) reached as far as South-East Europe. Conversely, spondylous shells and at the end of the Neolithic Age copper and gold jewellery from the Mediterranean or the Balkans and the Iberian Peninsular spread to Central and northern Europe.

Towards the end of the European Neolithic Age the first signs of the decline of the primitive society became apparent as a result of the ever increasing surplus, and the growing inequalities in property ownership. Clear evidence of the decline of primitive society are the sumptuous graves of "princes" which make a striking contrast to the more modest graves of the majority of the population; but these are already part of the Bronze Age, which began about 1800 B.C. In western Asia this development had already taken place at the turn of the 4th and 3rd millennia B.C. with the transition to the ancient-oriental class society.

THE BRONZE AGE IN EUROPE

There is thus evidence of developed Bronze Age civilizations in many parts of Europe and Asia at different times. Pottery, which already had a rich tradition, was the first indirect use of fire outside cooking, heating, and lighting for technical purposes. It thus contributed on the one hand to man's mastery of fire, and on the other it enabled man to produce tools for metalwork, such as clay pots, melting pots, and instruments for casting. The metal was extracted from the ore by using simple furnaces with a funnel and skillfully manipulating vents. Various casting techniques were used to produce utensils, but the lost-wax process was used for jewellery. The increasing mastery of metalwork techniques meant that experience and knowledge were all the more necessary. This was thus one of the first highly specialized branches of labour, and it played an important role in the development of the social division of labour.

The word metal is of Greek origin and means to look for, search, which refers to its scarcity. It was used initially only for a few utensils, as it was found in remote and often barely accessible places, or it was necessary to enter into expensive and lengthy trade agreements in order to acquire it. Stone tools were still used predominantly for land cultivation and the crafts. Thus burial gifts made from metal were always a sign of the high social position of the deceased, and certain objects, especially jewellery, were without doubt a sign of social prestige.

From the vast quantity of Bronze Age finds, the regional differences of which are not so much of a technical nature, but rather stylistic in character, some examples from Central and North Europe will now be given.

The Aunjetity Culture (named after the site in Bohemia, Únětice), the most northern culture of the early Bronze Age (1750–1550 B.C.), extended to Lower Austria in the south, to Poland in the east, and to Thuringia in the west, and produced metal jewellery which still had a relatively simple form. As with other early Bronze cultures the jewellery was similar in form and decoration to that of Neolithic times, which was then made of bones or minerals. To the south of the area covered by the early Bronze Age culture, which especially in its earlier phase was divided into local sub-groups, the decorative discs and brooches had strictly geometrical patterns, using mainly shaded zones, triangles, and concentric circles. In all areas of this culture gold jewellery in the form of simple rings made from twisted wire appeared relatively frequently in the earlier phase. "Princely graves" with generous gold gifts were found in Leubingen, Soemmerda district, G.D.R., in Xeki Male, Poland, and in mountain settlements in Bohemia and Moravia. These bear witness to a developed stage of social differentiation. This is particularly true of tribes living in border areas. They tended to be engaged in more war-like activities and therefore needed capable leaders. In other areas the funerary gifts do not immediately suggest such a clearly defined social differentiation.

The "Tumulus Culture" of the central European tribes which was formed at the height of the Bronze Age (c. 1600 –1300 B.C.) and evidence of which has been found over an area stretching from the Rhine right up to the Carpathian Basin, not only had the same burial customs but the material evidence they left behind also reveals a similar style. This is apparently rooted in the strong common traditions of the late Neolithic Age and the early Bronze Age. The craftsmanship and artistic quality of bronze casting and the work of the bronze smith had, however, become considerably more refined, and (with regional variations) had richer ornamentation. Apart from the decorations which came in at the same time as casting, other decorative techniques such as chasing and chiseling were introduced. The high standard of bronze casting can be seen in the filigree work, the disc and loop-pendants, the astonishing skill of the smiths in the wealth of jewellery with spiral discs.

In northern Europe bronze arrived relatively late on, but the art of working and using it was developed from approximately 1500 B.C. onwards, and reached quite a high standard. The earliest bronze objects such as brooches and rings used as hair clasps were imported from the Aunjetity Culture. Later bronze ore was imported (the Swedish copper mines were not opened until the Middle Ages) and was probably exchanged for fur, wool, food products, and amber, which came predominantly from Jutland.

By comparing finds archeological research has pointed to common cultural features within an area extending from the south of Sweden, especially the Schonen District, to the Danish Islands and the Jutland peninsular. The craftsmanship of this area later spread, largely due to intensive shipping, to Schleswig-Holstein, parts of North Mecklenburg and the north-east of Lower Saxony.

In numerous graves of the northern Bronze Age not only metal objects have remained intact, but also remnants from the clothing of the deceased. These give an insight into both the functional and decorative aspects of jewellery.

In the summer of 1935 research was carried out in Denmark on a woman's grave, a wooden coffin in a burial mound near Skrydstrupfeld, in the Haderslev district. Here a tall, slim, woman, about 27 years old, had been laid to rest dressed in a blouse, a belt, and an ankle-length pleated skirt. Her forehead was decorated with a ribbon woven from strands of wool; over her blond hair she wore a wig with a net of horse's hair; a golden spiral ring lying near each ear had once served as hair clasps; the neck and sleeves of the blouse were embroidered round the edges; a comb—which incidentally was nearly always found in both male and female graves—made of horn was in the belt. In other female graves the comb was sometimes used as a hair decoration. The buckles on the belt often took the form of big bronze discs with various spiral patterns, which were particularly highly decorated in Denmark and Sweden.

One woman's grave near Broholm on the Island of Funen contained a particularly impressive display of jewellery: on either side of the deceased's head lay an earring made of bronze-sheet with a ribbed decoration; a wide bronze collar which narrowed at the back of the neck was decorated in the same way (similar examples in Denmark and Sweden often had rows of spiral patterns). As in many female graves there was a dagger in the belt, the main buckle of which was flanked by four smaller ones. The deceased also wore undecorated spiral rings made of bronze wire on four fingers, and bronze bracelets on both forearms. It was not unusual for the women to wear anklets: this was the case with one woman found further south at Luebz in Mecklenburg. Her clothing did, however, include some details which did not seem to correspond to the "fashion of the day": she wore a leather waistcoat which was covered from the shoulders to the waist with narrow strips of innumerable little bronze balls. An ornamental bronze collar was draped round her neck and shoulders, a fibula with a bow-shaped clasp held the leather waistcoat together, and bronze rings at the shoulders and wrists completed the decoration. The abundance of metal jewellery in many female graves is evidence of woman's honoured position within the social organisation of the northern tribes.

The most important piece of jewellery for men was probably a good, functionable weapon, usually with rich decoration which was undoubtedly supposed to grant protection and strength to its bearer: sword and dagger-hilts with filigree design; inlays of resin, amber, horn or bone were common, as were pommels covered with a thin layer of sheet gold; scabbards for cut and thrust weapons had woodcarvings and other ingenious forms of decoration. Apart from this, men wore leather belts with either bronze buckles or double-button fastenings, which were originally made from wood or amber but later often from bronze. In male graves it was by no means unusual to find rings, bracelets, and wide arm rings with double-spiral terminals. The gold probably came from Transylvania or Ireland and had been traded from tribe to tribe.

As the civilization developed bronze artefacts became more common in the north, and as trade increased so, too, did the supply of gold. The traditional forms of jewellery began to lose their hold. In female graves (apart from those in Denmark) the heavy collar was gradually replaced by the more delicate choker and the big buckle gave way to smaller ones with a long pin.

After cremation became the general practice, the dead were given less and less gifts, and in the early stages of the nordic bronze civilization (13th–8th centuries B.C.) gifts became very rare indeed. Our knowledge of the jewellery of this period has been gleaned from numerous finds, which were uncovered in burial sites in large containers. These bear witness to the custom of equipping the dead for the after-life. The necklaces of this period were made of rings, cast in a round, hollow or flat shape, which were often linked with bronze pins to form a collar and were fastened at the back. These were later replaced by rings which twisted inwards and had hook fasteners and spirals at the terminals.

From the early Bronze Age onwards the fibula was a central feature of European jewellery; this was a decorative clasp, which was used to fasten cloaks at the shoulder or neck. It originally took the form of a simple needle made of wood, bone, horn, and later bronze; a thread was drawn through a hole bored in its head and tied tightly at its point. Man then used his creative powers to invent more practical and more decorative variations, until finally the decorative function predominated. About the middle of the 2nd millennium B.C. the thread of the fibula was replaced in North Europe by a bow-shaped wire, which the craftsman either twisted like string, or hammered out into a long pointed oval-shaped strip. This was the original two-piece fibula. The bow was consequently given different shapes and decoration, and the s-shaped and disc fibula were developed. Later many other kinds of fibulae were invented, and their chronology has helped archaeologists work out the date of the burials.

In southern Central Europe the one-piece fibula was worn, i.e. the pin and bow-shaped clasp were one piece. They were joined by a simple spiral coil, which also served as a spring. The end of the bow was either twisted upwards to form a loop, or hammered flat to form a rest for the point of the needle. This was the case with the violin-bow fibula, and the Peschiera fibula, which were common in the 13th century B.C. in the Po district, Sicily, in the area around the lower stretches of the Danube, and in late Mycenean Greece.

AUSTRALIA

As far as the cultural development of its original inhabitants is concerned Australia is the most backward of all the continents. Because of their isolated geographical position the Australian Aborigines, as they are officially called, lived for the longest known period of time (until after the Second World War in some districts of northern and central Australia) in a relatively early phase of a mid-Stone Age hunter-gatherer economy. In interrelated groups, the size and structure of which varied from a couple of hundred to several hundred members, according to the sources of food available, these people sought out areas which would offer them nourishment, moving according to the seasons. They would set up camp, and, depending on the circumstances, would stay there for several weeks.

The spiritual background to the art and thus to a considerable amount of the jewellery of these people, was the cult of the totem. During ceremonial feasts which involved the totem animal, especially the so-called fertility and initiation ceremonies, its movements and characteristics were mimicked in dances and songs. All ceremonies were carried out in strict accordance with ancient traditions. The ritual jewellery, too, was produced and worn exactly as laid down in the traditional rules, as ordained by the appro-

priate totem-hero. It was also usual for the jewellery to be supplemented by painting one's skin: scarification was used as a permanent decoration, and for ceremonies additional ornaments were painted or stuck on the skin.

Although the men and women—despite the often cool temperatures in winter—usually went around naked (only in South-East and South-West Australia was it usual to wear drapes made from kangaroo or opossum skin) and usually with no or very little jewellery, the ceremonial occasions were the only opportunities to wear sacred jewellery; the inhabitants of Central Australia used to paint their bodies with ochre, the sacred colour, with clay and charcoal, and they would stick the down of indigenous birds in patterns on themselves, along with threads of wild cotton. They used the blood from the arms or slashed limbs of the ritual "assistants" as adhesive. The headdress varied from region to region. In Central Australia so-called *nurtunjas* were common: they were poles up to 1 m long, with circles or slanting lines painted on them, or with down feathers stuck on to make a stripe-pattern. These poles were held on the head by tightly bound ribbons made from thick string: these, together with the heavily painted faces or feather decoration, gave the wearers an uncanny appearance.

An object called a *waningga* was usually stuck in the ground during a ceremony. Those taking part in the ceremony sometimes used smaller versions of the same object as a headdress. It was made from an oval wooden frame across which threads of hair or fur were stretched, and which was decorated with down and bunches of feathers. Wanninggas were common not only amongst the original inhabitants of Central Australia, but also in the western coastal area, and in the Kimberleys in the north-west.

Compared to these everyday non-ceremonial forms of jewellery seem simple. Hairstyles varied from tribe to tribe: some cut their hair short, some tied it in knots, some used ochre to divide their hair into brownish tufts. Some tribes used the tails of small animals, kangaroo teeth or shells as hair decoration. Threads of hair were plaited as neck and chest-decoration and chains made from seeds, teeth, sea and snail-shells were worn. Blades of grass and pieces of rush were also sometimes threaded on string and used as decoration. In Central Australia ochre-dyed string made from opossum fur, with kangaroo or any other teeth attached to it with resin, was commonly used. Ribbons made from rattan, a type of palm, were wound round their arms and legs in spirals or rings. Often a tiny loin-cloth, made from opossum fur, human or animal hair, emu feathers, grass, bast or bark, would serve rather as decoration than as clothing. The various stages in the life of the Australian, such as initiation, marriage, death of a relative, were also reflected in the jewellery customs. In North Australia jewellery made from shells was presented at initiation ceremonies; in some groups the nose was pierced at this ceremony, so that nose-rings could be worn; the female members of the group were entitled to wear hair-nets and ribbons made from opossum, kangaroo, and human hair only after marriage; widows wore a chain made from an opossum jaw as a sign of mourning. Shells had various uses, one of the main ones being jewellery. In shallow coastal waters such as those in North-West Australia and round the Cape-York Peninsula in the north-east, pearl oysters were collected and traded from tribe to tribe, thus penetrating deep inland. Some even turned up in Ooldea (Central South Australia). Whereas pearl oysters were used by some tribes in the north to make a kind of loin-cloth (members of the Caradieri tribe used to carve sacred patterns on them) which was tied at the hip with ribbons made from human hair, in Central Australia they were used as amulets with the supposed power to bring rain. They were also used as currency in the trade between the tribes. A popular form of jewellery for men was a disc-pendant made from haliotis and pearl oyster. They were often engraved and coloured with ochre. Some of them were supposed to possess magical powers. They were, as Spencer and Gillen put it, used by spurned lovers in order to "make the internal organs of a beautiful woman tremble with excitement".

MELANESIA

These western Pacific Islands, including most of the large South Sea Islands as well as New Guinea, were given the collective name of Melanesia (black islands) by the Europeans because of their inhabitants' dark skin. The Portuguese and Spanish first set foot on the islands in the 16th and 17th centuries, and were followed by the Dutch, British, French, and German colonialists who took over the islands, which until then were inhabited by tribes living in a primitive agricultural society.

Here, as with other peoples in the same stage of development, the jewellery customs were closely connected with important events in the life of the inhabitants: birth, initiation, marriage, death; events which brought about a change in the social position of those concerned. Certain ornaments were given as rewards to good warriors, others were worn to signify joy or mourning, or in honour of some ceremony. Characteristic of the ceremonial jewellery of these islands is the extraordinary richness of colour and design, which are parallelled by the proliferous and varied growth of the tropical rain forest. The jewellery was made exclusively from animal and vegetable-materials. Thus the face and upper body would be painted with soot, chalk, clay, ochre and coloured plant juices. One of the most important ornaments was the ceremonial headdress worn by the men. It was made from the gaily-coloured feathers of the paradise bird, parrot, and cassowary. Individual feathers served as nose decoration, or were combined with other materials to make splendid headbands. Brightly-coloured beetle-wings or even beetle-legs were strung together and used to make neck and arm-jewellery. Flowers, such as the red hibiscus blossom, were made into stunning hair ornaments. Wood, seeds, bast, nut shells and many other natural materials could be used for jewellery-making.

As was usual on islands and in coastal areas, sea and snail-shells were highly valued. If certain particularly popular types of shells were not to be found locally, whole trading expeditions were sent off to far-off islands to find the desired shells or to buy jewellery made from them. One of the most popular shells was the white ovula snail, which is 8–12 cm long; the shells were arranged individually or in group to make collar-necklaces. The nautilus shell as well as the giant *tridacna gigas* were carefully fashioned into expensive collars; the *tridacna gigas* was also used for armrings. Delightful collar-necklaces were made from polished tridacna discs with decorative polished tortoise shell on top. Smaller sea and snail-shells such as the nassa and cowrie shell were attached to string or plaited plant fibres and either made into collar-necklaces or into arm or hip-bands.

The jewellery did not vary greatly from one island to the next, yet slight individual variations in the workmanship or design are noticeable. The inhabitants of certain islands became masters in the production of specific types of jewellery. The combs made on the Salomon Islands were, for example, very popular, as were the wide tortoise shell bracelets from the north of New Guinea, and the trochal shell armrings from New Ireland.

THE PRAIRIE INDIANS OF NORTH AMERICA

Even before the arrival of Europeans in America the hunters and gatherers who lived on the prairie between the Mississippi-Missouri Rivers and the Rocky Mountains used to organize bison hunts. After 1600, when Spanish missionaries, soldiers, and settlers had set up horse-breeding ranches in the Rio Grande area, buffalo hunting soon became a specialized affair. By 1750 the northern tribes also had horses which had either been acquired through trading or had been stolen. Numerous tribes, which had previously been settler-tribes changed their whole way of life and began living in tents—tepees—and using light, transportable objects and implements, in keeping with their new situation. Changes in the social and political organization as well as in the religious sphere became evident; the customs of tribes with different traditions began to intermingle.

While small hunting groups went buffalo hunting in the winter, in the summer, because of the vital importance of these hunts to the life style of the people, all the groups within a tribe took part under one elected or appointed leader. Before a big hunt there were hunting ceremonies and buffalo dances to bring good fortune and success. Apart from being a source of food, the hunters' booty also provided material for tools, clothing, and jewellery. Leather, fur, horn, bones, and feathers were all worked with great craftsmanship.

There was no specialized production of these objects in the modern sense. However, the abundance of food meant that there was a relatively large amount of time free for the development of arts and crafts. Thus there were specialists who had particular skills and were therefore commissioned and paid to produce certain objects (such as bow and arrows). Generally, however, the production of clothing, weapons, and jewellery for their own use lay in the hands of the families themselves.

Signs of rank and the honorary headdresses showed the social position of the men in the hunting tribes. They were mainly evidence of their prowess in hunting and in battle. The honorary headdresses signified by their form and colour certain special achievements: coloured horsehair at the top of the feather signified that an enemy had been slain, other feathers signified the wounding or the swift tracking down of an enemy.

To go with their ceremonial dress the successful hunters and warriors decorated themselves with a kind of collar made of the claws of a grizzly bear or a chest plate made of deerbones. One- or two-strand necklaces of pearls, hollow bones, flat shells or the teeth of predators were common. Large decorative discs made of shell hung from short necklaces. The leather pouch with the indispensable dye for painting their faces hung from a belt or from a necklace. Ribbons, decorated with coloured hedgehog bristles, so-called quill-work—later replaced under European influence by glass beads—held their hair and decorated their upper arms and thighs. Armbands and decorative buttons on their belts were made of brass and silver— also introduced by Europeans—and spread by fur traders. The feather headdress with a long "tail" reaching right to the ground was the insignia of an exceptional warrior, often the chief of a warring group. The well-known form of feather headdress was most common among the Sioux but very quickly spread during the second half of the 19th century in the prairie region. Later it even spread as far as distant tribes like the Iroquois in the east and the Pueblo Indians in the south-west of the U.S.A. In some tribes certain office-bearers wore the so-called horn-cap—i.e. a large leather cap crowned with massive buffulo horns. In some eastern prairie tribes, so-called "deer-tails"—red or violet-coloured tufts of deer hair were worn as ceremonial decoration.

Women had a relatively large degree of authority and independence in many of the Indian tribes in North America. In the settler tribes they contributed to the supply of food by tilling the earth. In contrast to the honorary and trophy decorations of the men, the decorations worn by women had above all an aesthetic, decorative function. The festive dress of deerskin, later made of cloth, used to be brightly decorated with coloured glass beads by the Prairie Indians.

Elk teeth were regarded as particular treasures (the eye teeth of the wapiti-deer); women's festive clothing was often covered with vast amounts of these. Necklaces were not common. The ears were decorated with glass bead ornaments, animal teeth and the gleaming shells of the haliotis snail. Belts, bags and shoes (moccasins) also had glass beads sewn on them. Children's dress was similar to that of adults.

The attributes of the medicine-man are worth mentioning. He played an important role in the religious life of the Indians. He was expected among other things, to heal the sick and pass on information which he received from spirits in dreams and visions. His outward appearance displayed to the members of the tribe his close connection with other-worldly powers, which were worshipped in the form of animal spirits. Feathers covered his forehead, fur tails and a variety of hair tufts hung over his ears and shoulders, and between these the heads of birds, mice, and other small stuffed mammals peeped out. Sometimes he appeared in a bearskin costume or another form of animal covering (such as bison mask and fur drapings, or bird mask and feather coat).

AFRICA

There are many different peoples living in Africa, who, until the takeover by colonial powers during the last century, had reached various stages of development. The stage of development was determined by various factors, the main ones being the very diverse relations between the peoples and tribes of a particular region, the stage of development in the social division of labour, trade and migration of peoples, and climatic conditions. Other contributing factors were foreign economic, political and cultural influences, in particular from the Mediterranean area, and western and southern Asia. At the time of the colonial takeover there were peoples who were basically hunter-gatherers, such as the so-called bush men in the south of the continent, as well as the Pygmies. There were, however, also peoples whose social relations could be compared to those under the feudal system in medieval Europe. This was the case in Ethiopia, northern Nigeria, and some areas of the Sudan.

Numerous ornamental objects, which are attractive to Europeans, primarily because of their aesthetic qualities, are in fact trophies, awards, and orders of distinction. Peoples who were still living in a pre-class society or in the transitional stage before the early class society, adhered to strict traditions with regard to their forms of jewellery, and some of these still exist to this day. Thus a headdress or a pendant-necklace could mean that the wearer was a member of a certain community or it could be a sign of some achievement, which was highly revered under the given social conditions. Headdresses in particular were used to emphasize the status of a chief or other dignitaries within societies where social differentiation was already clearly developed. The chiefs of the Basengele in the Central Congo wore big discs made from copper or shells over their foreheads; others wore crowns made of complete wings, and shiny discs made from metal or shells.

The material and form of jewellery often have a symbolic value, or are connected with magico-religious beliefs. The liana, which attaches itself to, and climbs up other plants, is believed in many regions to symbolize faithfulness. The Pangwe in southern Cameroon fashioned engagement rings from it. Plants and roots which had proved to have healing qualities were often worn as amulets to ward off disease. Pieces of wood and nuts, as well as coconut shells polished into discs, were strung on thread. Because of their durability they were thought to symbolize determination, strength, and valour.

Women's jewellery, to a much greater extent than men's, had an erotic element in it, and was used as fertility charms. Lip-ornaments were primarily used by women. Thus the women in some tribes of the Zambesi and Njassa area of East Africa and in the Logone and Chari area of the Central Sudan wore large discs on their upper or lower lips. Some writers think that this distortion of the lips—the procedure takes place during the puberty ceremonies—was connected with a fertility cult. These discs may be an imitation of a hippopotamus' mouth—in ancient myths and religions the hippopotamus was connected with procreation.

Belts and other hip-ornaments also had an erotic significance for both men and women. Belts with heavily decorated codpieces or beaded aprons were worn by both sexes. The women in many tribes, particularly in the Congo area threaded strings of cowrie shells, the bringers of fertility, round their hips, and often joined several rows of shells to make a belt or corset. These are still worn today under their aprons or modern clothing.

It was not unusual for men's jewellery either to be an award for physical strength and personal valour or to encourage such qualities in the wearer. In some areas a bracelet made from rhinoceros tusk or rings made from the skin of an elephant's foot were thought to increase physical strength; a string of eagles' claws or eagles' feathers worn as hair decoration was supposed to make one keen-sighted; the skin and vertebra of the snake to give one agility. Amongst the most impressive male pendants were the rows of ivory and leopards teeth, which showed that the wearer had passed tests of courage. These were also thought to give one strength.

The development of the culture of the cattle-breeding nomad peoples of East Africa took place under very special conditions. Since they move with their herds over a certain, usually very widespread area, and only stop for a short time at any one place, their possessions in terms of utensils, household goods and artefacts cannot be many nor over-cumbersome. However, the traditional ideas about the cultural poverty of nomad peoples in no way correspond to reality.

The camel and sheep-breeding nomads of North-East Africa—from the bedouins and bedia in the dry steppes on the Red Sea down to the Somalis—transport domestic artefacts on their camels. The Somalis skillfully weave mats and baskets from the finest grasses and leaves. They carve bowls, spoons, and combs, with great craftsmanship. Jewellery in the form of easily transportable property, or often as war trophies is one of the artistic means of expression of the East African nomads. Metal jewellery is either produced by the peoples themselves, or bought from smiths in settler-groups or from traders.

Jewellery made from strips of fur and the manes of predators is also widespread. The Masai wear headbands made of lion's manes and bunches of ostrich feathers or of fur on the chin and cheek. They also wear rings of monkey fur round their legs. A heavy open bracelet for the upper-arm was possibly designed to emphasize the size of their biceps. In some eastern and south eastern African peoples men and women wear many metal rings on their arms and sometimes on their legs. These are often not just single rings, but spirals made from thick iron wire of considerable weight. In more recent times—in some areas even before colonial exploitation—glass beads were imported from Europe, and porcelain beads from Europe or Asia, for jewellery-making. In particular, bags, belts, and headbands are decorated with glass beads in colourful geometrical patterns.

Peoples in the most diverse stages of social development and with great cultural variety live in the West Sudan, where agriculture became widespread even in early historical times. In the villages the people lived together in family groups. In most cultures when the sons married they remained with or near to their father's side of the family. Thus, after several generations there arose large family farms, village quarters, or even whole villages where all the males as well as the females who were born there and had not yet married were related on their father's side. Before colonial rule several or just one or two of these family groups formed in some districts a political unit, however, a class society had not yet arisen. In other regions states had developed with clearly defined class differentiatons. The peasants had to pay tithes, and there were serfs or slaves. The material cultural possessions and thus clothing and jewellery vary not only from people to people, but also between the rulers and the ruled.

Metalwork, the production of domestic artefacts and jewellery made from iron, coloured and precious metals was widespread even before the formation of states. They had been developed as specialized crafts and as such had reached a very advanced level of craftsmanship.

Thus the metalwork of some of the western Sudanese peoples, who had never developed a class society shows great skill. These peoples include the Senufo who live in the triangle now occupied by the states of the Upper Volta, the Ivory Coast, and Mali; the great Bambara people who live further to the west; the Dogon in the north of the Republic of Mali and some other peoples who live in the Niger curve. The jewellery of these peoples which has been made from before the colonial period right up to the present day has been recognized to be of particularly high artistic quality.

One of the characteristics peculiar to the social development in many areas of the West Sudan was the formation of groups whose members were engaged in the same activities (as a result of the social division of labour). They not infrequently had their own settlements, married within the group, and were thus known in literature as castes. The smiths for one, who over many generations had gathered a multitude of experience, were joined up in groups such as these. Old and new skills were inherited and passed on within the group. Their ability to use fire and their mastery of metalwork techniques meant that in the eyes of those who did not have those skills, smiths became people who possessed secret powers.

In some areas there were similar groups of leather workers, weavers, potters, and musicians, but none of them were associated with magico-religious powers as in the case of the smiths. The social status and prestige of these castes varied greatly. The warriors and hunters were usually the highest ranking groups, followed by the smiths; the other groups did not enjoy the same prestige.

The metal jewellery of the Senufo people—mostly arm and leg-rings made from bronze using the lost-wax process—usually had a magico-religious significance. They also decorated themselves with tiny bronze models of rings, which were threaded and tied round the arm or leg. One Senufo explained this custom to a researcher; "if one is too poor to buy oneself big rings, one ties little ones round the ankle—that brings good luck".

Animal forms were widely used, mainly for finger-rings. Particularly popular, although, or perhaps because few are found in this area, was the chameleon. It appears not only on rings but also on pendants, and was obviously thought to be a holy animal. The natives explain that they make sacrifices to the chameleon, so that "the hens multiply and do not run away". The representation of other animals also had a deeper significance. "If a dog bites me and I kill him because of this, I must have a dog-ring made for me, so that the dog does not persecute me." Rings or pendants with representations of a cow, turtle, hedgehog, or crocodile, are supposed either to be lucky or to pacify an injured or dead animal (according to Himmelheber).

It was not unusual for bronze jewellery to be used by the secret organizations which were very widespread in Africa. Only members of the highest castes, the warriors and farmers, were allowed to join the exclusive secret organizations of the Senufo people, and only after they had passed painful tests and sacrifices. Thus before youths were accepted into the secret Lo-organization, they had to stay silent for eight days, and during this time they wore a "silencing-ring" in their mouths, with a small bull's head ornament, which was visible from the outside. The members of these secret organizations, acting on the authority of their ancestors' spirits, were responsible for discipline and morals within the tribe and for the upbringing of the young people.

In other areas in western, central, southern, and eastern Africa, metals, together with organic substances, or a combination of both materials were used for jewellery for centuries before colonial times. In western Africa jewellery made from copper, bronze, and iron, together with many works of art, were widely spread, especially among the peoples of southern Nigeria and Cameroon. Brass bracelets of highest fineness and artistic creative power belong to the masterpieces of the casting technique which were produced in the grassland of Cameroon using the lost-wax process. In eastern Africa jewellery made from iron predominated in many places.

Gold was used for many articles of jewellery and signs of dignity for headmen and dignitaries. This is the case especially in the district of the former Ashanti empire in present-day Ghana, in the former Dahomey empire and the state of Benin in southern Nigeria. Gold jewellery had also existed since ancient times in Liberia, furthermore among groups of population at the eastern African coast, whose culture was under Arabian, Persian, and Indian influences.

MESOPOTAMIA

About the middle of the 4th millennium B.C. there were city-states in the valleys of the rivers Euphrates and Tigris which lay like islands surrounded by vast areas populated by primitive tribes. Cultivators and craftsmen had parted ways with the cattle-owning tribes of the steppes and high plains, and had found new places to settle on the marshy land beside the big rivers. An economy based on cultivation and irrigation called for a more advanced form of political and social organization. A growing population and growing surplus, coupled with the more complicated task of looking after the common interest led to the formation of a new social structure with clear class divisions. The elders of the tribes together with the priests were responsible for dyke and canal construction, and they also knew how to calculate the time of the annual floods. They exploited their privileged position by allotting themselves land during the annual redistribution of the land. Thus the original role of leaders serving the community was turned into a form of government over the community: a small stratum of society, the prince with his priests and officials were separated from the majority of the population—peasants with no land, craftsmen, traders, slaves and small property owners with a small piece of land, a few tools or pack animals. The formation of an "elite" who were excluded from the work process made it possible for them to turn to more intellectual matters, which spurred on the cultural development. The beginnings of science were based on astronomy, mathematics, and the development of a script. Further technical developments led to better harvests: dams, reservoirs, and canals were built on the basis of the already specialized division of labour. Within the strongly fortified city boundaries, apart from religious buildings, public buildings such as warehouses and granaries were erected and a drainage system for the town was built.

In the artistic field sculpture as well as the ornamental arts were highly developed. The techniques used for these and the forms they took had an influence on the jewellery of these people. They developed a characteristically new attitude towards precious metals, the particular qualities of which, especially their softness, made them unsuitable for use in the production process as tools. Their brightness and splendid decorative qualities, together with the mystery surrounding their origin—the depths of the underworld, descended from the sun, moon, and stars—all this helped make them the epitomy of superfluity, rank, and even sacredness. In addition it was possible to use precious metals as a constant equivalent for necessary use-values. Only the rulers, who were thought to be descendants of the Gods were allowed to wear the holy metal in the form of jewellery. This was also true of particularly highly valued precious and semi-precious stones, which had been used since their discovery as amulets and talismen.

Later the individual city-states united to form large centrally governed empires—ancient oriental despotism—with a king from the ruling dynasty on the throne. During the first half of the second millennium B.C. Babylon became the most important state in the Near East and nearly all of the former Sumerian Mesopotamia fell under its rule. The class divisions became more accentuated: king, temple priests, court and temple officials formed the upper class; a type of middle class followed in the cities and included the rich workshop owners and land owners, as well as merchants in the developing area of foreign trade. The lowest class was made up of peasants, small craftsmen and slaves.

Skilled craftsmen who satisfied the upper class's ever-growing demand for prestigious luxury items also enjoyed a certain status. They now lived in their own town quarters, and specialized in certain fields. For metalwork there were melters, smiths for both rough and fine work and also for the production of jewellery from copper, bronze and gold.

Archeological finds displaying extremely fine workmanship are evidence of the goldsmiths' skill. The gold-work was usually incorporated with ivory, shells, bones, mother-of-pearl, or semi-precious stones, raw materials, which were still highly-prized well into the metal age.

The processes used to work the metals and the decoration were also those which had been handed down from ancient traditions: the hundreds of different possibilities of working gold were to be tried out only in a much later period. In accordance with the phase of technical evolution the sole method of working gold—admittedly a very sophisticated one—was that of hammering out a thin sheet of gold and cutting it into the required shapes. For three-dimensional objects such as helmets, hollow beads or figurines, the gold sheet was hammered into shape using a block made of wood or bronze. Fine parallel engraved lines or chasing completed the work which was, just like ivory, horn, or stonework, decorated with lines or dots.

The Sumerians were the most ancient inhabitants of Mesopotamia and they lived in the middle of the 4th millennium B.C. in city-states such as Lagash, Ur, Uruk, and Eridu. For a long time people thought that their culture had been lost for good. Although Pietro della Valle, an Italian traveller and writer visited the ruins of the city of Ur as early as 1625 and recorded his impressions on paper, it was not until 1854 that T. E. Taylor, then British Consul in Basra, finally identified the site as being that of the Chaldeans biblical Ur, when he found an ancient cylinder seal on the site.

Under the leadership of the British archaeologist, Leonard Wooley, systematic research was begun in Mesopotamia in 1922 and continued for many years. During their work hundreds of graves were found including the royal burial grounds of 16 princes and princesses, dating from the period between 3500–3100 B.C. The ordinary citizens were buried, according to their personal wealth, in coffins made either of terra-cotta, wood, cane, or rush matting; the poor had clay pots and the wealthier had gifts made from precious metals intended for the life after death. However, those royal graves which were still intact—most of them had been plundered by thieves in ancient times—displayed a multitude of burial gifts made from precious metals. The most famous is that of the Queen of Shubad, which Wooley uncovered in the winter of 1927/28. Her remains were covered by a robe made of innumerable gold, silver, lapis lazuli, carnelian, agate and chalcedony beads, bordered with gold cylinders, lapis lazuli and carnelian stones. The size of the queen's head-decoration would suggest that she once wore a wig on her head, which had long since disintegrated. On her head she wore three separate diadems, which were masterpieces of the goldsmith's art: round her forehead and the nape of her neck she wore a string of beads thickly hung with gold discs. Over this she wore a wreath of realistically designed gold willow leaves in groups of threes. The uppermost diadem was made from two rows of the finest gold beech leaves. At the back of her headdress there was a five-toothed comb with three upright gold flowers on long stems. Hooped earrings bent from a thin sheet of gold into a boat shape, as well as numerous necklaces of different lengths with beads made from semi-precious stones alternating with beads of gold, some with a rib pattern, others barrel or rhombus-shaped, completed the royal jewels. In the middle of one triple rowed necklace there was a flower ornament set in a gold circle. Three long gold hair pins with lapis lazuli heads and some amulets in the shape of animals—three in the shape of fish, and one with the figures of two seated gazelles—had been placed next to the queen's right arm.

The burial treasure also included gold and silver animal figures, goblets, tableware, and other valuables. With the queen there had also been buried serving girls, guards, dignitaries, musicians, ladies of the court, and drivers. Their skeletons were found by the archeologists in a pit before the burial chamber. They, too, wore ceremonial jewellery and rich clothing before they, during the funeral chants, presumably took some sort of drug and were covered with earth. Human sacrifices were reasonably common in many ancient civilizations, but no example can compare with the scale in which they were carried out here. This is a sign of the high, almost godlike status of the rulers and of their umlimited powers. In other Sumerian royal graves up to 80 skeletons were discovered. In one of them the women in the escort wore silver hair and ear-jewellery with bright red woollen dresses which had stone beads sewn on to them, in another they wore robes interwoven with gold. On their arms they often wore five rings joined together. The men wore ornaments on their wrists and upper arms, and it was quite common for men to wear ear jewellery, collars, rings and necklaces all made from precious metals.

Coloured semi-precious stones, which were highly-valued, reached Mesopotamia through trading links. Only the court and the temples could acquire these valuables and they represented a highly prized war-booty. The oldest known stone work in the form of seals (from the 4th millennium B.C.) was found in Mesopotamia. Cylinder seals dating from the middle of the 3rd millennium B.C. have pictorial representations of ritual scenes and temple buildings and were worn round the neck on a string. Besides stone work, the production of stone beads, pendants, and other luxury goods reached a high standard.

The various types of jewellery and the many techniques involved in their production meant that a highly developed goldsmith and stonework tradition with great expressive powers was established all over the Near East.

The many types of decoration in the 3rd and 2nd millennia B.C.—leaves and circular patterns, discs, interlocking rings, a clover motif, a many-leaved flower motif and animal shapes with obvious ritual significance also spread in the same or in a more elaborate form from Babylonia and Assyria to lands far from Mesopotamia. These basic forms can be traced in the art of western Asia over thousands of years, and the motifs travelled via the Mediterranean civilizations to Europe and Asia.

EGYPT

Our most comprehensive and detailed information about life in the ancient oriental world comes from the Nile valley, where the death cult was particularly strong, and where the climate was especially suited to the preservation of burial chambers and funerary gifts, which thus stayed intact over thousands of years.

In the Old Kingdom (3rd–6th Dynasty, about 2635–2155 B.C.), when power was concentrated in the hands of the godlike Pharaoh and his administration, technology, art, and science were already sufficiently developed to produce those monumental royal graves, the pyramids. The reliefs on officials' graves depict the wealth and possessions of the dead. Scenes depicting the market, ships, hunts, and dances tell us about Egyptian life, including the life of the peasants and craftsmen.

A state with a highly developed officialdom, based on peasant slave labour, already existed. The relatively small amount of jewellery left over from the Old Kingdom reflects the social hierarchy. The Pharaoh's jewellery was both symbolic of his power and was a means of state representation. However, the rulers and the nobility were not yet laden with jewellery to the same extent as in the New Kingdom. In the pictures the king wears various crowns, some of which take the form of a simple headdress, while others are made up of several separate pieces, all of which were supposed to have magical protective powers.

The main crowns worn by the godlike Pharaoh on official occasions were as follows: the tall "white" crown, which symbolized rule over Upper Egypt, and the "red" crown, which symbolized rule over Lower Egypt. The latter was a round cap worn on the back of the head, and ended at the front with a wire bent upwards. After the unification of Upper and Lower Egypt, a combination of the

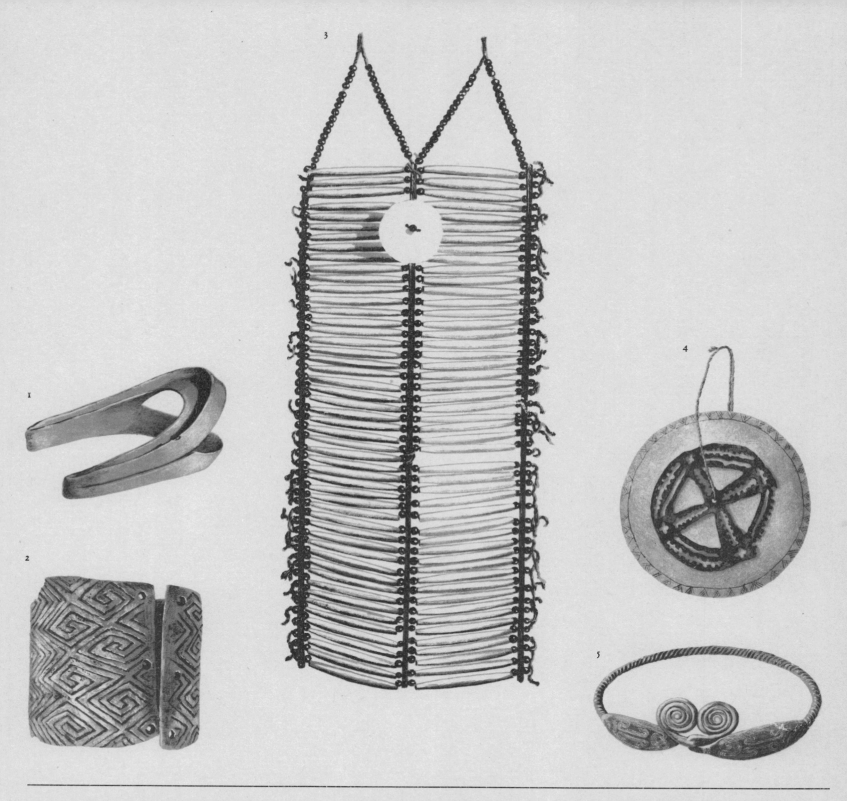

1 Armlet. Warrior jewellery of the Masai, East Africa.

2 Bracelet made from mammoth tusk with carved geometric ornamentation and holes for string. Paleolithic, Ukrainian Socialist Soviet Republic.

3 Chest jewellery of the Prairie Indians made from bones and beads. North America.

4 Tridacna disc with incised border pattern and tortoise shell mounting. Melanesia.

5 Bronze ring with decorated plates and spiral-shaped terminals. Bronze Age, Schleswig-Holstein, Federal Republic of Germany.

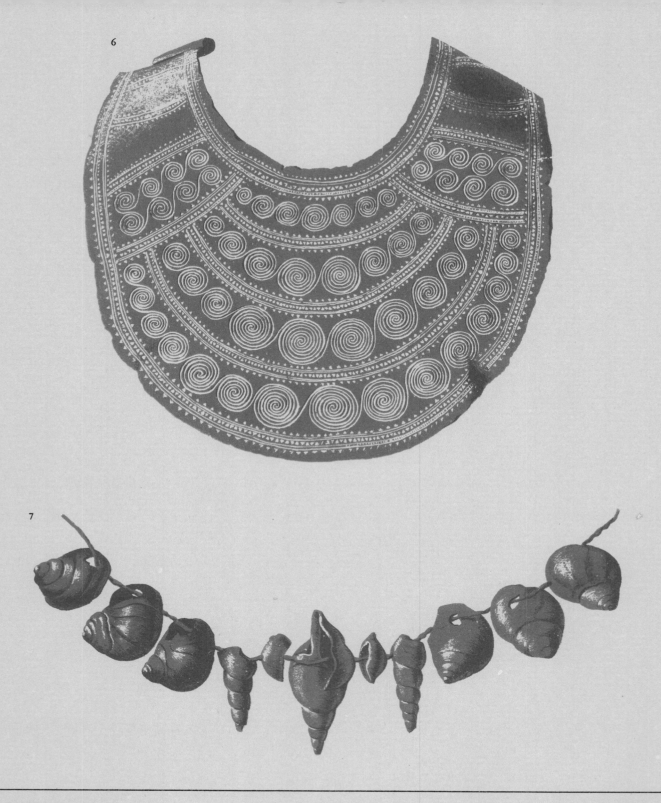

6   Collar with rich dot, line, and spiral patterns.
Northern Bronze Age, Gotland, Sweden.

7   Part of a chain made from snail shells. Paleolithic
Age.

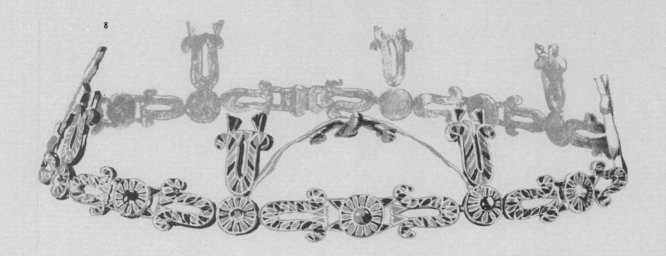

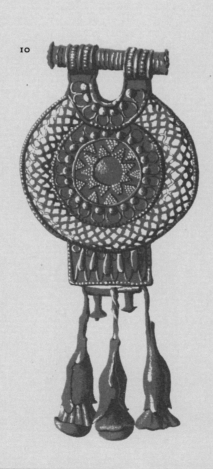

8　Diadem belonging to Princess Khemnet made of gold with inlay of carnelian, turquoise and lapis lazuli. Egypt, 12th Dynasty.

9　Bracelet with section of gold and coloured faience. Early Egyptian, *c.* 3000 B.C.

10　Golden earrings with faience inlay and cup-shaped pendants made from sheet gold. Egypt, 19th Dynasty.

11　Ring with scarab. Gold, lapis lazuli, carnelian, green feldspar. Egypt, 12th Dynasty.

12 Lip ornament, cast gold, in the shape of a snake with a mobile tongue in an open mouth. Aztec, Mexico.

13 Nose ornament. Sheet gold, in the shape of coiled and fully stretched snakes. Nazca-style, Peru, 8th or 9th century.

14 Chain made of gold with pendants. The eyes of the small mask are made from coral. Mochica culture, Peru, 4th–8th centuries.

15 Gold finger-ring with animal head. Mixtec style, Mexico, c. 1200–1500.

"white" and "red" crowns was worn as a symbol of the united empire. Another ancient and commonly worn crown was the *Atef* crown, a combination of the "white" crown and ostrich feathers. As a rule this was supported on ram's horns, often supplemented by a pair of bull's horns. The beginning of the New Kingdom saw the arrival of the so-called warrior's helmet, the "blue crown". It was shaped like a hood, painted blue, and decorated with small circles. To symbolize their power the Pharaohs wore on their foreheads the uraeus, an ornament made from gold and decorative stones, which was meant to be a threat to all enemies, just as a serpent was supposed to have helped the God Rê fight off his adversaries.

Various kinds of headbands have also been discovered in graves and on reliefs. In the 5th Dynasty a diadem was part of the royal attire. It was made of rows of gold and copper with two papyrus umbels placed opposite each other at the back of the head. Here as well the uraeus was worn over the forehead to symbolize the power and dignity of the ruler.

Another type of diadem was presented by the king mainly to men as a kind of reward: it was made of gold and had a simple loop at the back of the head. Also worn by men was the headband, usually made of copper and more rarely of gold, with two papyrus umbels placed opposite each other at the back of the head. The ends of the headband reached down over the back.

Diadems worn by the women during this period were decorated by a ring of papyrus umbels or flowers. They were also made of copper, sometimes of gold.

Amulets had always been worn as pendants on a thread or chain by both men and women. These could be anything from animal-teeth, shells, etc, to figures of animal or human gods. They were also sometimes inscriptions such as *ankh* (life) and *ib* (heart); symbols which for many centuries retained their protective significance. Decorative belts made from woven material or strips of gold covered with brightly coloured beads, were worn predominantly by men in the Old Kingdom. From the 4th Dynasty on-

wards men also wore the broad bead collar. This was sometimes combined with an amulet hanging from a chain.

The statue of Princess Nofret (4th Dynasty), which exudes both power and charm, was completed around 2560 B.C. and is now in the Cairo Museum. Her jewellery is characteristic of the female jewellery of this period: her thick black wig is surrounded by a band shaped like a wreath of flowers with red and blue rosettes and petals. The headband is painted white in an attempt to imitate silver, the "white" metal imported from distant lands which was the most valuable metal in the Old Kingdom, and was valued more highly than the indigenous gold. The Egyptian broad bead collar which Princess Nofret wears draped round her shoulders, was made in the Old Kingdom from a thick net of cylindrical beads made from lapis lazuli, turquoise, and carnelian. These were strung in alternating light and dark rows, and bordered by narrow rows of round silver beads. Drop beads hung from the lower edge.

Up to the 4th Dynasty narrow bracelets were worn by both men and women, but from the 5th Dynasty onwards they were worn exclusively by women, usually in sets. It was not unusual for both lower arms to be covered almost up to the elbow. The bracelets were made from sheet-gold, copper, or ivory. A set of 20 silver bracelets with *cloisonné* butterflies dating from the 4th Dynasty, was part of the burial treasure belonging to Queen Hetepheres, the mother of Cheops. From the 4th Dynasty onwards there were also wide bracelets which were worn on both wrists. These were made of several strings of brightly coloured beads, joined by a strap. Judging by the reliefs this type of bracelets became more and more fashionable from late in the Old Kingdom onwards, and remained a popular form of jewellery for both men and women until a much later period. Women also wore anklets and rings made from rows of beads: these were similar in form to the arm bracelets. The arm jewellery of the ordinary people was made mainly of sea or snail-shells, faience beads, or fresh flowers.

The materials which were considered most suitable and most pleasing for jewellery-making did not change for centuries. Even before the dynasties carnelian was a favourite. This was found in pebble form in the Arabian desert. During the 18th Dynasty (c. 1550–1300 B.C.) imitations were made from opaque quartzite set in red cement. Turquoise and malachite came from the Sinai peninsula (from one of the oldest mines in the history of mankind), the amethyst came from the Aswân district, and the Safâga district. Green feldspar was used most frequently for the jewels of the Middle and New Kingdom, but beads had been made from feldspar since the Neolithic Age. Jasper was also an indigenous stone, and was found in the area of Wadi Saga, Wadi Abu Gerida, and in the hills near Hadrabia, where it was mainly red in colour. Jewels were also made from milky opaque quartzite, clear rock crystal, alabaster, glazed steatite, and ivory. Later amber and coral were also used. Particularly highly valued was lapis lazuli, which was imported from the Middle Kingdom onwards from Syria and other countries in the Near East. Finds of lapis lazuli dating from the pre-dynastic period point, however, to earlier trading links with the countries to the north of the Kingdom.

Jewellery had been made from faience since the pre-dynastic period; this was a cheaper material used to imitate coloured stones, especially the popular turquoise, amethyst, and lapis lazuli, i.e. blue, violet, and green tones; there were, however, also white, yellow, red and multi-coloured variations. The beads were made from a mass of white or brown quartzite sand, which was covered with a coloured glaze. The Egyptians together with the inhabitants of Mesopotamia are thought to be the inventors of the ceramic glazes, from which they probably went on to discover glass at the beginning of the 3rd millennium B.C. Glass beads can be traced back to the Old Kingdom, but they were used on a particularly large scale during the 18th Dynasty. Coloured glass pastes were also used instead of semi-precious stones for less expensive jewellery, especially for imitations of turquoise which was particularly popular.

In the middle of the 5th Dynasty the Kingdom began to break up into warring princedoms, and a period of confusion, revolts, and social upheaval followed. "The nobility are full of complaints, while the lowly are full of joy", said a contemporary seer, Ipu-wer; "the most exquisite jewellery hangs round the necks of slave girls, while the ladies are dressed in rags".

After centuries of inner-political struggles the Theban Dynasty took over towards the end of the 3rd millennium B.C. and after a comprehensive re-organization of the state, the foundation was laid for a cultural revival during the 11th and 12th Dynasties of the Middle Kingdom (c. 2040–1785 B.C.).

Amenemhet I, the first ruler of the 12th Dynasty succeeded in protecting the land from any external threat by building fortresses in the north and south. Trading was taken up with the Mediterranean countries.

The art of the Middle Kingdom reached great maturity, and was in fact looked on by the Egyptians of later periods as a kind of classical period. The work of the goldsmiths, which is an organic branch of the visual arts shows in the 12th Dynasty complete mastery of their craft. The goldsmith had learnt how to arrange and shape rich decorative details without ever letting them remain mere shapes. In jewellery one becomes aware of a purity of style and correct use of materials which had not existed before and which was hardly ever achieved again.

On the whole the choice and variation of jewellery became greater and richer in the Middle Kingdom. Necklaces were usually made of single or several rows of threaded beads. The favourites were large amethyst, garnet or carnelian beads with a fastener in the shape of a falcon's head. These necklaces were held at the back of the neck by a so-called *manchit*, a counterpoise usually in the shape of a slender petal, which fell into the desired position, usually at the base of the neck.

Necklaces made with smaller beads usually had a combination of various stones, and often included amulet figures, or had amulet pendants. Gold and silver beads were soldered together from two embossed semispheres, often with a fine cylinder joining them in the middle. Larger gold beads were also shaped into knots, cowrie shells, or leopard heads. The soldering technique, now completely mastered, helped the goldsmiths to join separately embossed pieces of jewellery such as hollow beads or figures, which were made separately as two matching pieces, and then joined together.

On strap bracelets the strap lost to an ever greater degree its original function of keeping the strings of beads in place, and became a decoration in its own right. This development reached its peak in a later period, but the trend had its beginnings in the Middle Kingdom with the increased ornamentation and increased use of coloured stone inlays. The bracelets were fastened by loops which were interlocked, then held in place by a pin. Clasps and hinges were also known.

Decorative belts were made from a row of right-angled, metal jewelled discs. They were fastened by a buckle in the front, which was sometimes in the shape of a knot and sometimes an apron-like disc with drop pendants.

Rings came to Egypt from Crete after trading links had been established with the Mediterranean countries. One of the finds in the grave of Princess Mereret is obviously of Aegean origin. The signet ring appeared in the Middle Kingdom and has some typical Egyptian stylistic qualities: the stone disc-ring was in the shape of the scarab, the holy beetle with an inscription or a decoration on the underside, and was pierced through with a wire on the longitudinal axis, which ended in loops to fasten the ring at the back. This ring, the reversible scarab seal, was both functional and decorative. It was made from lapis lazuli, and from cheaper green stones, as well as from glazed steatite, faience etc.

Small right-angled or trapezium-shaped discs, so-called pectorals, made from painted wood or faience, had been worn since ancient times on a string or chain. They probably originally had a purely decorative function, but later they were used as amulets, and were decorated with religi-

ous or mystical scenes. Large pectorals have been found which date from the Middle Kingdom. In the middle they have the king's ring with the name of the ruler; this is surrounded by symmetrically arranged protective signs and symbolic figures, such as the falcon, which symbolized the Pharaoh, or inscriptions such as *ankh* (life), *djed* (endurance).

After the death of Amenemhet III (1797 B.C.) the empire once more dissolved into a period of internal strife. The battles for the throne and struggles for power caused the empire to be divided once more into numerous small provinces. There was a crisis in art and culture.

The Hyksos, nomads from the Near East, who conquered Egypt and ruled the kingdom from approximately 1785–1555 B.C. soon adopted the superior Egyptian culture. They also introduced a new item to Egypt's jewellery—the earring. Earrings had previously been looked upon as a barbarian piece of jewellery which was worn by the Nubians or the Asiatic neighbours, but from the Hyksos period onward it was worn by Egyptians, either in the form of a ring with a gap to insert the ear lobe, or in gold or silver spirals which were either clipped on, or inserted through a hole in the earlobe.

Towards the end of the 17th Dynasty (approx. 1650–1555 B.C.) which ruled from Thebes, the fight against the Hyksos was taken up by King Ahmose. He succeeded in driving the enemy as far back as Palestine. This was the start of Ancient Egypt's rise to become a world colonial power. The New Kingdom (18th–20th Dynasties, approx. 1555–1080 B.C.) was the most spectacular chapter in the history of Ancient Egypt.

Thanks to its military successes Egypt managed to expand its boundaries considerably: Thutmosis I conquered Palestine and Syria, and finally took over parts of the Sudan and made them into a province within his empire. However, his daughter and successor, Hatshepsut (1490–1470 B.C.) was more interested in the peaceful re-organization of her own country. Under her rule there began a period of cultural sophistication and of an increased regard for wealth and aesthetic values. This is reflected in the jewellery of this period. According to history naval expeditions were sent to the Somali coast by her to fetch such rare luxury items as long-tailed monkeys, sweet-smelling woods and incense, as well as gold, precious stones, and ivory. Her successor Thutmosis III (1470–1439 B.C.), one of the most famous generals of ancient history, colonialized Nubia, reconquered the countries in the Near East until his empire extended to the Euphrates.

There then began a period of increased cultural exchange, especially with the Mediterranean countries, and foreign trade flourished. The Egyptian fashions were swamped with imports from Palestine and Cyprus, while their own metalwork shows Cretian and Mycenean influences. Friends seeking favours from influential people would even give presents of foreign women for the harems, and the dress and taste of these women had a considerable influence on the development of Egyptian jewellery customs from the 18th Dynasty onwards. However, the Egyptian jewellery tradition was strong enough to assimilate foreign influences, without loosing its own character.

The jewellery found in the graves of three princesses, who belonged to the harem of Thutmosis III, and whose names, Menwi, Merti, and Menhet, suggest that they originally came from Syria, shows the oriental love for rich opulent decorations. They wear a gold cap on the top of their heads, from which hang long rows of gold rosettes. On their forehead, instead of the vulture or uraeus which only Egyptian queens were allowed to wear, they had a pair of small gold gazelle heads. Their jewels consisted further of earrings in the form of rosettes or discs with pendants shaped as grapes, buds, or figures, such as were worn by Egyptian women only 75 years later. On their collars they had instead of the usual decorative falcon-head clasps, lotus flowers. This motif was also used later on diadems.

Ladies of the nobility did not content themselves with bracelets on each upper arm, but also wore bracelets round their wrists, mainly strap-bracelets. Men preferred more solid bracelets: these usually consisted of two or three parts joined by a hinge.

In the military state of the 18th Dynasty men were obliged to prove their courage and valour on the battlefield. Amongst the battle-orders awarded by the Pharaoh was the "gold reward", "a visible sign of recognition". No soldier or officer forgot to have noted on his tombstone how often he had been given this reward. Amenemheb, for example, a general under Thutmosis III, received "for bravery before all men", two chain necklaces, four bracelets, a lion and two flies made of pure gold. (The fly, the symbol of aggressiveness and of the merciless warrior was considered a distinction as well as an amulet, whereas the lion with its long wavy mane of female hair symbolized the lion-headed goddess, Sachmet, who especially in the New Kingdom was much revered as the protectorate of soldiers.)

For six years archaelogists led by Howard Carter searched in vain for the "Valley of the Kings" near Thebes for the grave of Tut-ankh-amun. In the autumn of 1922 they finally stumbled on the entrance in a most unlikely place right next to the world-famous burial ground of Ramses VI. The mummy of Tut-ankh-amun had a mask of embossed gold. This was a mask of the king's head in the royal headdress with the uraeus and the head of a vulture above the forehead. Round the neck was a bead collar. The uraeus, vulture's head, and collar were all decorated with inlays of brightly coloured glass, lapis lazuli, green feldspar, carnelian, and other stones. Under the mummy mask there was a beaded linen cap with gold ribbons over the forehead. The lower arms were covered in priceless bracelets. There were precious jewels wrapped up in the linen cloths round the body—rings, belts, ornamental daggers, ear jewellery, necklaces, and bracelets.

In the New Kingdom decorative jewels and amulets were combined to such an extent that it was difficult to know which was which—there was almost an organized amulet production line, whose products were found in all the countries which fell under Egyptian influence. New motifs, obviously of foreign origin, were added to those drawn from earlier epochs. The bearded god of love, Bes, with his bow-legs and animal-tail was modelled in gold and was found not only above the royal bed, but was used for mirror-handles or for cosmetic boxes—the cosmetics were kept in his stomach. He was also found frequently on pendants, as part of chain necklaces or bead collars. Thoeris "the Great", was depicted as the pregnant hippopotamus, standing on its hind legs with the hieroglyph for protection on its hoof. This was the goddess-protectorate of the pregnant, and was found in miniature form in female jewellery. Animal figures such as the falcon, cobra, lizard, fish, bee, or grass hopper were believed to have magical powers and were often found in jewellery. Decoration was enriched by floral patterns, such as small leaves, lotus flowers, lilies, palmettes, grapes, rosettes, as well as drop and vase-motifs.

Gold was one of the earliest known metals in Egypt. It was usually found in alluvial deposits, but it was also mined. There were gold veins running through the mountain chains of the desert between the Nile valley and the Red Sea. The oldest source was in the district near Koptos, however, a far richer source was situated to the south in Nubia. Sesostris I (12th Dynasty) was the first to conquer this lucrative district. Not until the reign of Thutmosis I (18th Dynasty) did it become an Egyptian province, which it was to remain for 500 years. The Greek historian, Diodorus, who visited this district in the 1st century B.C. was obviously amazed at the methods used to extract gold: prisoners, chained, completely naked worked in the glaring heat of the Nubian Desert; they broke open the stones day and night. The big boulders were broken up into gravel and ground into dust in hand-mills. Women and children washed the gold out on big slanting plates.

Gold was used mainly to make sacred gifts for the temple, and to make implements and jewellery for the Pharaoh and his court. A royal decree reads as follows: "The gold, the body of the gods, is not for you (the ordinary people); it does not belong to you . . . anyone who chooses to ignore my orders will be persecuted by Osiris, Isis will torment his wife, and Horus his children. The highest court of the town, however, will pass judgement on him".

The goldsmith was entitled to work with this rare material and thus enjoyed a much higher social position than his colleagues, who worked with ordinary metals. From the time of the Middle Kingdom onwards the tombs bear not only the names of the aristocracy but, due to the rising prosperity of the middle-classes, painters, carpenters, goldsmiths, and other craftsmen could also afford to have a decent burial. Most of them probably still led a simple life, but some did manage to take the leap into officialdom. In the 12th Dynasty one man called himself on his tombstone "President of the Goldsmiths", and claimed that the Pharaoh had rewarded his son "even in childhood", and "had always shown him preference when new posts were to be filled". A well-known goldsmith in the 18th Dynasty claims with pride that he, as "President of the Artists in Upper- and Lower Egypt" was familiar with the "secrets of the gold houses", meaning the production of god-statuettes.

The goldsmith skills were usually kept within certain families, and passed down from generation to generation. The art of making wire, and working thin sheet gold was mastered relatively early. Out of the various decoration techniques used at this time: chasing, engraving, niello etc, the *cloisonné* technique was the favourite, as this suited the Egyptian taste for flat, strong colour effects. For the *cloisonné* work of the Old Kingdom the craftsmen cut out certain shapes in the gold backing and filled them with coloured semi-precious stones of the appropriate size and shape. Later the *cloisonné* method with cells was introduced: thin strips of gold sheet were soldered on to a strong gold backing: in the "cells" which were thus formed, stones or glass pastes were set and fastened with plaster. The granulation technique which was first used in the Middle Kingdom, presumably reached Egypt via the Aegean countries.

After 1080 B.C. the Kingdom was split once more into small states, and from the 8th century B.C. it fell under the rule of various foreign peoples. The influence of some elements of Hellenistic and Roman style on Egyptian art brought about the distinctive Greek-Egyptian and Roman-Egyptian styles, which brought many innovations into the traditional range of Egyptian craftsmanship.

In the later period the delight in strong colour contrasts gave way to a preference for duller colour tones. The jewellery reflects the feeling of tiredness and stagnation, and the old traditional designs are repeated over and over again.

MAYA

The ruins of the temples and palaces of the Maya culture can be found today, overgrown by tropical jungle, in northern Guatemala and the bordering areas of Mexico, El Salvador and Honduras. They are evidence of one of the most impressive cultures ever known, a culture based on a mode of production comparable to that of ancient oriental class society in its early stages, but which, however, knew only the means of production of the stone age. Metals were initially unheard of.

After a progressive formative era, the so-called classical phase of the cultural development in the Maya area began about the 3rd century A.D. Typical for this phase was the founding of cities as political and religious centres, which formed both the seat of residence for the priest-princes and a place of pilgrimage for the people. The corn-cultivators of the surrounding countryside visited the cult centres only for religious ceremonies; they took part in ceremonies and held a market there. Probably only members of the ruling classes, some privileged officials and craftsmen lived permanently in these cities.

The visual art of the classical period, especially the reliefs in temples and palaces, depict priest-princes and members of the court dressed in richly decorated robes with jewellery which was so sumptious that it seemed to try to emulate the luxurious growth of the tropical environment. In the so-called Palace of the King in Yaxchilán in contemporary Mexico priest-princes are depicted striding out in ceremonial costumes reminiscent of the baroque period:

on their heads they wear a tall headdress made of birds' feathers, covered with rosette motifs. On their chests they wear a kind of collar made of feathers or plaited ribbons with hanging tassels. Above this they wear a necklace, either a plaited chain or big beads. Their ear jewellery is either in the form of discs shaped as rosettes, or in pendant form. On their arms they have bracelets rippled either horizontally or vertically with inlays of beads or little bells on the upper edge. Richly decorated belts, rings round their knees and ankles, and rosettes on their robes completed the display of finery.

If their tombs are anything to go by, jade was the most valuable and most sacred stone for the Mayas. The Indians had always thought that jade had supernatural powers and it was used for the priests' jewellery and for statuettes of the gods. In 1952 archaeologists discovered the skeleton of a priest-king in a grave in Palenque (Mexico), one of the few graves to be found in a temple-pyramid (as a rule the Maya-pyramids were only built as bases for sacred buildings). The skeleton was surrounded by hundreds of jade beads and vast quantities of jade jewellery: the head was covered by a mask made from pieces of jade, and the chest by a pectoral. Ear plugs and rings on each finger were made from the same material. Hieroglyphs in the tomb suggest that they date from the period between 603–633.

In the mountain regions of southern Mexico, jade was found in loose rocks in the river abysses. The jade came in all sizes—from a tiny pebble to a piece of rock weighing several centners—and in every possible shade of green.

The technique of stone-cutting—like the art of featherwork—was probably taken over by the Mayas from the La-Venta culture, a kind of mother culture, which existed as early as 900 B.C. It formed the first big religious centre in Central America, and laid the foundations for the consequent cultural attainments of the Central American peoples: they had stone architecture, a hieroglyph script, a calendar system, and they were the first to use numerous techniques and skills which were handed down directly through the Mayas and other peoples to the Aztec culture.

Metals were, however, completely unheard of in Mexico and the Maya-territory until the 10th century. In the Maya culture a particular certain discrepancy can be felt between the great cultural achievements and the simplicity of the technical wherewithal.

During the 9th century the building of the classical Maya culture fell into decay, and building ceased in the temple centres. The reasons for this are thought to be an invasion by warring tribes from the north, the growing resistance of the oppressed people to the arbitrary rule of their leaders, and a combination of economic and ecological catastrophes. New religious and political centres were set up to the north of the Maya-territory, in the dry savanna land on the Yucatán peninsula. In the 10th century, according to Indian legends, the Toltecs were driven out of Tula and invaded Yucatán. A two-way cultural interchange followed. From the Toltecs the Mayas learned about metalwork, and from the goldsmiths in particular they learned how to use gold sheet for embossed work. The jewellery of this period, the so-called Maya-Toltec phase, was a mixture of styles taken from Maya and Toltec art. Research using a spectrograph has shown that the raw material, the gold, came predominantly from Colombia. Finished gold articles were also brought from Costa Rica and Panama.

In Cenotes, the holy lakes dedicated to the rain-god Chac Mool, researchers found numerous sacrificial gifts such as gold vessels, jewellery, even human skeletons. The Englishman, Thompson, who had drained in 1904–1907 the southern part of the Cenote of the Maya town, Chichén Itza, found along with articles made from jade many gold and copper articles such as goblets, masks, figurines, and jewellery. Most of them had been broken intentionally before the sacrifice. Analysis has shown that the articles date from a timespan covering more than 500 year . Even in the 16th century sacrifices were still given. The Spanish bishop Diego de Landa, who visited Chichén Itza in 1556, claimed that the Indians look on Cozumel, an island on the east coast of Yucatán, and Chichén Itza "as we look on Jerusalem and Rome, they go there with presents". They threw many things into the holy lakes, such as precious stones and other valuables, even gold. In 1441 the Maya-area was split into small warring city-states and thus became easy booty for the Spanish conquerers who invaded the country in 1541 under Mantejo.

PERU

The northern part of South America, with its numerous rivers rushing towards the coast had always been one of the richest gold sources in the world. According to legend gold was fished out of the rivers with nets in Rio Sinú (north-west Colombia) in the pre-Spanish period, in nuggets the size of eggs. In the gold territory of Carabaya (to the east of Cuzco) there were numerous alluvial deposits in the vast gold-ridden earth; this was the result of flooding caused by violent rainfalls. Only rarely was gold mined in Peru; where it was mined, simple one-man pits were used. On the other hand, copper and silver seem to have been mined in great quantities. Evidence of this are the old pits which have been discovered, up to 40 m deep.

The coastal area is mainly desert, and the river valleys form the only green oasises, however, it was in this area that cultures, primarily independent of each other, sprang up, each with characteristic art forms.

The centre of the Chavin-culture (c. 900–200 B.C.), the oldest higher Peruvian culture, was situated on the tributaries of the upper Marañón in the Andes. It was named after the main find, which was uncovered in a spot not far from the north Peruvian town of Chavin de Huántar, a former cult centre. The temple buildings, whose walls are covered with pictorial and plastic representations of a predator-god, housed the oldest gold work of the American continent—wide bracelets, chest plates, and coil-shaped ear jewellery—all of which were without doubt worn by a priest during ritual ceremonies. Stylistic research, in particular on the spread of the predator-god motif, shows that the Chavin art reached the coastal valleys of northern and central Peru.

Strings of beads made from turquoise, lapis lazuli, or shells as well as rings and ear ornaments made from bones were found outside the cult centre. In Cupisnique, among the finds dating back to the so-called coastal-Chavin culture, decorative plates were found made from shells with turquoise incrustation.

The first centuries of recorded history saw a climax in the artistic development of northern Peru; a climax which had its roots in the cultural heritage of the Chavin culture. Evidence of metalwork has been found mainly in the river-valley cultures, Virú, Santa, and Chicama, whose inhabitants also produced gold jewellery. As a result of military expansion these, as well as other coastal cultures, were fused into one big cultural unit, the so-called Mochica culture. The representatives of this culture were responsible for perfecting the irrigation systems, cultivating new kinds of plants, and building innumerable temples, which are perched on terrace-like pyramid bases.

Priest-princes and the members of the nobility, who showed a distinct weakness for pomp and splendour, formed a strong central power: they alone had the right to be carried in sedans, to wear certain articles of clothing, and to wear gold jewellery. They were responsible for the organization of the necessary social services, such as the organization of fields and canal-building, and, as privileged messengers of the gods amongst the people, they could order cult buildings and palaces to be built. However, judging by the vase illustrations, the Mochica art does seem more worldly and realistic than the art of the Chavin era which had a certain pathetic seriousness. The Mochica art depicts scenes from everyday life, often with an amusing realism: priests are seen making merry during hunts and games, and even erotic scenes are not infrequent. The effervescent choice and variety of motifs, inspired by a close observation of animal life, was also transmitted to jewellery making, and led to imaginative designs. The dominant motif in the Mochica art, as in all Peruvian cultures was the predator-god; a representation of the puma or jaguar, which as the strongest animals of the Andes region were revered as gods. The moon also, as the cool light in the night darkness, symbolizes growth and prosperity in the coastal regions where the sun blazes relentlessly, and is both a cult object, and a common decorative motif. The moon is thought to govern owls, spiders, snakes, the fox and the dog, which howls to the moon at night. The craftwork of the Mochica culture ranks amongst the greatest examples of the South American artistic achievements not only because of the variety and beauty of its motifs, but also because of the expertise it displays in the technical field.

The necklaces and collars found in the graves of the privileged members of society were mostly made from combinations of gold beads and idols—embossed hollow figures, or the lost-wax process was also sometimes used—alternating with flat or round polished beads of amethyst, emerald, turquoise, rose-quartz, rock crystal or shells. Tiny gold bells or gold pincers hang as pendants. Gold plates decorated with embossed work were worn as chest jewellery, and small gold ornaments were worn as dress brooches. Ear jewellery was made from circular discs with relief work or hollow figures on them, sometimes with precious stones used for *cloisonné* work. A cylinder-shaped keeper was inserted from the back through a hole in the ear lobe. The nobility had to have their ears pierced in early childhood. The headdress was also a sign of rank. A high crescent-shaped headband made from copper or gold with a representation of a predator-god was presumably the headdress of the priests, used as a sign of their office, and worn for ceremonial occasions. This headband and many others were supplemented by an artistic arrangement made from a combination of cloth and the bright feathers of tropical birds. The male "elite" also wore nose and finger-rings, as well as little gold discs over their finger-nails. In one grave the deadman wore a glove-like covering over his hands; each "glove" was made from seven pieces of sheet gold, with carefully shaped gold finger-nails. Certail feathers, furs, or animal-heads were probably used as a sign of rank.

The jewellery worn by the ordinary people was usually

made from copper, shells, or stones. Women wore chains made from pieces of shell, and necklaces made from lapis lazuli or quartz beads. In some areas the hair was tied in plaits and copper hair-clasps were worn. Women in higher social positions also had the right to wear the chief's emblems as jewellery.

The Nazca culture which existed at approximately the same time as the Mochica culture, was named after an archaeological site in southern Peru. The ornaments found there were cut from thin sheet gold and do not bear witness to any great goldsmith skill. The shell jewellery, mostly in pendant form, has, however, a wealth of colour and is extraordinarily beautiful. Stylistically it shows certain affiliations to the well-developed weaving and pottery work of this area. The Nazca style was fused with the art of Tiahuanaco, named after a cult centre on Lake Titicaca in the Bolivian highlands. Here pendants made from bone and shell were found with incrustation of gold, semi-precious stones, and contrasting shells in contrasting colours. These are worked in mosaic patterns to form religious pictures and symbols: these included a winged deity holding a club and a sling, puma and jaguar heads, or the face of some deity.

North Peru remained the centre of the goldsmith work. The classical Mochica culture was succeeded by the Chimú culture, the leaders of which started on an era of political and military expansion in Peru. In the 15th century, the climax of their rule—up to their defeat by the Incas—their realm included 15 river-valleys and stretched 900 km along the coastal area, approximately from Tumbes in the north, almost to present-day Lima in the south.

According to Chimú legend 18 kings ruled the land one after the other, and their mythical ancestors once landed on the coast on a raft. The ruling class and the nobility took tributes from the peasants and craftsmen. These were paid in the form of clothes, food products, utensils, and luxury goods; they (the ruling class) thus guaranteed themselves a good life. Archaeological digs have shown that the people were probably given planned accomodation in the big and small towns, and were housed in systematically laid-out enclosed housing districts.

In the ruins of old workshops within the former Chimú capital, Chanchán, gold and silver goods were found which are technically perfect: the lost-wax process, alloys of silver and gold, and of silver and copper were used. Researchers puzzled over the techniques used on some pieces of jewellery where strips of gold and silver were placed close next to each other, almost without a join: one chest plate, which has alternating strips of gold and silver was probably made by casting the gold and silver parts separately, and then joining them by carefully controlling the heat.

The change to a routine kind of mass production was without doubt a progressive technical development, but it proved detrimental in the artistic field. Chain pendants or dress-brooches, "tin rattles", were made from very thin gold sheet, which was hammered in a mechanical way over wood or stone moulds, thus making it possible to produce the same design umpteen times over. The decline in good workmanship meant a crippling of artistic creativeness: motifs and animal forms were borrowed from the heritage of the rich Mochica culture: they became less and less imaginative and soon the traditional ones were just repeated over and over again.

The Chimú territory was annexed arround 1465 and became part of the giant Inca empire, which at its peak, under the rule of Huayna Cópac (1493–1527) encompassed present-day Ecuador, Peru, Bolivia, northern Chile, and western Argentina. The highly organized state apparatus, whose clear social differentiation bore the features of a class society, was run by leaders, who were throught to be the embodiment of the greatest deity, the sun, and who introduced the solar-cult into all its conquered territories.

The Spanish chronologist, Cieza, reported that the Incas took Indians from the conquered peoples: Indians who were "skilled in metalwork and took them to Cuzco and the provincial capitals. There they made jewellery, and anything else demanded of them, from gold and silver." The crafts and plant cultivation had not been clearly separate fields in past eras, but in the Inca empire they were quite separate. There were, however, no free craftsmen, as in the Aztec empire, who could produce goods as they desired and sell them at the markets.

Particularly skilled craftsmen, goldsmiths, mosaic and feather workers, were even forced to work for two to three months a year to satisfy the needs of the court in the Inca capital-city of Cuzco.

Chiefs, nobility and gods had exclusive rights over gold and silver, known in Indian mythology as "sweat of the sun" and "tears of the moon". Government decrees ordained that all gold, including that which was won from the new well-established mines, was to be delivered to the capital. Any attempt to remove the gold from the capital was punishable by death. Considering the bounty of precious stones in this land it is no wonder that the Spanish, who conquered the Inca capital in 1532 under Pizarro, landed themselves a rich booty of precious stones. Chronologists report of a "garden of the sun" in the holy temple of Cuzco where golden lizards, frogs, snails, trees, and lamas with shepherds stood glistening in the sunlight amongst golden hillocks. When the last Inca-chief, Atahualpa, gave himself up as prisoner, he was covered in layers of gold jewellery, carried on a gold-sedan, and accompanied by members of the court, also decked in sumptuous jewels. Indians who were "skilled silversmiths and casters, worked at nine melting furnaces at once" and melted down most of the Inca booty into a more transportable form so that it could be shipped back to Spain. Only a few of the original pieces which were sent to Spain have survived the centuries. Most of them were either melted down later, or adapted to suit contemporary taste.

MEXICO

"The gold and precious stones do not fill me with wonder, yet I am amazed at how the artistic work by far surpasses the materials available. With eyes full of wonder I have seen thousands of shapes and patterns which are simply indescribable. I have truly never seen any before which so attracted the eye and drew it towards it by the sheer force of its beauty"; so wrote Petrus Martyr d'Anghiera, the first royal historian of the new world, in the 16th century. Dürer expressed similar wonder at the sight of the booty brought from Mexico. And indeed, over the centuries before the conquest of Mexico there had developed an aesthetically and technically mature art, and the craftsmen there produced the most beautiful jewellery in pre-Columbian America.

Highly developed cultures with theocratic societies were probably first formed in the mountain plain of Mexico and along the central and southern Gulf coast. Others then developed in the first centuries of recorded history in Oaxaca in the south, on the top of a hill which the Spanish named Monte Alban (White Mountain). Tribe migrations and cultural overlapping painted a very diverse cultural picture, but the Mixtec-Puebla culture towered above the others because of the sophisticated craftsmanship of its products. This culture had its centre in Cholula, which was both the capital city and a place of pilgrimage.

The Mixtecs whose tradition dates back to the 8th century A.D. were the creators of artistic picture scripts. They produced the most sophisticated ceramic work in the whole of Central America and shone in all fields of the goldsmith and feather crafts. They were admired for their jade and onyx carvings, and for their careful bone and shell carving.

The Mixtecs replaced the Zapoteks as "people of the cloud land" in the highlands of north-Oaxaca. They took over the Zapotek cult centre on the tip of Monte Alban in the 14th and 15th centuries and used the tombs for the burial of their own dignitaries. On January 9, 1932 the Mexican archaeologist Alfonso Caso found among the remains of an older Zapotek burial ground in one of the subterranean chambers, in the so-called grave 7 the skeletons of nine Mixtec noblemen. These were surrounded by more than 500 precious burial gifts such as gold and silver artifacts, bone-carvings, jewellery with pearls, semi-precious stones, and mosaic work.

Among the finds were some large pectorals which have since become famous. For example, the "pectoral of the universe" which has cosmic symbols depicted on seven pieces of relief work joined by rings. The separate parts are done in so-called cast filigree work, a more sophisticated form of the lost-wax process, which was a speciality of the Mixtec craftsmen.

Gold or copper rings made by this process were in their time very valuable and a popular export-good. They have been found in far-away places such as the Cenote near Chichén Itzá, near Guasave in Sinaloa, in Honduras and in the highlands of Guatemala and El Salvador. Some of the rings from grave 7 have small pendants: one is in the form of a bird's head holding a disc with little hanging bells in its beak. Rings of this kind were worn on a raised hand, one of the gestures which contributed to the dramatic appearance of the Indian nobility.

The Mixtecs showed a keen sense of the acoustic in the effects they used, especially for necklaces. In grave 7 a chain was also found made from bits of gold shaped into jaguar molar-teeth, and a long little bell was attached to each individual tooth. Similar ornaments were made from arrangements of gold miniature turtle shells, or bead necklaces made with semi-precious stones, both with bells. Other jewellery included earrings, lip and ear-plugs, bracelets, gold feathers and headbands such as a gold mask of the god, Xipetotec, "our god of the oppressed workers", the protector of seed and plant culture, and also the god of the goldsmiths. He was always covered with the skin from the face of a sacrifice, which was supposed to symbolize the new skin of the spring-like nature. His sacred jewellery also included a nose pendant in the form of a butterfly, and large round earrings.

It is not yet entirely clear where the goldsmith skill in Mexico was derived from, however, since there is no evidence of a gradual development from simple work to more sophisticated products, it seems plausible that they acquired it from the inhabitants in the south of the country. It is, however, still amazing with what skill the Mixtec crafts-men first caught up with, then overtook their teachers; how they learnt to combine form and function, while making the valuable material stretch as far as possible (Mexico had in comparison to Colombia and Peru relatively little gold), and how they developed their own simple yet luxurious artistic style.

A large number of metalwork techniques had already been fully developed. Copper and zinc alloys (bronze) were used for utensils and tools. On the other hand, *tumbaga*, a mixture of gold and copper which was first discovered in Colombia and Central America, was used mainly for jewellery.

One of the various gold plating methods known and one which shows great inventive power is the so-called *mise en couleur* technique which was used in Colombia and Central America. According to Spanish reports the *tumbaga* object was immersed in certain vegetable acids which caused the copper on its surface to dissolve, leaving behind a thin gold film, which when heated and polished energetically, gave a realistic gleam. Using a similar process the Mexican gold workers removed, presumably with the help of salt and clay-earth, the silver from the surface of gold objects, as Mexican gold had a high silver content. Another gold plating method involved covering a simple cast object with a layer of wax, working in the details on this layer, then, using the lost-wax process, pouring on the metal.

The Mixtec craftsmen were also well trained in hammering, soldering, smelting, rolling wire, and knew how to use such decorative techniques as chasing, granulation, real and artificial filigree.

In 1506 parts of the Mixtec territory fell under Aztec rule. The Mixtecs were such skilled craftsmen that they had a great influence on the artistic development in the post-classical era. This period thus became known as that of the Mixtec-Puebla culture. The Mixtecs not only left their mark in the further development of creative art within their former territory, but also had a considerable influence on other areas, for example Cholula. The Spanish, who held their first terrible bloodbath in Cholula, were, judging by their reports, extremely surprised at the beauty and cleanliness of the town, and at the clothes of the inhabitants with all its trimmings, embroidery, and jewels.

The Aztecs, the last of the Nahuatl-speaking hunter and gatherer tribes, which presumably came from the north Mexican Plateau and moved southwards in several waves, settled about 1370 on a marshy island on Lake Texcoco: the same place where the Spanish were 150 years later to admire the splendid capital city of Tenochtitlán, the ruins of which lie under the present-day Mexico City. The Aztecs were extraordinarily gifted in military and organizational matters, and were feared by other tribes because of their cruelty and their bloody cult. They also showed a great talent for assimilating progressive cultures and borrowing from them. Thus the Aztecs went about conquering large parts of Mexico. They did not, however, build up an empire, as the Incas did, but formed rather a state made up of a loosely held confederation of principalities, often situated far apart from each other. The important strategic points and traffic junctions in these areas were manned by Aztec garrisons. The Aztec chiefs, supported by a powerful nobility made up of warriors and officials, formed a privileged class, whereas the ordinary people still lived partly in the traditional primitive matriarchal society. There was the section of society which was relegated to forced labour, and also the slaves who "belonged" to their masters and could be sold. The inhabitants of the conquered provinces had to pay considerable taxes. Thanks to the trading links with the south the Aztecs learned to appreciate in their new homeland the brightly coloured feathers of the tropical birds, especially the green tail feathers of·the quetzal, which had the same value as gold, turquoise, and jade, and were worn as ornamentation only by these in a high social position. From old accounts it can be established that jewellery material of this kind either flowed into the capital in large quantities from the conquered territories, or it was acquired through trading. The high valley of Mexico did not have any gold or precious stone deposits. From a conversation between Cortés and Moctezuma, recorded by the chronologist Bernal Diaz, it can be concluded that most of the gold came from Zacatula and Malinaltepec on the Pacific, and from Coatzalcoalco on the Gulf of Mexico. A total of approximately two tons of crude gold, nuggets, and slabs was imported every year, including deliveries from areas not mentioned above. According to the accounts turquoise was acquired mainly from the present-day states of Guerrero and Veracruz.

The pomp of the court and religion meant that the crafts were well supported. When the Spanish arrived the crafts were organized in a kind of guild system, and divided into different skills; each guild was resident in a certain town quarter. The Spanish priest, Sahagún, who made a careful study of the customs of the land and wrote them down in the *Codex Florentino*, notes a difference between "gold-workers" and "gold-casters" and goes on to say that "some are called smiths. Their sole function is to hammer the gold into a thin sheet with a stone. And there are some who do the finishing touches. These are the real masters of their craft. There is also evidence of feather, mosaic, and metalworker colonies in Azcapotzalco, now part of Mexico City."

In contrast to the theocratic period, the craftsmen now formed a secular class within the city metropolis, and enjoyed more social prestige than the peasant farmers. Their handmade tools included stone-hammers and chisels, obsidian-knifes and bone-drills, and less frequently copper pipes and knifes. The skills were passed down from father to son, but before the son could take up his craft professionally he had to sit a state examination. The craftsman put up his goods for sale on the market, and the Spanish were full of praise for the size, variety and organization of the Tlatelolco market.

The illustrations in the *Codex Vindobonis*, a Mixtec hieroglyph script, which was about 170 years old at the time of the Spanish conquest, give us some idea of the Indian customs and beliefs. Thus, for example, the jewellery worn by the upper class was subject to strict regulations according to position and place of birth, even the Gods had their own particular ornamentation. Any upgrading of social position or prestige was accompanied by the right to wear certain garments, pieces of jewellery, and hair styles. The Aztecs called this *tlahiutztli*, which means "what one is judged by". Abuse of the regulations recording ornamentation was severely punished.

Warrior-chiefs wore the so-called stone pillar hairstyle—the hair was tied up vertically over the crown of the head, and eagle or heron feathers stuck in it. Important dignitaries were entitled to wear the stone-pillar hairstyle with two tufts of quetzal feathers, which hang down in a dignified fashion over the shoulders and back. The warriors of the Totonac and Tarasc tribes wore large discs on the lower lip, the Aztecs, however, preferred smaller, button-like discs made from obsidian, agate, or rock crystal, while the inhabitants of Tlaxcala and Huexotzinco tried to put fear in the hearts of their enemies by wearing curved tusk-like lip jewellery.

Upper class women wore clothes with gold braid, necklaces made from jade beads, ear jewellery made from coral, pearls, jade, and in their hair they wore bright ribbons. Apparently it was for a time considered fashionable for the upper class Aztec women to file their teeth down to a point, then to dye them a dark colour; paint their faces yellow and tattoo them, preferably using the symbol of *Macuilxochitl*, the god of flowers and games, as a motif.

The jewellery of the chief was identical to that of the fire god, *Xiuhtecutli* (god of turquoise), since the chief was thought to be the embodiment of this god on earth. His diadem, a headband with a triangular forehead piece decorated with turquoise incrustation, was characteristic of fire and sun gods; it could, however, also be worn by the highest ranking officials if they were of royal descent. In the picture script this diadem signified "master", "prince". The ceremonial piercing of the king's nose, lower lip, and ears, so that he could wear the decorative gold and turquoise nose, lip and earplugs, was part of the royal co-ronation ceremony and was performed in the presence of all the gods and priests. The royal attire also included gold-plated wrist-straps with inlays of precious stones, as well as a wide bracelet for the upper-arm, made of shells, and with a large long dangling bunch of quetzal feathers. In war the chief wore clothing and jewellery bearing the sign of the god, Xipe Totec: he wore a crown and a short mantle of pink spoonbill feathers, which symbolized the skin of the sacrifice, and he had an apron of quetzal feathers.

The Spanish were extremely impressed by pieces of Indian gold jewellery, which, similar to those from Peru, had alternating strips of gold and silver. Even Benvenuto Cellini (1500–1570), the famous Italian goldsmith, tried in vain to reveal the secret of the technique used to fashion a silver fish with gold inlay, which had probably required several casting processes. It is reported that at the Tlatelolco market the goldsmiths' wares included objects with movable parts, such as fish or birds with rotating sections. Finds such as a gold pendant which was unearthed in Chinantlilla, Oaxaca, bear witness to the extraordinary skills of the craftsmen just before the Spanish conquest: a mobile jaw was found attached to a golden skull. with two rows of bells hanging from it. At the slightest movement of the wearer, presumably a priest, the jaw would open and close to the accompaniment of the light tinkling of bells. Other little masterpieces include lip ornaments which were pushed through a hole in the lower lip, and fastened by a kind of button at the back; on the front there was an eagle's or snake's head with a moving tongue. Ornaments of this kind were undoubtedly a great hindrance when speaking, apart from their obvious psychological effect. However, we learn from the Spanish missionary Fray Francisco de Burja that "... it was considered a virtue, a princely quality, the greatest sign of nobility and authority not to exchange many words."

TROY

The history of jewellery in the Aegean begins with the numerous finds from the second settlement level of Troy, on the Asia Minor coast, dating from the period between 2400–2300 B.C., i.e. an early Bronze Age settlement.

In the course of a long drawn-out series of excavations no less then nine settlement levels, one on top of the other, were uncovered on the mound of Hissarlik, where Heinrich Schliemann began his digs in the 1870s and 1880s in the hope of finding Homer's Troy. The seventh level, and indeed the first section of this level, which dates approximately from the 13th century B.C., was the scene of the so-called Trojan war, which was the historical basis for Homer's epic poem, the "Iliad", written in the 8th century B.C. Therefore the reasons given for the Achaeans attack on Troy, as given in the Epic can be dismissed as pure legend. The capture of Helena, the Achaean spartan princess and daughter of the gods—the most beautiful woman in the world—by Paris, the Trojan prince, was undoubtedly a poetic embellishment of the true story. The real background was the fight for naval supremacy in the eastern Mediterranean, especially for access to the Black Sea, which could be blocked by the Trojan stronghold at the foot of the Dardanelles.

Schliemann, an expert on, and an ardent admirer of the Homer Epics, was a pioneer in the field of using archaeology to shed light on the cultural history of the ancient Aegean Bronze Age. He set to work with the enthusiasm of the trained autodidact. He originally thought he had found the Troy of the Iliad in the second settlement level, where numerous finds seemed to tally with the descriptions given in Homer's epic, or so he thought. However, it was the splendour of the jewellery in this layer which revealed his error.

When Schliemann found a vessel in a niche in a wall, filled with pieces of gold jewellery; he assumed this was the treasure of the Trojan King Priamo in Homer, and thought it may have been worn by the beautiful Helena herself. The jewellery was first wrapped up in Frau Schliemann's apron (Frau Schliemann was his constant companion and assistant) to prevent any robberies, then packed into baskets and covered with vegetables with the excuse that Sophia Schliemann preferred the vegetables from Hissarlik to all other kinds. The jewellery was later presented to the Berlin Ethnological Museum, but has been missing since the end of the 2nd World War. Schliemann did, however, dress his wife in one of the headdresses and necklaces, and thus a photograph of the jewelled head and shoulders of the beautiful Sophia Eugastromenos-Schliemann has been preserved.

The jewellery taken for that of the beautiful Helena dated, however, from a much earlier period than that of Homer's heroes. It was more than one thousand years older, and is thus the oldest known example of Aegean metal jewellery. It bore all the marks of a fully developed bronze-age goldsmith art. Gold was won in almost all parts of the Mediterranean area either from mines or from rivers, and was familiar to all the peoples of the Ancient Mediterranean world from an early age onwards. The technical standard of the gold work corresponded to that of other bronze age cultures in the same stage of development. Sheet gold and gold wire remained for a long time the basic elements for the work of the goldsmiths in the Ancient Mediterranean world.

Sheet gold, produced without using heat, by hammering

and embossing, was given the desired shape with the help of a wooden mould or by working it into grooves in a stone form.

Gold wire was the basic material used for two closely related techniques, filigree and granulation. As the gold pieces from Troy's second level have shown, these two techniques were often used on the same piece of jewellery. The filigree work of the ancient world was done with gold wire which could either be straight, twisted, or in little grains. The goldsmith either worked the wire, without any tools, on a gold background, or he rolled the wire round a wooden pin. For granulation work tiny particles of gold wire were melted into small balls by adding coal dust, then in a second stage they were again sprinkled with coal dust, and in a third stage melted on to sheet gold. Early granulation work from the 3rd and 2nd millennia B.C., still has light strips of wire or furrows to keep the grains in place.

Chasing was also practised, as was the use of a punching tool to imprint a pattern, which could then be used as a stamp to give an exact replication of a certain motif. Examples of this include the spirals, double spirals and rosettes, the most popular ornamentation motifs in Troy.

Three of the diadems with pendants attached to them at the front were made up of more than 1500 individual parts. Some of the ear jewellery shaped in a basket or boat-like form had loosely-attached chains or rattles; others were simple gold spirals, which were clipped onto the ear lobes. The hair jewellery also had a spiral form. Bracelets and dress pins were usually less fancy than the hanging pendants commonly found on head, ear, and neck-jewellery. The rich array of individual parts must have made a charming whole, and the combination of numerous little discs and rattles must have veiled the wearer in dazzling, tinkling splendour. Not long after the flower and leaf-headdress of Shubad in Sumer had been completed, the early Bronze Age Trojan jewellery began to develop a distinctly different artistic trend, an individual, independent sense of beauty in the ancient Agean, which left its mark on the jewellery of the Cycladic and Helladic lands.

Jewellery reached a high stage of development once more in the Cretan-Mycenaean culture, when the techniques for its production had been mastered once more, and it was given new artistic life. Most of the jewellery of the Minoan culture an Crete dates from the 17th century B.C., on the mainland the Mycenaean goldsmith work began to develop in the 16th century B.C.

CRETE

After new technological developments had allowed sea travel to gain in importance, the eastern Mediterranean area, with its numerous islands and coastal settlements, became to an ever greater degree the gateway between the Orient and Europe. The Minoan culture on Crete became, thanks to its central position in the Aegean Sea, a bridge between oriental and European culture. On this island with its favourable climate and wealth of natural beauty and fertile land, traces of human existence can be found dating back to the Paleolithic Age. Later, from 2100 to approximately 1400 B.C. it experienced an unparalleled flourishing in the Bronze Age. The Greeks were still speaking of it 1000 years later. They called ancient Crete "Island of the Fortunate", although they can only have seen the ruins of its former glory, since about 1400 B.C. the whole Minoan culture was wiped out by a major catastrophe, which has not yet been totally explained. Presumably a volcanic eruption on the island of Thera, 1,200 km to the north of Crete, together with a marine earthquake whose tidal wave swept the north coast of Crete played a leading and terrifying role in this catastrophe.

We know today thanks to the excavations of clay-slab archives which give bills, receipts, and other financial reports, that Crete owed its rise at the end of the 3rd millennium B.C. to a strong centralization of its economy, which dealt among other things with exports to Syria and Egypt. The prerequisite for this extensive trading was a strong fleet and unchallenged supremacy in the eastern Mediterranean. Thus the Cretan towns and palaces remained completely unfortified. In towns like Phaistos and Knossos 50,000–60,000 people lived round about the palace: people in influential positions along with the top officials lived in big houses, the others lived in smaller and some in very poor houses on the peripheries, as was usual in the early class societies of the ancient Orient. The palace played an over-proportional role in the people's lives: everyone was involved in the running of the palace, and it is probable that the beginnings of slave ownership were present.

The most common themes in the jewellery are obviously of a cult nature. Scenes with figures predominate on the signet rings: finds from the ancient palace of Phaistos, which date from about 2000 B.C., often show, apart from hunting, bull-fight, or dance scenes, a priestess or mother-goddess receiving homages. Two axes or bull's horns are usually represented as well: their exact meaning is not yet clear, but they probably symbolized some deity or the presence of some deity. Doves, snakes, and pillars were also common motifs for jewellery. A pendant found in a grave near Mallia, dating likewise from around 2000 B.C., consists of two hornets facing each other, holding a disc ornament with their legs. Shell, sea animal, and insect motifs were found mainly on gold dress pins. The holy symbol of the bull's head occurs again and again on decorative discs and ear jewellery.

In the maternity cult, (the mother goddess was honoured as goddess of the trees and mountains, of man and animals, of life in general) one can see a dear expression of the great respect paid to women in this very probably matriarchal-run society. Women are the main subjects of pictorial representations: they are depicted as priestesses, doing acrobatics, or being driven in elegant chariots. On frescoes found in the palace of Knossos women are depicted sitting between men in spectator-galleries or boxes—possibly during a ceremony or the ritual bullfight. They are dressed in open bodices and layered skirts, with artistically curled hair styles, laced with strings of beads. They wear an ornamental headband or diadem over their foreheads, and rings or chains of beads round their neck and wrists. On other wall paintings boys and girls wearing ornamental headbands pick flowers in a country scene full of blossom, butterflies, and insects. The so-called prince with the feather crown on a wall painting in the southern part of the palace of Knossos wears an arrangement of tall peacock feathers on top of his wreathe-like headdress.

Sport, games, holidays, the animal and vegetable world, ritual ceremonies in the open air—these are the motifs which came up again and again in the arts and crafts. War, booty, and conquests do not seem to have been so important to the Cretans. From the picture "Minoan Peace" it can be seen that although the Cretans did in fact take over the war chariot of the Hyksos, which could have been a real form of military advantage, they then proceeded to deck it out elegantly, and use it to take their women on joy rides.

From the 17th century B.C. onwards a centralized empire with extraordinary economic power had existed, with leaders sitting in Knossos and Phaistos. Thus in 1500 B.C. (approx.) new palace buildings were erected, the palace of Knossos being the most sumptuous.

According to legend King Minos, the mythical founder of Cretan naval supremacy, son of Zeus and Europa, had the Knossos labyrinths built and kept the man-eating minotaur in them. This was a monster with the head of a bull, and the body of a man. As a tribute, Athens had to send seven youths and seven maidens every years to feed the minotaur. When Heinrich Schliemann climbed the mound of Cephale near Candia in 1886, he was convinced that he would find the palace of Minos under the mound. 13 years later excavations were carried out under the direction of Arthur Evans and it was confirmed that a vast building had once stood in this place, which showed certain similarities to a labyrinth, in that it was impossible to work out the vast lay-out of its rooms. Its size alone—20,000 m²—shows its importance within Crete. Apart from being the seat of residence of a priest-king and housing all cult buildings, as well as the administrative and technical centres, its biggest hall was devoted to important economic buildings, such as shops, stores, market buildings, and workshops.

The highly stylized, yet elegant floral motifs, which sometimes give the appearance of having been carelessly thrown together and which are found very commonly in frescoes, are also to be found in jewellery: they were initially spiral patterns, and were later developed into leaves, petals or palmette motifs. Lilies also appeared, and, much later, papyrus motifs. Amongst the finds extracted from the ruins of Knossos was a gold pendant in the form of an exact replica of a duck. The pendant dated from approximately 1500 B.C. The lines of its wings and tails are formed by the so-called "groove"-granulation technique, an early form of granulation: the gold granules are held in long grooves.

One of the main contributing factors to the flourishing of the empire, and to the variety of Cretes culture from approximately 2000 B.C. onwards was its far reaching contacts with other countries, especially with Egypt. The simultaneous economic flourishing in the Nile valley and on Crete, from 2100–1720 B.C., was certainly not coincidental. The large number of Egyptian goods found on Crete and vice versa would indicate that the exchange of goods was not limited to luxury items for the ruling classes. To a more modest degree a broad section of the population had their share of Egyptian goods, as is seen by the finds of numerous Egyptian scarabs, in the form of pendants, rings, or seals. Possibly sailors brought these as souvenirs from the far-off land. On the other hand there is evidence of a wide selection of Cretan exports in Egypt. Egyptian frescoes show Cretan envoys carrying vessels from their homeland and underneath is written "The people of Crete bring presents". The numerous princely funeral gifts in Egyptian burial tombs also show that the exports included luxury gold jewellery.

MYCENAE

There is some archaeological proof at least of some aspects of the Greek legend about Theseus, who killed the holy bull of King Minos, and thus freed Athens from the need to pay its yearly tribute to Crete. It has been proved that the Greek mainland was once under Minoan influence, and even formed a branch of the Minoan culture around the turn of the 3rd–2nd millennia B.C., which today is known as "Helladic". Around 1900 B.C. the Achaeans invaded this territory from the north. These were tribes who still had a primitive form of society. They, however, by no means wiped out the superior Helladic culture of this captured land, but rather took over the native production techniques along with the Cretan influences inherent in the native art; they did not, however, take over its basis, the Minoan palace economy. Instead of this the Achaean aristocracy became the ruling class. There were no groups of houses in various shapes and sizes around freely accessible palaces, as in Phaistos or Knossos: here the ruling princes and their families had strongly fortified castles built for them and their successors, and from these they ruled the mainland, in Mycenae, Tiryns, Athens, and elsewhere.

Crete, with its firmly established cult of motherhood, held on to the remains of its matriarchal culture. This was expressed, for example, in the greater freedom enjoyed by woman and in the luxurious culture, which had woman as its central point. In contrast, the valiant warrior came to the fore in the Mycenean princedoms. The relations between these two very differently based societies must have soon become friendly, not only because the legend claims that the Cretan princess Ariadne stood helpfully aside to let Theseus kill the minotaur in the labyrinth at Knossos, but also because Mycenean art seems undoubtedly to have been able for centuries to unite decorative elements of both a matriarchal and patriarchal nature. This is seen to a certain extent in the Mycenean jewellery.

When in 1876 Schliemann, still on Homer's trail, discovered the first Achaean fort, Mycenae, in the Argolis (according to the "Iliad" the seat of the Achaean army general Agamemnon), he found, amongst other things, six princely graves from the 16th century B.C. within the outer wall. They contained as burial gifts gold ornaments such as diadems, necklaces, death masks, bracelets, chest and finger jewellery weighing almost 15 kg: a find which was unparalleled in the Aegean. The supposition that the gold was given to the Achaeans as a reward for helping drive the Hyksos out of Egypt is still within the realm of the possible. When jewellery first began to be developed, the Egyptian elements of the death cult were probably borrowed. One such element is the custom of covering the upper body of the dead princes with masks.

This custom was completely ignored for female burials, and the less valuable jewellery kept more to the Minoan tradition. Thus gold rings were found with unmistakably Minoan cult representations; on the other hand ornaments such as the huge rosette-earrings made from and precious stones have completely lost their Minoan refinement. A dress pin, 21.5 cm long, made from silver with gold inlay displays in its bulkiness a taste which is totally alien to the Cretan elegance; however, the ornamentation still relies essentially on Minoan influences; arm and head decorations made from thin sheet gold have embossed patterns of spirals and concentric circles. Gold decorative discs (in one grave alone Schliemann found 701 of them) have apart from spiral patterns, rosettes, or geometric motifs, the traditional Cretan representations of stylized sea animals and insects. (Evidence that these ornaments were put into mass production with the help of stamps is seen in the fact that they spread throughout the whole trading area of the Cretan-Mycenean culture: to Cyprus, Rhodes, Syria, and the Asia Minor coast.)

The Mycenean goldsmith often used various metals for one objects, thus combinations of gold with silver, bronze, iron, tin, or copper occur in the funeral gifts of both men and women.

On one heavy armband made of gold, silver, and gold foil, gold leaves were arranged round a copper centrepoint to form a many-leaved floral ornament. Schliemann also found amber beads from the Baltic in some graves.

In full accordance with the position of the man in a patriarchal-based culture, it was male-jewellery which particularly developed. The high social position of one of those buried in Mycenae can be seen in the chain he wears over his armament with two massive gold eagles. His princely array also included a helmet made from boars' teeth, a real masterpiece of Mycenean show armour, similar to that which, according to Homer, was once worn by his hero Odysseus. 40–50 wild boar were needed, to get the required number of tusks for the ivory carvers to fashion them artistically, dye them purple, and sew them onto a leather helmet. The goldsmiths supplied him with a gold support and a bunch of horse hair was placed in this on top of the helmet, and must have once fluttered boldly in the wind.

To complete his outfit the distinguished Achaean required above all the expensive cut-and-thrust weapon, which was always placed in his grave. The simple functional bronze sword was covered with gold, silver, electron (an alloy of gold and silver, first used by the Egyptians), or niello, in representations of hunts or fights; one even had a representation of a Nile landscape with papyrus. Numerous show-swords and daggers like this were found in Mycenean male graves, but it is still not clear, whether they were designed more as decoration than for any functional use.

The archaeological finds point to a considerable deterioration in the relations between Minoan Crete and the Mycenean mainland about 1450 B.C. After the catastrophe hit the island and the fall of the palace-based economy around 1400 B.C., the Achaeans took over its cultural heritage for a short time. The culture was now centred round the Mycenean forts of Peloponnes, but also spread to the islands in the Aegean Sea. This cultural unit was given the overall title of "Minoan-Mycenean". There is some evidence to suggest that the Knossos Palace was now used as a military and administrative centre, and houses with Mycenean characteristics suggest that it became an Achaean settlement.

By the 13th century B.C. Mycenean jewellery was considerably different from Minoan; the final collapse of the Mycenean culture was heralded by a decline in the goldsmith art. About the same time, during the 13th century

B.C. the Achaean fortdwellers on the mainland strengthened their already highly fortified walls. They had obviously recognized the first signs of the so called migration of the Aegean peoples. However, their fortified walls could not withstand the Dorian offensive in the 12th century B.C. The Dorians, related to the Achaeans through their ancestors and their language, pushed their way southwards from the Balkans, and took over important parts of Greece for their new settlements, either suppressing or driving out the native Achaeans. By about 1000 B.C. the last tribes had settled in what was later to become Greece after the Dorian migration. When they settled they were living in the late primitive society, and they introduced a government of military democracy. With this, then the Mycenean epoch the last phase of the Aegean Bronze Age came to an end, and with it the history of ancient Agean jewellery. Meanwhile, parallel to the development of the new Iron Age, the scene was being set for the rise of Greek civilization.

GREECE

After the land, later known Greece, had been taken over, there was, judging by archaeological finds, a low ebb in cultural life lasting over 100 years. The reason for this was, without doubt, that a new ruling class had brought with them and imposed their own social relations, i.e. that of the last stage of the primitive society. However, production, based on iron, experienced a new upswing which lasted until the beginning of the 9th century B.C. Within a short space of time the immigrants had learnt from the captured people the essence of house and ship buildung, sea travel, clay preparation, pottery, and presumably many other things, for which we have no archaeological proof; the immigrants did, however, as excavations in the big religious centres of Greece have shown, take over the cult centres of the captured people and tried to oust the former deities.

However, what the Greeks did take over from the dying culture was done in such a way that they always gave the impression of experimenting with a new beginning; this was because they confronted whatever they found and examined it in detail before using it. Therefore there is no Greek jewellery with an ancient Aegean tradition. The examples we have of jewellery, ceramics, and sculpture, as well as metal tools from the 9th and 8th centuries B.C., rather bear witness to an ingenious, consciously achieved combination of form and decoration, a unified independent style, which bears no relation to any of the previous cultures and which is called "geometric" because of its tectonic-geometrical structure.

The jewellery, heavy and technically simple, has as decorative motifs a zig-zag pattern or meander lines to modify the sharp edges; rhombus and circles are also used, as are ray-like linear designs, simple stars and dots done in chasework.

During the Iron Age, bronze was still initially used for most of the jewellery. The real beginnings of the Greek goldsmith art took place in the 8th century B.C. Typical of this is the embossed sheet gold from Attica, Eretria, and Corinth. The very abstract figures depicted on these late-geometric examples are either pressed onto the sheet gold by means of a mould, or raised from the back by punches. Animals which are obviously cult figures such as birds, horses, and even groups of human figures were represented, often in hunting scenes or scenes related to sea travel. A golden headband, decorated with maidens during a round dance, is a reminder of one of the numerous motifs, which are (according to Homer) supposed to have been used by the god Hephaistos, an expert in the art of the goldsmith and weapon-maker, for the splendid armour of the hero Achilles (Iliad, XVIII, 590–606). The Homeric epics "Iliad" and "Odyssey" were written at the same time, i.e. in the 8th century B.C., and both were derived from old myths. It is thus no wonder that contemporary jewellery should be described in them. Homer gives descriptions of female jewellery; for example, Hera, the wife of the most powerful Greek god, Zeus, says that she wraps herself in her exquisite robe; in her best one and that; "she fastened it over her breast with golden clasps and her waist with a girdle from which a hundred golden tassels hung. In the pierced lobes of her ears she fixed two earrings, each a thing of luminous beauty, with its cluster of three drops."

In the 8th century B.C. there was a potters-quarter in Athens, where the ceramic workers lived and worked together: metalwork and the art of the goldsmith had probably also developed as crafts. During the 8th century B.C. the crafts and sea trading both experienced a rapid development—the city became the centre for state institutions, and thus also the cult centre for the surrounding area: the Greek city-state developed, the polis, and became the instrument of the ruling nobility, who through sea-trade were given the possibility of acquiring and using foreign slaves. In Attica, for example, the running of the state was in the hand of nine archons, elected from the nobility, together with other representatives of the high nobility. They were a class apart from the farmers and artisans who together made up the demos, the people.

The lively trade with the Orient which began to develop in the young city-states meant that they were increasingly open to oriental influences. In the world of art the Greeks gave expression to the confrontation with oriental design in the 7th century B.C. in their so-called orientalizing period, which came after the geometric style. As far as jewellery is concerned, the increased contact with the east brought new life into the form, just as the geometric period was coming to an end. This was initially especially true of the Greek islands in the Aegean Sea, which were geographically nearest to the Orient. Numerous pieces of jewellery come from these islands: many embossed chain-pendants, which have oriental motifs such as lions, griffons and other mythical animals as well as various ornamental designs. The islands inhabited by Ionic Greeks were still the leading islands in the 7th century B.C., particularly in stone engraving, the glyptic. The gems cut mainly on Melos from green steatite show in their demons and animals a living synthesis of oriental and Greek design. Such a synthesis was to occur again and again as the Greeks continued to confront the world of the Orient.

The orientalizing period, which finally came to an end in the latter part of the 7th century, seems to have continued to play a role in the consciously out-dated traditional attire favoured by conservative circles, since Thucydides (c. 460–400 B.C.) reports, that not only the long oriental linen robe, but also rich gold hair ornaments, were commonly worn in Athens by the older generation of the aristocracy until just before his time. It is, of course, also possible that this fashion reached Athens by another route: from Asia Minor through the Ionians.

By about the middle of the 7th century B.C. Peisistratos, the leader of the ambitious class of slave-owning merchants and artisans had already deposed the ruling aristocracy in Athens. Trade with the Black Sea countries and Egypt was increased, bringing more grain and more slaves, and Attica became an economic and cultural centre, and took over the government of the Greek city-states. In the first decade of the 6th century B.C. the Solon reforms finally led to the abolition of slavery for debt in Athens. This resulted on the one hand in the increased use of imported slaves and on the other hand in a growing self-consciousness amongst the population (now legally divided up into strata according to their income), in the struggle between the traditional nobility and the people, who were now beginning to be liberated. This awareness was, of course, only possible for the free man, the full citizen. The favourite subject in the visual arts was now man in his prime, naked, in the ideal age of the young god Apollo, which at this point made the break-through to the Archaic style. These Archaic youths, called *kouroi*, hardly ever wore jewellery, or at the most simple round ear-discs which gave the ear an ornamental curve, or an inconspicuous smooth choker, which formed an organic part of their physique. It is hard to imagine, given this striking ideal of beauty, that Greek men apparently possessed a large amount of jewellery in the 6th century B.C. They presumably limited themselves more or less to carved stones, since, thanks to the Egyptian-Phoenician influence the scarab reached Greece at the beginning of the 6th century B.C. However, no great care was taken over the design of the beetle, and the stone cutters threw all their energies into the engraving. Most popular were representations of male figures and scenes from myths. Stones with the mark of the craftsman have been preserved from the Archaic period, which points to the high value placed on these gems at this time.

Society was run by man; the most important role for the respectable woman was that of mother and mistress of the house. Apart from courtesans, prostitutes and slave girls, women only appeared in public for the numerous processions and cult events during the big religious festivals. If one were to believe the later ancient Greek comedies, they used these big feasts as an excuse to get out of the house they then set out, supposedly to the festivals, with flowers in their hair wearing long saffron robes and white lacing-sandles, perfumed, being very liberal with their coquettish glances, and decked in jewellery. However, from what the visual arts tell us about the archaic women, it seems that it was never fashionable in Greece to be laden with jewellery; even when worn with an expensive intricately folded female robe, the jewellery was always an organic part of the whole outfit. In spite of this, distinguished ladies and leading courtesans undoubtedly had expensive jewellery, chosen, perhaps, to match their garments, as the goldsmith art blossomed in the archaic period, and after the colonizing period new centres were set up. These were in western Asia Minor, on Rhodes, and also in the Balkans, as is seen by the finds at Trebenice. Archaic jewellery developed as a craft, however, mainly in Greece itself, in the Greek city-states, of Sicily, in southern Italy, and played a considerable role in the development of Etruscan jewellery, which was technically the furthest developed of this period.

During the classical Greek period—after the Persian wars in the 5th century B.C.—numerous costly pieces of jewellery were fashioned in the Greek colonies in southern Russia. These were made by Ionian goldsmiths working there. Along with the ingenious earrings, interlocking gold necklaces, also directly imported from Attica, were the most popular forms of jewellery on the Black Sea coast.

The female jewellery of the classical period consisted primarily of the traditional hooped or disc-shaped ear ornaments, with pendants in the shape of grapes, anchors, pyramids, and flower motifs as form variations. For the first time as well, narrow earrings were worn with hanging gold ornamental terminals, usually encompassing a woman's or a ram's head. Inventories of temple-treasuries confirm that jewellery was by no means scarce in the classical period: necklaces, bracelets, anklets, belts, ear and finger-rings, and dress-pins are all mentioned in the lists of sacrificial gifts. Herodotus has left us with a curious tale about women's dress-pins in the classical period: women apparently had to conform to the wishes of their menfolk with regard to their jewellery. Herodotus writes that after the unhappy campaign against Aegina (568 B.C.), the wives of the fallen warriors of Athens surrounded the only survivor of the campaign, and, for some reason or other, stabbed him with their dress-pins. The men of Athens, more outraged at this deed than over their defeat, immediately forbade the then conventional Dorian dress, the peplos, which was fastened at the shoulder with a fibula, and used their legal powers to force all the women to wear the Ionian dress, the chiton, which did not require a fibula. The results of this action shed some light on the discord between the Greek city-states: according to Herodotus, the Argives and Aignets decreed in protest against the unpopular Athenians, that all their women should keep the peplos, and further that they should have their dress-pins made one-and-a-half times longer. They were then obliged to give these symbols of local patriotism as offerings to the gods.

In the classical polis, wreaths of natural leaves and flowers were a sign of office, and of the inviolability of the wearer. The myrtle wreath was worn mainly by city elders and orators. The men did not even go to a drinking bout without donning a fresh wreath. The laurel, an aromatic, healing plant, was dedicated to Apollo, and was used to symbolize victory. It was also given as a prize to the winners in sport competitions. It was a great honour, especially amongst the Lacedaemonians and Athenians, to be presented with the citizen crown, originally a crown of fresh olive branches, but later made from thin gold foil.

The ring had a particular significance, although in Homer it is not mentioned once. It was, however, already being worn in Greece and the colonies by the 7th century B.C. The oldest rings imitate the reversible Egyptian scarab ring in their form (a clue to their origin), but in the 5th century B.C. blue chalcedony rings were popular: like the beetle they were convoluted but with a smooth surface. We know that stone signet rings were very popular even in the 7th century B.C., as a law, passed in 594 B.C., decrees that ring engravers are forbidden to keep copies of the signet-rings they sell, in order to prevent these being misused by others. In the 6th century B.C. Ionian wire-enamel rings with oriental plant motifs also appeared. However, most of the rings before the 4th century B.C. were made entirely from metal, except for those precious stones mentioned above, which continued to be highly valued from the 7th century onwards. Top officials in Athens received a ring in the classical period as a sign of office; when Cleon (born in 422 B.C.), an Athenian politician, was forced to resign from his post, the Athenians demanded that he give back his ring; ambassadors and envoys showed their rings as a sign of their trustworthiness. With the beginning of Hellenism Alexander the Great was supposed to have placed the signet ring of the defeated Persian king Darius on his finger as a sign of his power, and on his death-bed he passed it on to his successor, Perdiccas.

Apart from this functional aspect, the ring was also associated with mystical powers. The Greeks and later the Romans wore the ring on the fourth finger of the left hand, because it was thought that a fine nerve ran from this finger straight to the heart. Silverrings with a gold stud in the front plate were worn as protection against evil looks; there were rings with goodluck messages, and so-called "capsule rings": rings with a front plate which could be opened and shut. According to the Roman, Pliny, (23–79 B.C.), both Demosthenes (384–322 B.C.) and the Carthaginian general, Hannibal, wore a ring with a capsule of poison under the stone. According to legend, Gyges, the king of Lydia, even possessed a ring which could make him invisible.

Throughout the Mediterranean antiquity right up to Roman times all precious stones were called *gemma* (bud, precious stone). Glyptic, the ancient stone cutting craft, flourished during Hellenism, from the 4th century B.C. up to the early stage of the Roman Empire. There were some radical changes in stone-craft at the beginning of Hellenism: engravings were done on amethysts, garnets, prase, carnelian, chalcedony and sardonyx, and it became fashionable to wear stone rings.

The craftsman, in comparison to the representatives of the intellectual world, the thinkers, philosophers, politicians, even architects, did not enjoy much prestige in the Greek city-states (which partly explains why Hephaestus, the divine smith and patron of craftsmen, is depicted as dark, ugly cripple). However, in the Hellenistic period the prestige of some particularly skilled craftsmen rose considerably. Onesas, Skepas, and many other stone cutters signed their work. Alexander the Great had his portrait cut in stone, and the name of the stone cutter in Alexander's service, Pyrgoteles, has gone down in history.

There were other changes which made themselves felt in the form of Greek jewellery from the 4th century B.C. onwards. Whereas the jewellery of the classical period was still characterized by a balanced form, and was made exclusively from gold, Hellenistic jewellery became more resplendent, and was overloaded with a multitude of ornamental techniques.

Great technical innovations and an unimaginable amount of new artistic forms seemed to go hand in hand, and there were obviously no technical obstacles which the goldsmith could not overcome.

The filigree technique began to win increasing popularity, while granulation fell increasingly out of favour. It was obviously considered worthwhile to heighten the effect of gold by combining it with other coloured materials. Up to now, damascene work and enamel had been used for this purpose, but under the uninterrupted oriental influences which jewellery was exposed to during the reign of Alexander and his successors, the Diadochi, coloured stones were used more and more frequently in gold jewellery.

This development took place while Greek classical culture was slowly fading into the background. By the end of the Peloponnesian wars Athens was wrought with internal and external strife. The endless internal struggles during the first half of the 4th century B.C. led to fierce commercial competition between the individual polis. They were now beginning to feel the absence of any possibility for further economic development, since there was no way of opening up new markets, and consequently production was brought to a standstill. The polis-organization of the Greek city-states had now in every way outlived itself.

Alexander of Macedon, raised on Hellenistic principles by Aristotle and a Greek in education and thought, had crossed the Hellespont in 334 B.C., defeated the Persians, and conquered Phoenicia and Egypt. He was recognized as pharaoh by the Egyptian priests and in 331 B.C. he also ascended the throne of the Persian Empire as the successor of the Achaemenidae Dynasty. He led his troops through Iran and parts of North India, before he finally died from a fever in Babylon in 323 B.C. He had not succeeded in founding his world empire and the Greek polis organisation was replaced by the new territorial states of the Diadochi, Alexander's successors. While on the one hand Alexander's conquests had considerably extended the sphere of influence covered by Greek culture and art, they also opened Greece once more to the ancient oriental cultural influences and these new impulses were expressed in the new world of hellenism. By the time of Alexander's death the way had been paved for a unified Hellenistic culture in the Mediterranean world, and the result was a kind of internationalizing, even of jewellery, in the Mediterranean area. All the hellenized lands developed a taste for valuable materials which had previously been either totally or almost unknown: these included carnelian, turquoise, garnet, and malachite, and later on amethyst, rock crystal, and a kind of chalcedony which the Greeks called plasma. Amber regained its former popularity, and Indian pearls and ivory were particular favourites. Numerous archaeological finds have pointed to the variety of form, the colourful combinations of materials, and above all the wealth of jewellery in the hellenistic period. Finds excavated in Thrace, Asia Minor, Egypt, Sicily and Italy, as well as those in Thessalia, Macedonia, Central Asia, Transcaucasia and the Black Sea territories south of Russia display a distinct unity of style, despite occasional concessions to local traditions. The finds are similar not only in their high standard of technical skill and precise workmanship, but they also shared some elements of form which to a certain extent may have been connected with religious-mantic or superstitious beliefs. A popular motif of this type is the Heracles-knot (which brings good health): a reef knot used mainly for necklaces, bracelets or courtesan amulets (worn round the thigh). Persian-style animal heads had been used previously as terminals for neck and arm-jewellery in some areas which had once been under Persian influence, for example, the Black Sea and Hellespont, but in the hellenistic period they became downright fashionable. Most popular were the heads of the ibex and the lion, the royal animals of the Achaemenidae Dynasty, but the ram's head, a symbol of fertility and wealth, and the head of a goat or antilope were also used as motifs.

Because of their rarity, durability, and beauty, magical forces were attributed to precious stones; there is evidence that this was true even in ancient Babylon. Such ideas seem to have been held by the Greeks for a long time, since at the beginning of the 5th century B.C. the Greek, Onomakritos, wrote in the form of an instructive poem the first "stone book", an invaluable handbook for the goldsmith of the ancient world, as he always had to find the appropriate lucky stone for his customer. Thus the diamond, which was still rarely used at this time, was called "adamas", the relentless, because of its durability, and was supposed to bring its wearer power and strength of character; the ruby was supposed to bring energy and luck in love; the sapphire brought harmony and health into the house of the wearer; the emerald depth of feeling and fame; the turquoise endowed one with fearlessness and invulnerability. However, in the Hellenistic period these beliefs, which had previously been held in separate individual areas, became generally accepted for the first time.

The cultural life in the states under the Diadochian Dynasty was centred round the distinguished courts, where poets and artists found food and patrons, and learning and the arts underwent a rapid development. One development which was not exactly fortuitious for jewellery, was the development out of the classical Greek forms of a peculiarly naughty taste for eroticism, for cute little dancers, niks, or for love scenes from ancient legends—often used as much for sentimental reasons as for decoration.

Ear jewellery, in particular, became a medley not only of decorative little twirls and chains, but of every possible shape and size of figurines. The ear disc with the inverted pyramid had been around since the 6th century B.C. In the 4th century B.C. small golden tassels were attached to this basic form, and they were soon replaced by pendants in the shape of figures, for example, eros, dancers, sirens, birds, or even a Pegasus. In the 4th century B.C. the pyramid-shaped central pendant was often replaced by a vase-shaped form. About the same time crescent-shaped pendants were introduced from Asia. These were attached to a round ear disc, and had a medley of fine chains and little balls hanging from them. Later the selection of ear pendants with figurines became even greater: sphinxes, winged sea horses, or capricorn goats dangled from twisted wire. The simple hoop earring made from smooth or granulated wire was also still worn with a human, lion or goat-head fastener on the lower end.

The necklaces were often exquisitely elegant and were not rarely composed of thousands of tiny individual parts. Thin twisted gold wire was worked into a supple network, often with garnets at the crossing points and edges. Gold tassels were also often hung from necklaces made from supple twisted gold wire with a Heracles-knot in the centre. Chains of gold beads were also usually composed of several

flexible parts, and decorated with various filigree designs. Apart from the traditional motifs such as fruit, birds, animal and human heads, necklace pendants now included buds, flowers, spear-heads, amphorae, and theatre masks. Variations of the basic hoop bracelet were the most popular form of arm jewellery: some had vine-tendril decorations done in filigree work, some were made from sheet gold cylinders with spiral engravings, and decorated with small animal-head terminals made from sheet gold; there were also flat gold bands twisted to make a spiral, mostly in the shape of two snakes whose tails were tied in a Heracles-knot.

Dress-pins were also often crowned with an animal-head, or an erotic figure, a bird, or a representation of a god, all made from sheet gold.

The belts were often composed of rich ornamental plaited chains with medallion-like decorations, and clasps in the shape of the Heracles-knot. They also had rich stone inlays, and decorative pendants made from twisted gold wire.

The oriental diadem, taken over by Alexander, and consequently worn by the Hellenistic rulers, was resplendent with inlays of precious stones and coloured glass. It replaced the Greek wreaths and headbands. The Greek jewellery, however, had lost in the Hellenistic period the character and simple form which formerly distinguished its goldsmith art.

SCYTHIANS

The Scythians were a number of nomadic or semi-nomadic husbandry tribes with similar cultural traits, who inhabited the vast Eurasian steppes, which lie between the Danube and the Yenisei, from the 7th–3rd centuries B.C.

Herodotus, himself an Ionian from Halicarnassus in Asia Minor, gave in his historical work exhaustive accounts about the Scythians of the Black Sea area. These were partly based on his own experiences during his travels, and partly on reports (which were not always very reliable) from Ionian warriors. The Ionians had lived in settlements on the

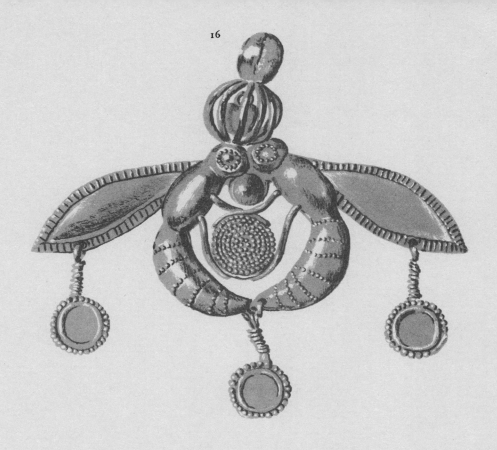

16

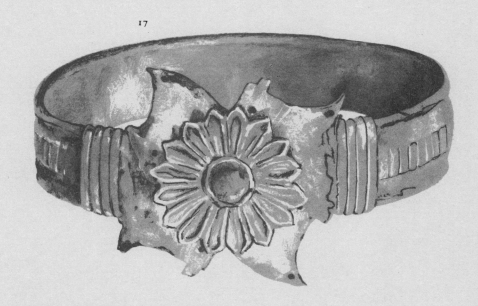

17

16   Gold pendants in the shape of two hornets from the Necropole in Chrysolakkos. Mycenean. 17th century B.C.

17   Bracelet. Gold and silver. Mycena, 1550–1500 B.C.

18 Finger-ring. Geometric style. Gold with granulation. Greek, 1000–700 B.C.

19 Gold comb with representation of Scythians in battle. Solocha, U.S.S.R. 4th century B.C.

20 Gold granulated decorative disc with sculpted female heads. Greek, 8th–7th centuries B.C.

21 Chain made from hollow gold beads with granulated pendants. Greek, 3rd century B.C.

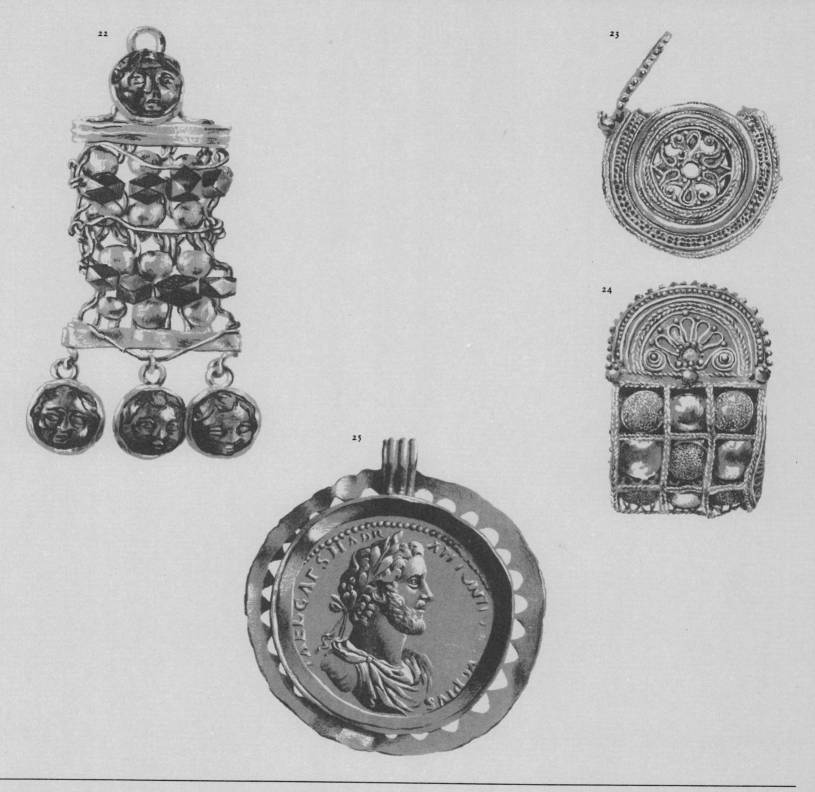

22　Gold pendant with cut stones. Roman, 3rd century B.C.

23, 24　Front and side view of a basket earring, gold with granulation. Etruscan, 2nd half of 6th century B.C.

25　Coin with the portrait of Hadrian (A.D. 76–138), used as pendant.

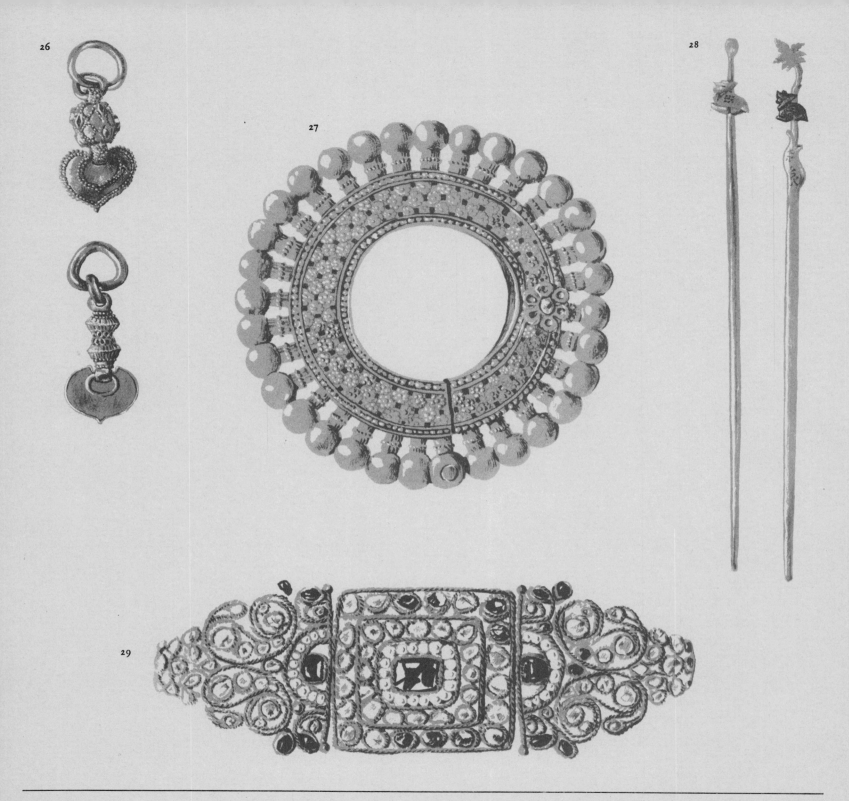

26 Gold earrings with granulation, China, T'ang Dynasty, 8th–9th centuries.

27 Silver anklet, India, probably 19th century.
28 Hair pins made from bones. Japan, probably 2nd half of 19th century.

29 Three-section clasp made from gold filigree, set with beads, rubies, emeralds, and diamonds. India, probably 19th century.

northern shore of the Black Sea, right next to the Scythians, since the 7th–6th centuries B.C. Herodotus differentiates between the "agricultural Scythian", "the wandering Scythian" (nomadic) and the "royal Scythian", thus clearly defining the prevailing economic and social divisions.

In the 8th century B.C. Scythian tribes ruled over parts of western Asia for a certain period of time. The contact with the more advanced culture of this area had a long-term effect on the consequent cultural developments of the Scythian tribes.

Under the influence of the western Asian culture as well as that of linguistically related Persian tribes, the Eurasian Scythian culture developed at the beginning of the 6th century B.C. with its centre round the area to the north of the Black Sea. It was open to other cultural influences through the increasing contact with the antique world, and this had a particularly strong influence on the life style of the upper classes. There were lively trading links with Greece, and Greek goods, mainly luxury goods were traded for corn, animal products and slaves. Excavations have shown that the Greek craftsmen were adept in catering for the taste of their customers, and the goldsmiths could adapt their work to suit the Scythian ideas on form and decoration.

Because of their innumerable military adventures the leaders of the Scythians formed a military elite, which gained more and more recognition, power, and wealth due to its importance within the military-run communities. The members of this elite were buried in earth mounds which contained burial chambers, so-called *Kurgans*, and were given rich funerary gifts—women, servants, horses, weapons and luxury goods. Although these *Kurgans* had been plundered by robbers even in ancient times, there were still some left untouched which could be used for research. Archaeologists are still discovering today valuable finds which have been added to the collections of Soviet museums and which are greatly admired for their high artistic and material value.

Animal representations are very common in Scythian gold jewellery as a result of the long tradition of animal husbandry: game animals, predators, bulls, griffins, were probably thought to possess magical powers. Domestic animals are also depicted, as are scenes from the life of a warrior, and scenes from life in peace time.

In the lower stretches of the Kuban archaeologists uncovered seven *Kurgans* which, because of their similarities, were called "the Seven Brothers". Three of the *Kurgans* had been completely plundered, however, in one, dating from the 5th century, a skeleton was found with the remains of a leather collar, covered with iron and bronze scales, some of which had a covering of sheet gold. Over the skeleton's chest lay a silver chest plate, also partly covered with sheet gold, and with representations of a hind deer, a suckling calf, and underneath a bird in flight. Around his neck the dead man had worn a solid, twisted gold ring, called a *griwna*, a string of cylindrical gold beads and a chain with oval gold beads and pendants. On and around the skeleton lay innumerable tiny stamped gold discs, which had once been attached to the clothing.

Finds from the Chertomlyk burial mound to the north-west of Nikopol on the lower stretches of the Dnieper give us an idea of what sort of jewellery the upper class Scythian women wore. A woman's skeleton was found here laid out on the remains of a spaceous bier. On her forehead she wore a golden headband with floral patterns. On both sides of her head were gold earrings and all round the skull lay 49 little gold discs in the shape of flowers and rosettes. There were also seven gold buttons which had once formed part of the head decoration. Another 57 square discs were found next to her head and body all with the same relief—a goddess, flanked by a Scythian and an altar. These discs were originally used as decoration for a long purple veil. She wore a massive open gold ring-necklace with lion figures at the terminals. Wide, smooth gold bracelets with just a groove for decoration were worn on both wrists, and on every finger was a ring.

During the 4th and 3rd centuries B.C. the Hellenistic influence also increased in the Black Sea area. On the Kerch peninsula a skeleton was found wearing an exact imitation of a wreath of olive branches such as was worn by the dead on the Greek mainland. Other graves had twisted bracelets with rams' heads and richly decorated earrings with chains, pendants and other Hellenistic traits. This was actually true of all jewellery which was fashioned within the area affected by Hellenism. These forms of jewellery were found mainly in the western settlements, but the old tradition of animal motifs continued to be popular in the east, especially in Siberia, right up to the north-west Chinese border, for a long time to come.

ETRURIA

Prosperity and a love of splendour are what the jewellery which the early Etruscan overlords left in the tombs of their dead suggests. Most finds come from tombs dating from the first half of the 7th century B.C., when the Greek orientalizing style was in full swing, and the Etruscans were also particularly open to oriental influences.

The Etruscans entered the stage in the 8th century B.C. in Central Italy between the Tiber, the Arno and the Tyrrhenian coast, in the area now known as Tuscany. Before Rome extended its rule over the whole of Italy, the Etruscans were the only power which in the 7th and 6th centuries B.C. formed a cultural entity on the peninsula. The origins of this people are unknown. They were a seafaring and trading people and from the 8th to the 6th centuries B.C. their use of all the shipping routes of the Tyrrhenian Sea to Sicily, Sardinia, Corsica, as well as far away parts of the western Mediterranean remained unchallengend. Their culture was probably shaped by a mixture of native traditions and various outside influences and style elements, from lands as far away as Asia Minor.

The peak of Etruscan power was in the 7th and 6th centuries B.C. after they had conquered more land in the south (including Campania and Latium) and the land beyond the Apennines up to the eastern Alps in the north. The basis of Etruscan political organization was the city-state, which was originally governed by lukomons, overlords of the religious, judicial, and military spheres. In ancient reports twelve independent city-states are mentioned in the Central Etruscan area and these formed a kind of confederacy. The Etruscan-occupied territories in Campania and the Po valley formed another confederation of twelve city-states. From the 6th to the 5th centuries B.C. republics were declared in the individual cities such as Tarquinia, Caere, Vulci, Chiusi, Volaterra and others. These were ruled by a minority of patrician families which kept a check on each other. These oligarchies did not disappear until the 4th–3rd centuries B.C. when the Romans succeeded (after the Etruscan break-up) in conquering one Etruscan city-state after the other. The official incorporation of Etruria into the Roman Empire was finally carried out under Augustus Caesar.

Being a seafaring and trading people in the Mediterranean the Etruscans came in close contact with Greek art. This can be seen in their numerous imports of Greek works. The Etruscan art also went through, always a little later, the same stylistic periods as Greek art, so that one can follow the development from the orientalizing period to the archaic, the classical and then finally the hellenistic period in Etruscan jewellery.

However, the secret of the Etruscan artistic skill was not the ability to borrow styles from others. They managed to take foreign elements and give them an unmistakably Etruscan flavour. This is true of all stylistic phases in Etruscan art. In the technical field the goldsmith's granulation work is the most impressive example of this ability to produce an independent style. Early examples of granulation had already been found in Elam, Troy, Crete, and Mycenae from about 2000–1500 B.C., and the technique was also used by the Egyptians and Greeks. The Etruscans, however, were the first to perfect this complicated and precise artistic skill. After the decline of the granulation technique in late antiquity, the skill was lost to the world.

Since the end of the 19th century both technicians and theoriticians in the goldsmith trade have been trying with growing success to master the granulation technique once more. However, the ancient technique for producing the little gold granules necessary for granulation is not yet totally understood. It seems most probable that they were produced in the following way: true gold particles were melted in pulverized charcoal to form small balls, and after they had solidified these were then heated in coal dust below melting point; thus the surface of these balls was coated with coal dust and was easier to melt. As a result one could melt the granules directly onto the prepared sheet gold, and their surfaces, which now melted more quickly than their cores, served as an adhesive. The Etruscans had already mastered this technique in the 8th century B.C. It was also about this time that they finally stopped using the granulation techniques which had been used up till now in the east, i.e. groove or bar granulation, and learned how to form lines with the granules, without any aids, and with the greatest of precision. They used the granules to portray various ornamental designs and figures on the gold background; such as those seen on the unique Etruscan jewellery of the orientalizing period. At the peak of Etruscan power, in the 7th and 6th centuries B.C., the Etruscan goldsmiths produced their most important works, i.e. the jewellery of the orientalizing period. Excellent examples from this period were found in tombs in Caere, Palestrina, and Vetulonia, and date from 680–650 B.C.

The richest find was the "Regolini-Gelassi tomb" in Caere, named after its discoverers. Here a distinguished Etruscan lady by the name of Larthia was buried: her name was found engraved on six silver goblets. The extraordinary wealth of the Etruscan jewellery in this grave points to the high social position of this woman. We, of course, do not know her exact position, but there seems to be sufficient proof to suggest that she ranked very high in Etruscan society.

The jewellery was almost totally undamaged: gold spirals once served as hair decoration; there was a chain with gold-framed amber pendants; a belt fastener in gold and as well as numerous gold fibulae and gold lotus flowers attached as decoration to her shoes. Particularly fascinating for us today are a pair of sheet gold earrings which are about 7 cm wide, and 10 cm in diameter: this corresponds approximately to the space between the earlobe and the shoulder. Such earrings have also been found on female statuettes from Caere, so there is no doubt that they were used as earrings and not bracelets. The magnificent earrings are decorated with embossed figures: on the outer frieze the ancient oriental patroness of animals is represented with a palmette tree, standing between griffins and male figures: in the centre are groups of three patronesses standing between palmette trees. The decoration is done almost completely in granulation work and the embossed work is surrounded by a granulation line, in a technique which is otherwise completely unknown. While these decorative pieces alone suggest that the deceased enjoyed a high social status, the two most unusual pieces from the treasure, the so-called Regolini-Gelassi fibula and the golden pectoral, can leave no doubt in our minds as to her social position. The pectoral, 42 cm high and almost just as wide, made from embossed sheet gold, was originally slightly convoluted and backed with copper. It is shaped like a bib, and the whole surface is covered with narrow friezes lying parallel to each other which depict mythological animals in the orientalizing style. The individual friezes are separated from each other by rows of pearl-shaped chase-work studs. The Regolini-Gelassi fibula, on the other hand, is modelled on a purely Italic form, i.e. the disc fibula with transverse plates. This basic form is elevated into a monumental version, noteworthy for the alternating use of relief and plastic work. This unusual 32 cm long fibula with its valuable decoration was worn by its owner, who was once presumably some kind of priestess, either on the shoulder, or on the head above the forehead.

In the Larthia tomb, and also in other less resplendent burial tombs, the finds suggest that the Etruscans were in lively contact with other Mediterranean cultures—Egypt, Phoenicia, Assyria, Cyprus, and Greece. Imported originals from these countries, such as Egyptian scarabs, molten-glass beads or faience discs were executed in metal by the Etruscan craftsmen, and thus adapted to suit Etruscan taste. Necklaces were usually executed in the "semi-solid" form, presumably modelled on Egyptian examples: large metal components were joined together with loops or hinges; men, however, usually wore the solid choker, the torque. A purely Etruscan invention is, however, the *bulla*; this capsule, which could be of great or little value, contained a healing or a lucky object, a type of amulet worn by men, women and children. The *bulla* was worn alone or in rows as pendants on necklaces and bracelets and remained popular up till Roman times, with only minor changes to keep up-to-date with the changing fashions. Even early examples made from embossed sheet gold which were produced mainly in the 7th–6th centuries B.C., show orientalizing representations of scenes, all technically perfect, from Greek god and heroic myths. These were obviously part of Etruscan education, and had perhaps already begun to leave their mark on the Etruscan religious beliefs. Amber chains in the orientalizing style composed of figures—seated monkeys and women with long hair—alternating with disc and drop-shapes, were found mainly in the Vetulonia tombs, and it is probable that there was a workshop here in the 7th century B.C.

A new Etruscan invention, the so-called basket earring for women, was added to the repertoire of Etruscan jewellery during the archaic period, which is reflected in Etruscan art from the 6th century B.C. until the middle of the 5th century B.C. The "basket"-earring is the term used to describe the earring made from sheet gold originally in the form of a flat square, later bent into a half or two-third cylinder shape. A crescent-shaped plaque is attached to the front, especially to the front of swollen "basket" earrings. The ornamentation on this peculiar and completely independent Etruscan innovation was always extremely rich; the curved surfaces are usually divided into two parts, and the foremost decorated like a chessboard with squares filled alternately with shiny and matt granules. The half-cylindrical shaped earrings often had additional ornamental figures. Bracelets were very popular and usually took the

form of simple gold bands, with or without granulation. Some, however, such as those found in Vetulonia, were made from thin strips of sheet gold and decorated in open filigree work. It is clear both from finds and paintings that rings with stones or embossed gold relief-plaques were sometimes worn on every finger, even on the thumb. No ring, however, was ever worn on the middle finger, which was also left ring-free by the Romans, who called it the *digitus Impudicus* (the unchaste finger). The archaic dress-pin kept the indigenous fibula shape with the long pin-covering (hood)—decorated with animal figures and ornaments in granulation work—and the curved pin head. The head was now often given the shape of a lion or sphinx, or decorated with several sphinxes. The favourite chain-pendants were plaque-like lion's heads, god-masks and figures decorated in granulation, and particular favourites were palmette-shaped ornaments, which were arranged on the chains individually or in groups of up to six palmettes.

Although simple gold diadems are represented on finds dating from about 500 B.C. (such as that worn by the goddess of death from Caere; now in Berlin), it is still considered unlikely that these formed a normal part of a woman's jewellery. In the tombs gold wreaths and diadems first appear amongst burial gifts dating from the Hellenistic period.

The Etruscan classical gold jewellery again bears witness to Greek influence, but once more masterly worked into Etruscan style. From the middle of the 5th century onwards small busts were made in Vetulonia in the early-classical style. These were pressed in wafer-thin gold foil and served as medallions. A chain from Vulci consists of 16 punched gold discs with alternating representations of sileni and maenads. Discs of this kind or in a similar form often change the shade of gold or the motif on one chain. By 500 B.C. rings were also often decorated with masks; for example, in Orvieto three small masks were soldered onto a strip of gold which was twisted into five spirals. During the 5th century B.C. Greek forms of earrings reached Etruria; small plaques decorated with flowers; horns made from sheet gold joining in lion's heads; or simply rings with pyramids made from gold balls and the rings with the usual crescent-shaped or boat-shaped lower part, which stayed in fashion until the 3rd century B.C.

During their classical period the Etruscans had already lost much of their power and wealth due to the rise of Carthage to a sea power and the significant expansion of western Greece. They finally lost their independence in the hellenistic period. These developments were expressed in due course in all aspects of life, not least of all in jewellery.

Their technical mastery in all the arts and crafts was maintained, but the typical Etruscan stylistic elements were swamped by the more uniform art of the hellenistic Mediterranean. The change which jewellery went through in all Greek cultural centres in the period after Alexander the Great, also left its mark on Etruscan jewellery.

Characteristic of this period is a proliferation of over-resplendent ornaments and motifs; for example, the basic disc earring of the classical period was now elaborated on in the 3rd century B.C. and had not only busts of women wearing wreaths of flowers hanging from them, but also bulky chain-work with various figure pendants. Apart from the famous Hellenistic diadem from Perugia, another piece of princely splendour has been found dating from the end of the Etruscan civilization; a headband in the shape of a laurel wreath, fastened at the back of the head by a gold chain. Above the forehead in the centre of the wreath is a representation of Lasa with a mirror and alabaster in her hands and a cosmetic box next to her. At the joins between the laurel leaves are semi-circular gold discs with representations of Glaucus, the merman, holding dolphins in his hands.

The heritage of the Etruscan goldsmith art was to come to the fore again later, especially in Rome.

ROME

In the early years of the Republic precious metals were by no means common in Rome, and gold finds from this period are few and far between. Those that do exist are rings of Etruscan origin. With the growth of Roman power and the capture of the gold and silver mines throughout the whole Mediterranean area, both the supply of and demand for valuable jewellery grew steadily, and continued to increase parallel to the rising standard of living and growth of luxury, until in the late republican period the supply and demand had reached almost the same proportions as in the time of the empire.

Even in the early republican period the Romans had to come to terms (in the cultural field) with their neighbours: with the Greeks in lower Italy and with the Etruscans, whose cults, art, and way of life were beginning to have an influence on the old traditional Roman style. After the takeover of the Etruscan city-states, more and more elements of Etruscan culture filtered into Rome. After the conquest of the greater Greek cities in lower Italy in the 3rd century B.C. Greek luxury infiltrated Rome although it was at first passionately rejected by the representatives of the austere old-Roman life style. When the Greek motherland finally fell into Roman hands in the 2nd century B.C., Greek influence in the visual arts knew no barriers, and Hellenistic jewellery became fashionable everywhere. In the early empire period Horace (65–8 B.C.) looked back on this earlier period and wrote: "Hellas, conquered in battle, was victorious over the wild conquerors, and brought the arts to the peasants of Latium". At this time the leading schools of philosophy were still in Athens, and Horace was one of the numerous distinguished youths who were sent abroad to study Greek philosophy and poetry. On the other hand, leading representatives of science and the arts came directly to Rome along with an army of skilled artists from Greece and the eastern Greek provinces. They proceeded to exercise a great influence on the style and techniques of the Roman art and crafts until well into the empire period: until the 2nd century B.C. They were given many commissions to work on using the gold from the generous war-booty and from the mines in the conquered lands.

There are various telling anecdotes which stem from

this time, and which show us how the traditional old Roman ideas on virtue were determinately held on to, and how the infiltration of a less austere way of life, a love of jewellery, and a need to adorn oneself were resisted. In particular, that memorable day in 192 B.C., when women beseiged the Capitol in Rome and even addressed their menfolk, i.e. the consuls and praetors, has gone down in history. (Titus Livius: Roman history, chapter 34). The women achieved the annulment of the Oppic Law which was passed in 215 B.C. during the second Punic War (218–201 B.C.) and decreed that "women should therefore not adorn themselves with gold, precious stones, or flowers in their robes, but should display instead modesty, respect for their husbands, love for their children and our existing laws; should show their pride in our weapons, victories and triumphs". In the meantime, however, victory had long since been achieved, prosperity grown, and since 214 B.C. Spain, a wealthy source of gold, had been under Roman rule; thus the law had become expendable from the material point of view. The politically moralizing tone used in the consequent debate in the senate, (in keeping with Roman Law, only attended by men) to discuss the right to satisfy the demands of female vanity is a source of amazement to the present-day onlooker. In connection with this, the famous conservative consul Cato gave a general warning on women: "What will they demand when they have rebelled against everything, one thing after the other? As soon as they begin to be your equals, they will be your superiors!" In reply the tribune Valerian, who stood up for women's rights, is supposed to have declared: "If you cannot bear to see the women in jewellery, and would like to do something great and worthy of a philosopher, then go and cut off their hair, give them a petticoat and a mantle, arm them, and put them with God's blessing on horseback and lead them, if you like, to Spain". The senate granted women the right to wear jewellery and fancy robes: gold wire could now be used without any restrictions for weaving and for embroidery. The members of the aristocracy could now, and indeed did so without shame, dress to distinguish themselves from the other members of the female sex who were of less noble origin. On the other hand, the ideal of the virtuous wife, whose real "pearls" were her children, husband and fatherland, still held weight in the most distinguished circles of the old nobility, and was embodied in Livia, the wife of Augustus, at the beginning of the empire. From the republican period the shining example of Cornelia, Mother of the Gracci, is held up through the centuries before Livia's time. She, the wife of a consul who was in office in 177 and 163 B.C., was asked by another Roman woman, laden with jewellery, to show her jewels. She then proceeded to show her two sons saying they were her most valuable gems.

In the first centuries of the Republic the most important male decoration was the signet ring, and its ever-increasing value could be used as a gauge for the overall development fo Roman jewellery. At the very beginning the signet rings were made from iron and had rather a functional than decorative purpose. Envoys were given a gold ring at the expense of the state as proof of their trustworthiness on missions. The envoys could keep the rings but were not allowed to wear them, as gold rings were still used primarily as a sign of rank amongst the nobility, i.e. nobles from birth. As the war booty began to bring in more and more precious metals this regulation became more lax, and towards the end of the 3rd century B.C. gold rings were also worn by patricians and legates. The pro-consul also presented gold rings as awards for outstanding civil or military services. Later on, everyone, even a former slave, who had managed to collect a certain minimal amount of property and thus climb up the social ladder into the class of the knights, the lowest rung of the nobility, had the right to wear a gold ring. In keeping with an old tradition the emperor wore an iron ring. Married couples also exchanged plain iron rings to symbolize the purity of their feelings. Slaves were forbidden to wear gold-rings, and they thus preferred the gold-plated iron ring, which was known as the Samothracian ring. Towards the end of the Republic expensive gem rings cut by Greek master-craftsmen were worn, the favourite stone being sardonyx. The luxury of the early stage of the empire brought with it another innovations; namely the compact signet ring made completely from one of the stones which were valuable at that time—mainly from chalcedony, but ivory, jet, and amber were also used. During this period rich men and women would cover every finger, except the middle finger with expensive or not so expensive gems.

The *bulla*, the amulet capsule, originally worn on a string, but later worn as a pendant on chain necklaces or bracelets by men, women, and children was undoubtedly of Etruscan origin. It was worn in the more traditional families until the time of the empire.

A typical Roman decorative award was the bracelet, usually made from silver and sometimes called *armillae* or *dextralia*. These were given as rewards to soldiers. One soldier by the name of Licinius Dentatus boasts of having 16 such awards. Another sign of distinction were chain necklaces, which hung right down over the chest. Torques had the same function in the empire period. These chokers, with an opening at the front, had probably been taken over from the Celts.

At the beginning of the empire period the Roman women often wore long decorative hairpins, and later sometimes a hair net made from gold thread. Fibulae made from both valuable and baser material had always been available, but in keeping with Roman dress, had never been of any great significance. On the other hand, bracelets were abundant and were worn according to the fashion of the day, either on the upper or lower arm. Their forms—snake-like spirals with green stones for eyes, hollow rings with animal heads as terminals—kept their hellenistic affinities for the longest period of time.

Chain necklaces were often made from a wide network of coloured stones set in almost invisible gold mounts (one necklace from Pompeii was made from alternating emeralds and mother-of-pearl). Other chains took the form of collars with a combination of numerous pendants. From the middle of the 2nd century A.D. onwards coins were used increasingly for decorative purposes. They were worn as pendants, often held in a gold frame of open filigree work, or they were taken fresh from the mint, joined together to make whole chains, and complemented by the favourite stones of that time: emeralds, opals, and beryls.

The earrings worn in the early empire period were a variation of the familiar Hellenistic grape-form: they were often made from garnets (later emeralds) combined with the equally highly valued sea pearls, or from amethysts or plasma, a leaf green variety of jasper. The swelling hoop earrings, sometimes with an animal head, continued to be worn for a long time to come, while the intricate hanging earring, called *crotolia* (the rattle) also gained in popularity. It was composed of little metal rods hanging from a round hoop with little balls made from precious stones, sea pearls, or glass—depending on the financial circumstances of the wearer—attached to the lower end. In the 3rd century A.D. it became customary to decorate the upper transverse band, which held the pendants, with ornamental vine tendrils. In contemporary literature the Roman women wore earrings which "tinkled like bells" (Pliny), or they were seen as "fools, who thought they were not torturing their husbands enough, if they did not have two or three inheritances' worth of earrings dangling from each ear." (Seneca).

It is worth mentioning that real pearls, which were usually used for ear jewellery, originally reached Rome in the form of war booty, but later the bulk of them was transported over a dangerous trade route from the coasts of southern India, Ceylon, and the Persian Gulf, and sold for fantastic prices. Towards the end of the Republic, Caesar is supposed to have presented Brutus' mother, whom he treasured above all else, with a single pearl worth six million sesterces. Not until the conquest of Alexandria in 30 B.C. were pearls available in Rome in greater quantities, and used for jewellery. Pliny reports that Lollia Paulina, one of Emperor Caligula's wives, was seen at a festival wearing pearls and emeralds; her hair, ears, neck, and fingers covered in jewellery; and carrying with her all the necessary documents to prove that all her finery was worth a total of forty million sesterces. Men as well seem to have fallen under the spell of the pearl: Nero (37–68 A.D.) is alleged to have possessed a bed decorated with pearls, Caligula even had pearl-embroidered slippers, and the son of a rich actor opened up a pearl, as Cleopatra had done in Caesar's time, drank the liquid and claimed that "he found the taste extraordinarily pleasing". These articles were, however, by no means the norm: they were, on the contrary, considered great exceptions.

The materials used for the jewellery of the less well-off were still primarily glass, then coral and later on amber, which was originally considered valuable, but which was consequently imported from the North Sea and Baltic Sea coasts in such quantities that it no longer merited the attention of the rich. Imitations of precious stones were also a cheap alternative for the less well-off. Glass pastes often made the prettiest of gem imitations, even if they served to fatten the wallets of dishonest business men. Pliny was of the opinion that of all dishonest activities the imitation of precious stones was the most profitable, and told how colourless crystal could be turned into imitation emeralds, carnelian into sardonyx. Alabaster pearls looked almost real when covered with a coating of silver lacquer.

A high percentage of the population was employed in Rome's highly specialized craft sector. The bigger enterprises had a factory-like organization: under one management an article went through various specialized departments before its completion. In the jewellery sector modellers, casters, polishers, gilders, and chisellers were employed, as well as other skilled workers. Even for more sophisticated jewellery which was usually executed by individuals there were still specialists for pearl-work, and precious-stone carving and polishing. We have evidence that guild-like organizations existed, for example, amongst gold and silver workers, ring makers, gold beaters, and gilders. The division of labour demanded that craftsmen specializing in one skill live close next to each other, and thus they congregated in streets or small colonies or even occupied a whole town quarter.

Over half of those employed in the crafts were slaves, and only a few of them managed to become really skilled or to gain any prestige. On the tombstone of one slave it is said of the deceased that "he was proficient in making necklaces and mounting bright sparkling stones in embossed gold". Another had the following homily written on his tombstone: "He was always surrounded by large amounts of gold and silver, but he never allowed himself to lust after it."

The preference for new production techniques did much to contribute to the development of an independent Roman style of jewellery in the late antiquity. A clear break between hellenistic and classical jewellery was made particularly in the use of colour; through the liberal use of *cloisonné* work, and also with the so-called *opus interrasile*, openwork done in sheet metal (a filigree-type of pattern was fashioned with a chisel). This decorative technique was used for bracelets, necklaces, and especially for mounted medallions, the medallion becoming more and more important in the jewellery of late antiquity. An irregular arrangement of various stones on a very narrow mount or without any mount at all was also characteristic of the polychromy of this period; the stone was held by a pin pierced through it. On the other hand, a wide ribbed mount was also used for single stones. In the 4th century A.D. the *opus nigellum*, or the niello technique, was reintroduced. This process involved preparing grooves in the metal and filling them with pulverized silver sulfide, which was, depending on the mixture, either dark grey or black. The patterns thus achieved stood out very effectively against the shiny metal. The niello technique, like the many-coloured champlevé technique, retained its popularity until well into the Byzantine period. The Byzantines also took over the luxurious oriental pearl which was most common in the jewellery of late antiquity, and as far as can be judged from the remains of this period, it must indeed have been a very great luxury. Particularly highly valued were compositions of identical pearls, either arranged on strings or on ear plugs.

Many of the diverse techniques and traditions of Roman jewellery turned up again in Byzantine workshops, however, the western Roman cameo-cutting disappeared from the scene after the division of the empire under Theodiosius I at the end of the 4th century A.D. The magnificent cameos of the empire period were the most outstanding products to emerge for centuries.

The art of elevated relief work had first blossomed under the Ptolemies during the Hellenistic period, but it reached its zenith at the beginning of the Roman Empire. Cameo portraits as well as pictures in relief work showed scenes from legends, cults, and everyday life. The Roman state-cameos, usually made from several strata of sardonyx, had symbolic figures and portraits of emperors worked into them by using the many-coloured layers. There is a whole series of magnificent examples of these cameos, starting with the *Gemma Augustea* in Vienna and finishing with the *Theodosius-Cameo* in Trier, from Augustus, the first Roman Emperor, to Theodosius, the last of the overall rulers in late antiquity: his reign saw the first signs of the development of the eastern Empire of Byzantium.

INDIA

The Indus-Valley, or the Harappa Culture (named after the site of the first finds) flourished over a relatively large territory: it spread over the land bordering the River Indus—i.e. all of present-day Pakistan, and large parts of other countries in this area. The beginnings of this culture can be traced back to the 4th millennium B.C., but it first flourished in the 3rd millennium B.C., and in the middle of the 2nd millennium B.C. it suffered terrible destruction, either as a result of a natural catastrophe, or of a war: there is, as yet, no definite explanation for the destruction.

Excavations were first carried out in the 1920s by British archaeological teams, which were later joined by Indian ones (J. Marshall, E. Mackay, M.S. Vats, D.R. Sohni, and others), and which have produced evidence of an uninterrupted history. The towns, which were based on agriculture, trade, and the crafts, were probably united in the 3rd millennium B.C. into one centrally-ruled empire, which was administered from two capital cities: Mohenjo Daro ("Place of the Dead") in Sind, and Harappa in the Punjab district. The excavations have brought to light the excellent lay-out and planning of these towns, which are unsurpassed in the cultures of this period.

Tools were found in special town quarters for craftsmen, mainly made from copper, but some from stone. Raw materials and finished goods belonging to the gold and copper smiths were also uncovered, as were those of the bead makers.

The bead makers formed an important contingent amongst the craftsmen. Their skill and long tradition which dated from Neolithic times, was now mastered to the level of virtuosity, and led to the production of little works of art made from semi-precious stones and terracotta. With the help of sophisticated chemical-technical processes the beads were given brilliancy, colour, and decoration.

The craftsmen knew how to cut stones in accordance with their organic structure, so that they were shown to their best advantage. They also filed and polished relatively hard stones such as nephrite and quartz. The brown-red colour of carnelian was heated until it became bright red. They heated crystal with soda and copper added to it, until certain temperatures were reached, and their surface began to shine and to take on a shimmering turquoise-blue colour. Tiny, pierced, and glazed beads for necklaces were made from soap stone. Here—as well as in Mesopotamia—the first articles and beads made from faience with a lead glaze were found. The bead makers of the Indus valley were possibly the inventors of the attractive etching-pattern found on numerous carnelian beads from north-west India, such as were also found in ones and twos in Troy and on the site of Ur. The white, mainly geometric motifs were formed by using a chemical process involving alkalines. The stones were finally heated in red-hot coal so that the pattern was left imprinted.

Beads from the Indus valley, which probably developed into a production centre, travelled far afield, considering the traffic communications at that time. There were probably routes along the coastline, over the Persian Gulf, or over land through Baluchistan and southern Iran to Mesopotamia. Stone beads, however, did not only have a decorative purpose, but were also obviously used, due to their beauty and the ease with which they could be handled, as a kind of currency in commercial dealings (the coin had not yet been invented).

Some engraved gems, used as seals, were worn in the

Indus valley as pendants or amulets, and were undoubtedly of Mesopotamian origin, while others, excavated in what was formerly Elam and Ur, came from the Indus valley.

Research into India's early history is still, relatively speaking, in its early stages. Information on the jewellery customs of this period is relatively hard to get hold of since no burial grounds have been found within the area covered by the Indus valley culture—until recently the Indians cremated their dead. Apart from workshops which have been pieced together by archaeologists, Indian sculpture—although stylistically full of contradictions—has offered us some material to work on.

The steatite bust of a bearded man, perhaps a priest-prince in the 3rd millennium B.C., shows that he wore as jewellery a flat headband with a central circular-shaped ornament over the forehead, and a similar ornament on his upper arm (armrings were a sign of royalty in the ancient Orient). It seems feasible that this jewellery was executed in a similar way to the contemporary sheet-gold work in Mesopotamia and Egypt. A stylistically completely different bronze figure shows a dancer wearing a choker with a three-part pendant as well as numerous bracelets. Similar examples have also been found in the original, as have gold beads, composed of two half-beads soldered together; gold discs with a hollow tube soldered onto them so that a string could be inserted, such as were also worn in Mesopotamia. Large numbers of rings made from gold, silver, or copper wire were obviously made in the Indus valley, and worn either as bracelets, finger or earrings. Jewellery which hung from a string was worn round the neck, wrist, ankle, or on the ears and fingers, and often combined with semi-precious stones; jade, jasper, carnelian, agate, and amethyst being the favourites.

The varying value of the jewels, and also their varying artistic qualities, would lead one to suppose that there were very definite class differentiations. The upper class could choose from selected pearls, necklaces, chest plates made from gold and semi-precious stones—often made from valuable material imported from abroad—whereas the ordinary people had to content themselves with amulets, bracelets, and strings of clay-beads.

Peculiar to the Indian mentality is the stubbornness with which they have hung on to some of the specifically Indian types of jewellery dating from the distant past, and still wear them, without any modification, to this day. Examples of these specifically Indian pieces of jewellery are the cone-shaped headdresses, made from gold, silver, copper, or faience (these are attached to the hair by loops inside them), and chains of tiny black beads alternating with gold-work, such as were found in Mohenjo Daro and which are still worn today in this area (the chains are worn at wedding ceremonies). The ancient Indian chain belt, which went out of fashion 700–800 years ago, is also to be seen on a terracotta figure found in the Indus valley. It is composed of six strings of carnelian beads alternating with metalwork. At the terminals of the belt there are round and triangular plaques made from copper, gold, soap stone, and coloured clay.

The area around the lower stretches of the Indus has been desert since the time of Alexander's Indian campaign (end of the 4th century B.C.), as a result of some change in the climate. However for thousands of years before recorded history this area was covered in forest and swamps, and inhabited by elephants, rhinoceroses, and tigers. These animals, along with the main motif, the bull, are therefore often represented on seals and in ornamental art.

The relatively simple ornamental forms used in the Indus valley were later to become a source on which the rich diversity of genuine Indian fairy-tale-like decorative forms was to draw on.

India's culture was not restricted to the western part of the subcontinent, but spread over a wide radius, covering all the surrounding territories: Sri Lanka, Burma, Thailand, Cambodia, Vietnam, parts of Indonesia, Nepal, Tibet—all fell to a greater or lesser degree under India's influence.

The effects of an extraordinarily stable slave-owner and feudal system in the core of the country on the extremely varied Indian arts and crafts were interesting. Unmistakable features of a primitive culture could be kept alive for a long time because of the unparalleled respect for tradition. Thus new impulses which came with every new epoch served to enrichen art, but the old traditions still remained unchanged. The characteristically Indian caste-system made no small contribution to this state of affairs.

Until well into the 18th and 19th centuries there was a clear division between the extremely refined court culture in the towns, the seats of the ruling dynasty at this time, and of its aiders and abetters, and the old Indian village community, where the inhabitants were employed solely in agriculture and in the crafts. The crafts were likewise split in two: as a result of a more rapid development of the productive forces, a clear specialization process took place in the towns, whereas in the country the universal craftsman produced amazingly sophisticated work with relatively simple tools.

The old folk epics, myths, religious and philosophical lessons which have been handed down from early history —from the 2nd millennium B.C.—have been embellished and exaggerated over the years, and have the most longterm influence on all of the cultural spheres right up to the present day. Brahmanism with its ideas on mysticism and migration of the soul, as well as Buddhism with its theory of continuous change, and the Noble Eightfold Path to redemption, had a considerable influence on the decorative motifs and ornamentation and made a contribution to the abundant wealth of Indian forms.

At about the beginning of the 3rd century A.D. the transition from a pre-feudalistic social structure to feudalism began to take place in India. The era of the Gupta-Dynasty (320–about 500) with its seat in Pataliputra is considered the classical age of Indian culture, a time when art and science blossomed. After the Gupta period Brahmanism and the caste system advocated by it gained in strength. After the growing stagnation in the post-Gupta period the confrontation with Islamic art after the conquest of northern India by the Moslems (11th–14th centuries), came as a

breath of new life for the Indian crafts, and had a longterm influence on them. New impulses from central and western Asia, which were especially strong during the Mogul period (1526–1858), were also successfully and imaginatively assimilated into the Indian forms already in use.

"India, the treasure trove", with its "rivers full of precious stones", as Pliny described it, has indeed been renowned since ancient times to be a land overflowing with precious metals, pearls, and minerals. The pearls found in the waters between southern India and Sri Lanka were transported by merchants from Phoenicia and Babylon to the Mediterranean area. Amongst the oldest finds in India are fragments of jewellery made from alabaster, chalcedony, carnelian, agate, onyx, steatite, and amethyst, minerals, whose value was equal to that of precious stones. All diamonds in antiquity came from the river beds of India, as did the rubies, emeralds, and sapphires. According to ancient accounts, even Emperor Nero used an eye-glass made from an Indian emerald to watch the gladiator fights. In some areas of India precious stones can still be found, such as the area around Broach in West India where agate is found, Punjab, where serpentine is found, and Gujarat, where amazonite is found. Turquoise, onyx, and rock crystal are found all over the country. Recently jade from central Asia, lapis lazuli from Afghanistan, rubies from Burma, Thailand, and Sri Lanka have found their way over trade routes first to India, then further westwards.

The wealth of valuable metals and minerals, as well as the love for decorative ornaments, which often show affinities to the country's prolific tropical vegetation, were probably the main contributing factors to the tendency of both men and women, rich and poor, to adorn themselves from tip to toe with colourful jewellery, as had been the case from early historical times. Until recently jewellery was also still looked upon as an investment, a bank account for the wealthy, and the goldsmith often played the role of the banker. As early as 300 B.C. Megasthenes who as Bactrian envoy stayed at the court of Magadha in the time of Chandragupta, expressed his astonishment at the great discrepancy between the elaborate jewellery and the simple life-style in India, a contradiction which even today is seen nowhere as crassly as in India.

One of the commandments of Indian religions is to cremate one's dead and not to give funerary gifts. This has meant that only a few original pieces of jewellery more than 250 years old have survived, however, Indian pictorial art and passages from old Indian literature help to fill in a few of the gaps. Comparisons with the jewellery forms and production techniques used by modern masters are also helpful. The vast variety of Indian crafts, resulting from the various social, religious, and ethnic influences, has led to an enormous amount of different jewellery forms, only a small number of which can be examined here.

The poet and scholar Kalidasa (*c.* 600 A.D.) has provided us not only with records of this period, which are valuable from the point of view of the history of civiliztaion, but also with some clues as to the ornaments of this time, most of which are still known under the same name today. He mentions a headdress called a *cirdamani*, made of precious stones; the *muktajali* was a hairnet made from precious stones and pearls, which, as is shown by contemporary art, was placed over flattered and parted hair; *kirta* was the name given to a tiara for kings; *mani-kundala* was ear jewellery made from rubies; chokers made from coins were called *niska*, and a string of beads in a certain form was called *muktavali*. Even today most of the pieces of jewellery in India are named after flowers. Some pieces of jewellery are worn by the more tradition-conscious Indian women only on certain occasions and on a specific part of the head or body: there are particular forms of jewellery to hold one's hair together, earrings are differentiated according to form and material, and for nose ornaments there are special rules as to whether they may be worn singly or in pairs. There are similar rules for most kinds of jewellery; whether it is to be worn on head, forehead, ear, nose, around the neck, or round the waist, ankle, finger or toe.

Armrings worn round the upper arm, in ancient times the prerogative of royalty, were later worn by everyone, but especially by men. In some regions, especially in the south of India, it is still usual for the bride to be given a choker, called a *thali* on her wedding day: this she wears until her husband dies. However, nowadays it is often sufficient to exchange wreaths of flowers. In the northern parts of the country every married Hindu woman is obliged to wear a toe ring and a glass bracelet. A nose ring seems to be obligatory for Hindus, and for some Muslims, and should preferably be worn at weddings (in Punjab and Gujarat ivory rings are most popular). In Bengal women are obliged by their religion to wear an iron ring round their ankle. *Kingini* is the name given to a chain of hollow gold beads with metal granules inside them. These were supposed to protect children from evil spirits, and probably also helped to keep an eye on them. The Hindu middle classes still wear gold jewellery with religious symbols as a kind of talisman. Apart from these symbolic ornaments there is also a vast number of ornaments with a purely decorative function, or whose original symbolic meaning has long been forgotten.

Another must for women, from ancient to modern times, but today only in the country, has always been ankle jewellery in the form of ornamental metal rings, some with pendants or little bells, and some hollow with little balls inside which rattle with every movement. In the first centuries of recorded time (around the middle of the 3rd century) massive rings, sometimes two or three on top of each other, were worn not only by members of the upper class, who enjoyed a life of leisure, but also by serving girls, who had to carry baskets from the market, as well as wear these heavy ornaments. From the 5th century onwards ankle rings were given a slightly curved form which followed the shape of the foot, and in later times they were sometimes worn singly, sometimes in pairs; some were decorated with a jewelled buckle, some with chain network and medallions which linked the ankle ring with toe rings.

The sensual power and cultured beauty which emanate from the old Indian sculptures and paintings, are also present almost without exception in the delicately modelled representations of jewellery. If one is to judge from these works of art, neither men nor women wore any clothing above the waist, right up to the arrival of the Muslims: it seems that seductive jewellery was all that was worn. The female figures especially, naked, yet sophisticatedly and generously decorated with jewellery which served to emphasize their waist lines, suggest certain affinities (in spite of a visible refinement) to the mother cult and fertility cult of past primitive communities. In fact, matriarchal customs were preserved longer in India than in any other country and came into conflict with the patriarchal-inclined town cultures, which began to develop in the 1st millennium B.C. The feminine element was dominant in all jewellery with an erotic slant, even in men's jewellery, which was apparently quite common. As in the case of stone-age idols, the belt, above all, had an erotic function: The old Indian chain belt had been fashioned in the time of the Indus-valley culture, but in the course of its long history it was given various new forms and decorations. During the Maurya period (c. 322–185 B.C.) it was composed of several rows of chains, which were joined under the navel by a clasp or plaque. The figures of the tree goddesses (courtesans?) on the pillars of the Stupa of Bhutesar (2nd century A.D.) wear wide open-work hip belts, decorated with floral motifs, which look like skirts they have grown out of. In following epochs the decorations were of more or less intricate character and took the form of strings of rosettes, square or round sections, chains alternating with heart-shaped or oval plaques, bells, and pendants hanging from a large clasp.

In the second half of the 10th century, in late Hindu art, elements of decadence become obvious in the way ornamentation is overdone: jewelled pendants intermingled with innumerable long loops and tassels dangle from arrangements of numerous chains, and often reach right down to the middle of the thigh. Not until the time of Mogul rule was the chain belt gradually replaced, in accordance with a change in dress style, by the Mogul sash. The pendants, however, remained in use, one of them being the *dekhani* box, a little rectangular box made from bronze, and decorated with little chains, filigree discs, and leaf-shaped ornaments. Men wore belts with long cord tassels, bells, and metal balls as a counterbalance for their knives and daggers.

There were slight changes in the jewellery customs after the Mohammedan invasion in the 13th century, when women began to wear tight corsets, and neck and chest-jewellery was no longer worn next to the skin, but on top of their clothing. This tendency became even more noticeable in the Mogul period. New cultural influences came from the north, from the home of the equestrian peoples, mainly from Persia and Turkistan. Men and women wore jodhpurs, riding cloaks, and overcoats. The robes were buttoned up to the neck (by no means comfortable in India's hot climate), and this meant that jewellery, apart from finger-rings, was worn on top of one's clothing, usually on turbans or shoes. Only a modest amount of jewellery was now worn, however, upper class jewellery consisted of highly expensive, often giant-sized precious stones, as well as numerous strings of beads.

The precious stones were not, however, as they were in Europe, cut using faceting, but were always cut *en cabochon*. This made them less luminous, but on the other hand heightened the colour effect, making the colours stronger and more harmonious.

The strong ties to nature found their clearest expression in the ornamental forms of Indian jewellery. The oldest motifs, which were used especially for ritual jewellery over thousands of years, show a spiritual relationship to the cultures of western Asia, with elements from Sumeria, Assyria, Mycenae, and the Hittite Empire: lions, bulls, and half-human, half-animal figures predominated. The peacock, originally used for the coat of arms of the Maurya rulers, remained a favourite, along with other bird species and innumerable floral elements. The lotos blossom, an ancient symbol for life-giving water, was even mentioned in Brahman poetry as a simile for the redeemed soul, which rises out of muddy depths towards the light. The lotos blossom was the most widely used decorative motif which was supposed to bring luck, until it was replaced by Islamic decorative motifs. However, it never completely disappeared from the scene. External influences are to be found mainly in the new ornamental motifs, which were, however, always creatively incorporated into the range of traditional forms. Some of the finds from Taxila, a town in the north-west of India, which blossomed in the 1st century A.D., show certain Hellenistic affinities. They include many-tiered necklaces made from gold beads, delicately plaited links and medallions, on whose surface Indian elephants or peacocks in gold embossed work are depicted strolling between flowers; earrings and other chain necklaces are overloaded with stones, gold ornaments, and bead pendants, in keeping with the indigenous taste. Hellenistic stylistic elements went through an extremely original synthesis with the Indian decorative forms, but lost their influence after the disintegration of the ancient world and did not leave a deep impression on the traditional Indian decorative arts.

The deepest inroad into Indian ornamental art was made after India's confrontation with the Islamic world. Since the 11th century the Mohammedans had conquered large parts of northern and central India. The attempt to force the Islamic culture on the Indians was unsuccessful. However, India's culture had begun to stagnate under Brahmanism, and now, the crafts in particular were given new impulses in both technique and style, which have retained their influence up to this day. The slightly degenerate, delicate motifs of the late Hindu period were happily combined with Islamic designs which had strong luminous colours, and with them impulses from Persia, which had already been converted to the Islamic religion, were also assimilated. Stylized animal representations in Persian style were very popular, since human representations were forbidden by the Islamic religion. The bracelets from this period are decorated at both terminals with lion or elephant heads and the flat hair ornaments have a peacock's head over the forehead. A particular favourite was the combination of a star and a crescent moon. This combination had in fact been used in India before, but never to the same extent as now.

Persian taste also left its mark during the Mogul period, and had a considerable influence on miniature painting, as well as on the carpet-like intricate decorative styles used in metal and stonework, with delicate leaves, tendrils, flowers, and the tree of life. One of the Mogul jewellers' specialities was the incrustation of precious stones on a gold-backing: they fashioned subtle floral patterns with jade stalks and flowers made from garnets, rubies, and diamonds. These were used as decoration for dagger hilts medallions and brooches, which were used not so much to display the brilliancy of prize jewels, but rather the grace of exquisite jewellery.

The gold-enamel work of the Mogul period is also famous. Champlevé was the technique used most frequently, usually in shades of green or red. The less expensive silver enamel was used mainly for blue and green ornamentation. Even the reverse sides of jewellery were decorated with delicate flower, bird, and plant-motifs or with religious symbols done in carefully executed enamel work. In Jaipur the tradition of gold, silver and copper enamelling has been continued until this day.

The Indian arts and crafts reached a technical and artistic climax under the Mogul rule, with its luxurious, representation-conscious court. Skilled jewellers enjoyed great prestige, and were not only well paid, but also received food and board. That respect was paid to their skill is seen in the fact that the Moguls Akbar (1542–1605) and Jehangir (1605–1628) were accustomed to visiting their jewellers' workshops in person.

Buddhist legends report that even prior to and during Buddha's life (c. 550–480 B.C.) the crafts were organized into 18 guilds. Because of the rapid development in the towns specialization within the crafts took place relatively early, and was supported by the fastidious demands of the court. However, in the country the craftsmen had, as a rule, always been a caster, engraver, chiseller, enameller and stone-mounter all in one. On top of this he even today often makes his own tools. His implements consist of a blow-pipe, an anvil, files, a hammer, chisels, and engraving needles. His products are in the most cases more the result of his skill and patience than the products of his tools. Nevertheless, at the beginning of recorded history there was already a highly developed tradition in the most important precious metalwork techniques embossing, niello, filigree, the lost-wax process, enamelling, and various ornamental techniques.

According to legend, the crafts were originated by Vishkavarma, "the master of the many arts, master of the 1,000 crafts, carpenter of the gods, architect of their heavenly palaces, designer of all jewels, who invented all ornaments, the first of all craftsmen". Every member of the old Indian village community, the centre of the traditional crafts, remained true to this their religious assignment, and held on to the old techniques and ornamental forms which had been passed down to them. The techniques and forms themselves were never the main consideration but were rather subordinate to mythical-social considerations, and to legal rulings such as rulings on the criteria for good and bad work, on illegal possession etc., which were laid down in the law book of the *Manu*. Various foreign influences have already been mentioned, but for thousands of years these were successfully integrated into the prevailing techniques and motifs: hardly any direct changes ever took place because of them. This stability was supported by the rigid caste system, which meant that the son was strictly bound to the profession and caste of his father. Only the members of one caste would live within one village. In the eyes of the Hindu, craftsmen and artists were engaged in "baser" work, only their products were recognized to have social value; the creators had none, and always remained anonymous. Many craftsmen and artists from the oldest sections of the population, wanting a better social position, gave up their profession when they became Hindus.

After the decline of the Great Mogul Empire in the 17th century there was also a crisis in the arts and crafts. However, given favourable conditions, worthwhile traditions, were preserved in the country and in some parts of North India. Despite the growth of European cultural influences, the traditional forms of jewellery—not least of all because the national arts and crafts receive state support—have managed to survive in present day independent India.

CHINA

After the unification of local tribes into small state organizations, the fertile loess plain watered by the central stretches of the Hwang Ho, the Yellow River, became the home of Chinese culture in the 3rd millennium B.C. It was later to have a lasting influence on Korea, Japan, Mongolia, and other areas of eastern Asia, and finally on Europe as well. From these small beginnings emerged the giant "Middle Kingdom" or the "Blossom of the Middle" as Chinese poets used to praise their land, content in the knowledge of its central cultural position. The kingdom expanded in all geographical directions, not by use of arms, but rather in a peaceful manner, through agricultural colonization. It did, however, suffer from attacks by neighbouring peoples, and also fell for both long and short periods under foreign rule, but it always made a rapid recovery after blows of this kind, and held on to the firm foundation of a tradition-linked culture with firm roots in the life of the people. Foreign conquerors, who chose to stay in the land, were soon converted to the Chinese way of life.

The break-up of primitive society and the formation of small states with a class structure took place in the 2nd millennium B.C. Bronze was discovered round about 1400 B.C., and bronze work reached a technical and artistic zenith about the middle of the 1st millennium B.C. Tools and ornaments dating from Neolithic times, however, continued to be used for a long time to come.

Research into China's early history is still in its initial stages. Three early dynasties are mentioned in Chinese history books: the Hsia dynasty (for which there is not yet any archaeological evidence), the Shang Ying dynasty (16th–11th centuries B.C.) and the Chou dynasty (11th century-256 B.C.). Up till 1899 the Shang Yin dynasty was thought to be more or less legendary. However, excavations in Anyang, the site of the former capital city of Yin, in 1928–1937, as well as excavations carried out in the 50s and 60s not far from this site, produced evidence of a fully developed town civilization. Research workers confirmed that in the 2nd millennium B.C. fortified towns were in existence, that carriages were driven, and that a script had been invented. There is also proof of the existence of deities and of ancestor worship, but, as yet, not detailed research on this has been carried out.

In royal graves rich funerary gifts were found next to the human remains of former rulers; these included a large number of richly ornamented bronze implements, sculpture, ceramics, and jewellery made from bone and stone, especially ornamental amulets, beads, buttons, pendants, and plaquettes made from jade. The earliest precious-metal finds in these graves, which one can put a date on, are delicate fragments of gold and silver-leaf work, which had probably been designed as inlays for various bronze objects. Since 1950, workshops, which obviously once belonged to bronze-casters, bone-carvers, and potters, have been excavated not far from these sites, in present-day Chengchow.

Gold first became the most highly valued material at a much later date, although there is evidence that it was mined in the mountains to the south-west of the kingdom, in Szechwan and Yünnan, from a relatively early stage onwards, and that it was found in rivers as well. During the first dynasties, however, jade was the most highly valued material. It was probably transported over a long trading route from Turkistan, or from Lake Baikal. Articles made from jade were placed in the graves of dead rulers, as this stone was believed to bring the soul into a harmonious relation with the cosmic forces, and to protect the body from decay. Everything holy or worthy of respect in old Chinese literature was likened to jade: the residence of the Supreme Ruler of Heaven was made from jade; his name was the "jade emperor"; the goblet which was used by the mythical Hsia kings to partake of the ritual sacrificial drink was made from jade, not from gold. In the book "An Explanation of (ancient) Symbols and an Analysis of (the complete) Chinese Characters", written by the scholar Hy Schen in about 100 A.D., the following definition is given under *jü* (jade): "Jü is the most beautiful of all stones. It is distinguished by five virtues: its luminous yet warm glow symbolizes charity; its transparency, which reveals to us the colour and vein of the stone, symbolizes honesty; the purity of sound and penetrating ring it produces when tapped symbolizes wisdom; its durability symbolizes courage, and it is hard and not easily damaged, like justice."

The hardness of jade (hardness 7–8) proved to be no obstacle to the stone cutter at the end of the Neolithic Age, nor to the stone cutter of consequent eras: they cut jade into thin slabs, filed it into round shapes, pierced holes in it, engraved it, and carved motifs in flat relief work. Their tools were made first of stone, then later of metal. It was perhaps the difficulty with which this unmalleable material was mastered which made it so valuable, and made it into a medium of the supernatural powers.

Finds from the 2nd millennium B.C. already have decoration built up in a very strict formation. The main motifs are geometric designs and animal figures. The motifs were drawn from the world of mysticism and religion, and seem to be related to the ancestor and fertility-cults. They included stylized reptiles, birds, forerunners of the dragon design, the horned *taotie* mask, and were usually set against a background of small spiral or criss-cross patterns. These early forms of ornamentation, drawn from the wealth of Neolithic motifs are characteristic for the implements and jewellery produced in the Shang Yin period. They also remained, despite later ornamental innovations, the basis of all motifs and were found in miniature art right up till the 19th century.

In the Eastern Chou dynasty (8th–3rd centuries B.C.), at the height of Taoism and Confucianism, the early phase of the Huai epoch, named after sites in the Anhwei province, gained in significance for the decorative arts. Together with early bronze mirrors, metal belt-clasps are the most common burial gifts. The belts come in various forms, but several of them have a long tongue-shaped main plaque in common, with a dragon's head as a hook. They also have a flat or concave lower half with a stud to attach them to the belt, to balance out the curved upper half.

Characteristic for the style of the Huai epoch are belt clasps with geometric stylized, animal-like ornamentation reminiscent of masks or cicadas figures. They often have fine bead-like background pattern, similar to granulation, yet not cast separately. The contrasting effect produced by a dark bronze background (sometimes iron, but few made of iron have survived), and gold and silver-inlays was, judging from the number of such finds, obviously very popular. The precious metal, usually thin strips of gold or silver, was hammered into grooves already engraved in the work. Casting was also practised, using precious metals and the lost-wax process, but it was still closely linked in technique and ornamental detail to bronze casting. Few of the ornaments made from thin gold leaf, which had been hammered out and given a relief design (worked from the reverse side), have been preserved. The relief was placed over a wooden or bronze mould and this was an early form of gilding, which was first used for belt-hooks and for small pieces of jewellery.

Amongst the various material combinations which occur in individual finds dating from the 4th and 3rd centuries B.C., and which bear evidence of a particularly high standard of craftsmanship, are a long silver belt-clasp with inlays of glass and jade, and a jade pendant, with monster-heads made from gilded bronze. Both of these were found near Guweitsun in the Honan province. Glass-inlays in bronze work were not unusual, but turquoise, jade, and malachite-incrustations were obviously preferred for gold ornaments during this period. An exception in its combination of materials and in the representation, in metal, of a mythological figure in human form, is a gold belt-hook combined with glass, with a representation of the Taoist deity Hi Wang Mu. However, it should be said that there are still many gaps in our knowledge of old Chinese goldsmith work, and that archaeological finds in this field have been few and far between.

China's transition to a decentralized, local, autarchic, feudal economic system took place during the Wei (386–549) and the T'ang dynasties. The latter witnessed a blossoming of the arts, especially of gold and silversmith work, as a result of the favourable political and economic climate.

Even at the time of the powerful Han Empire (206 B.C.–221 A.D.) carefully executed, sophisticated pieces of jewellery were produced, the decorative motifs of which—long-necked dragons, birds, cloud scrolls (slightly asymmetrical curves), cat-like figures with wings and horns, lizard-like mythical animals—seem even then to have established themselves as the basis for the peculiarly Chinese style of decoration. Some motifs, for example the lion, a pair of doves—which were worn in particular by the women of this period on long hair pins as head-jewellery—were obviously inspired by the animal-style of the steppes-nomads. Floral motifs first appear in Chinese ornamentation after the middle of the 5th century, and were obviously introduced through Persian influences. Indeed, the whole of the second half of the first millennium is characterized by an inflow of numerous foreign artistic impulses.

Out of all the numerous towns, which throbbed with activity during the T'ang period, Canton alone had 10,000 foreign inhabitants: Mohammedans, Christians, Jews. In the merchant colonies of the towns it was mainly Persians, Arabs, and Iranians who were responsible for the lively foreign trade, conducted partly via caravan routes, partly by sea connections, and which involved primarily Byzantium, India, and the Islamic Empire. After Persia had been conquered by the Mohammedans in the 7th century, a particularly large number of Persian emigrés poured into China, and it was presumably they who awakened in the Chinese their love for gold and silver work, since the art of working precious metals already had a long tradition in Persia, especially during Achaemenid period (c. 700–330 B.C.), and later under the Sasanian dynasty (226–651 A.D.).

The metropolitan atmosphere of the T'ang period, the tolerance towards foreign influences, the love of the exotic, all left their mark on the craftwork of this period. New metal techniques were used, including very delicate filigree work, sometimes even combined with granulation. New ornamental motifs, such as flowers, tendrils, types of birds, all of which had up till now been characteristic of Iranian art, were now used in the T'ang period to a much greater degree in Chinese jewellery. Other such motifs were palmettes, foliage, mythical figures, vines, lotos and acanthus heads, and stylized scrolls, usually strictly symmetrical. These new motifs were however, merely embellishments: the specific character of Chinese representation was left unscathed. All innovations were adapted to suit the Chinese taste, and were often even intermingled with old, traditional ornamental animal motifs, such as the peacock, phoenix, tiger, and dragon. This was the case with one silver-comb backing which dates from the 7th or 8th centuries: in a delicate raised decoration, stylized peacocks are depicted strolling between blossom. On one piece of hair jewellery from the Kemp collection, the largest collection of old Chinese metalwork (Ekvesund, Sweden), lotos flowers are combined with a silber dragon and two flying mandarine ducks—the Chinese symbol for married bliss—on a fine mesh of silver wire. A ring-punched background for the motifs is typical for all metalwork of this period, including jewellery.

Amongst the few pieces of jewellery which have been preserved from the T'ang period, hair ornaments seem to predominate. Their forms vary from the simple U-shaped silver hair-pin to the plaited gold-wire one, and to the precious jewel in the shape of a lotos flower, with inlays of turquoise beads. Other hair ornaments have a phoenix bird perched on a slender pin, cut in silhouette form from gold foil, and often decorated with filigree, granulation or turquoise. The phoenix, originally the emperor's emblem, was considered a lucky symbol, and was to remain an important element in China's wealth of decorative motifs. Hair ornaments with extremely intricate phoenix representation, modelled from very fine gold wire, probably date from the later phase of the Northern Sung dynasty (960–1127), when goldsmith work went through a period of great refinement. They were also decorated with kingfisher feathers. On the frescoes at Tun-huang women are depicted with elaborate hair-styles, decorated with giant fan-shaped ornaments which encircle their heads like haloes, and are obviously gold diadems combined with flowers and feathers. On the horizontally-inserted hairpins mobile pendants can be discerned. Hair jewellery was also worn by men, albeit in a more modest form.

Neck jewellery often consisted of interlocking rings which were in turn interspersed with beads and filigree ornaments, or stones cut *en cabochon*. Strings of beads or precious stones appeared later on. Chain belts with engraved gold plaquettes and jewelled inlays, and large clasps are reminiscent of similar belts of Indian origin. Bracelets, ear jewellery and ornamental combs, both expensive and inexpensive, were also very popular.

According to ancient sources, it was a magnificent display indeed when the emperor travelled through the streets of Changan. The "son of heaven" had five carriages decorated with the imperial emblems, the tiger and dragon: one each made from jade, gold, leather, expensive wood, and one with ivory-inlay. The men of his entourage were dressed in silk gowns, and carried swords with ivory or crystal hills, and wore belts with inlays of carved jade, lapis lazuli, ivory, or horn. The women apparently wore a large number of more delicate ornaments. When the royal procession had passed, there remained, apart from a cloud of perfume, valuable articles, which the ladies had lost: lapis lazuli necklaces, golden hairpins, tiny jewel-studded shoes. Contemporary literature gives an account of the luxury in the royal courts during the T'ang period: there were beds made from gilded wood, gold and silver tableware, bowls made from jade, agate, and gold, and there is nothing to suggest that these were by any means rarities. Not much, however, has survived, but in Japan, which at this time had close contacts with China, about 3,000 artifacts have survived, including jewellery. These stem from the treasury of Shōsōin in Nara, a legacy which the widow of Emperor Shōmu dedicated to the buddhist temple, Tōdaiji in 756 A.D. Amongst the treasure were fragments of a ceremonial crown as well as a mirror with the first example of *cloisonné* work in eastern Asia on its back. According to Chinese sources, this technique was first introduced into China in the 14th century. The terms *ta-shih-yao* (Arabic goods) and *gugaiguojao* (goods from the land of the demons) suggest that they were of foreign origin.

The period between the end of the T'ang dynasty and the beginning of the Ming period (1368–1644) was a time of political and economical confusion, and although there was a blossoming of the arts at this time, hardly any jewellery has survived. In fact, from the later stages of the Southern Sung dynasty (1127–1279) onwards, there seems to have been, as there was in the visual arts, a tendency to fall back on convention and tradition; a tendency which was based on the firmly established class structure of Chinese society. This meant a certain stagnation with regard to the forms of jewellery: old traditional forms were revived, and the choice of forms was narrow. This tendency took place at a time when China was increasingly shutting itself off foreign influences, and developing an unsympathetic, even disapproving attitude towards the merchants' activities, although the merchants, by opening up new foreign markets had made no small contribution to the cultural and technical development of the country. A navy expedition, organized by Dscheng He, a very influential eunuch in the imperial court, consisting of 62 ships and 27,000 men, was sent off to fetch precious stones, coral, gold, amber, rhinoceros horn, kingfisher feathers, perfume, turtle shell, and other popular luxury articles. It was consequently heavily criticized by contemporary Confucian scholars and literay figures as "vain"; they advised Dscheng that he should rather turn to tradition. The scale and significance of this expedition, which took its crew to Sumatra, Sri Lanka, Persia, as far as the African coast, received no recognition whatsoever.

Under the Ming rulers the backward-looking views became even stronger: nostalgia, especially for the "golden age" of the T'ang period, became a national pre-occupation. The backward trends in the arts were expressed in the field of jewellery through the use and refinement of old traditional techniques, and the revival and domination of old Chinese symbols. Thus a gilded silver crown, which once belonged to a princess and which was found in the Honan province is an agglomeration of lucky symbols: two dragons form a "chou", the symbol for long life: peony flowers symbolize female beauty, happiness and wealth; dragons, phoenixes, and fruit symbolize success and longevity. Head and hair jewellery of this and later periods often became, even amongst women from the middle classes, a silent, yet very expressive medium of a symbolic language. Young, marrigeable girls wore, according to their financial means, hairpins decorated with precious stones, glass pastes, or flowers, and every colour and form-combination had a certain meaning: irridescent insects, for example, made from jade were placed in the bride's wreath, and were supposed to mate in the wreath of flowers, and thus increase the seductive powers of the wearer. The heroine of a novel written in the Ming period wore the "hairpin of marriageability" for two years before she met her future husband.

An example of male jewellery with symbolic meaning is provided by the description of the hero in the novel: "The Dream of the Red Chamber", which was written about 1757 under Manchu rule: the young boy, Bao jü, a member of the noble elite, puts on his jewellery before he goes on a visit to princes. Around his neck he wears a necklace of precious jade arranged in gold mesh; attached to his silver belt, embroidered with beads he wears a fan, mythical seals, and various gold, ivory, and wood pendants, which are "impregnated and laden with the powers of Tao". One such pendant takes the form of a golden unicorn with emerald inlay. His forehead is decorated with a string of gold, and two dragon figures grasping at a bead, a thread is woven through his hair, and attached to this glisten four large beads and eight sacrificial emblems.

Amongst the relatively rare finds of Chinese jewellery number the burial gifts found in the grave of the Ming ruler Wan-Li (1563–1620) and his wives. In the autumn of 1950 their burial chamber was excavated and the burial gifts revealed. Archaeologists found Wan-Li wrapped in a long dragon robe; his hair was plaited in a pig-tail, and hairpins were used to hold his magnificent headdress in place. An iron helmet with gold inlay, a gold-plated weapon, arms, robes, and shoes, and a belt with gold and jade inlay were also found in the coffin. In the women's coffins sophisticated decorative pins were found, together with a headdress made from gold, silver, and precious stones, and other articles suggesting expensive tastes. On one pair of gold earrings a rabbit was represented in a symbolic fashion: according to Taoist legend the rabbit was supposed to grind the herbs of immortality to dust.

Solid pieces of jewellery cast in gold were still common during the Han period, but not so much later on, and in keeping with the fashion of that period, mostly took the form of belt clasps or hooks. A golden clasp with two curved S-shaped dragons, as well as a small dress-pin in the form of a gracefully shaped swan with a curved neck have been preserved. The latter, smooth and clear, without any surface decoration is a masterly example of the art of simplifying typical characteristics of the subject and managing to give an effective representation.

Gold leaf covering had been used since ancient times, and had probably always been worked in the same way: the craftsman laid the sheet gold between sheets of specially strong paper, made from the inner grain of a type of giant bamboo. The shapes were then cut out and fixed with laquer to the article in question. The Shensi province developed its own speciality: gold ornaments of the type described above were attached to the finest carefully processed sheepskins, and used as decoration for luxury dress fabrics.

Gold leaf used on metal objects was usually given an elegant design which took the form either of birds, scrolls, spirals and coiling dragons. Cicadas, the ancient symbol for the liberated soul, were also used as motifs. Besides, gold-leaf gilding, a type of hot gilding also seems to have been in use from the 2nd century B.C. onwards.

The granulation technique, which first came into more general use when China had come into contact with the Hellenistic World during the Han period—the granules had a diameter of 0.5–1 mm (in Etruria 0.14 mm), and were thus comparatively large—was also used in later years. The technique was increasingly refined and was often used in combination with filigree work. From the 14th century onwards the enamelling techniques were also mastered, *cloisonné* being the main one used, followed by champlevé and painted enamelling.

Ornaments made from "kingfisher jade" are typically Chinese: tiny pieces from the breast feathers of the rare species of kingfisher, the *feitsuei* were fixed to cell-like compartments in gold or silver ornaments. The silky, intensive blue of the feathers outshone the enamel. Kingfisher jade (this is also the name given in Europa to the most valuable kind of jade) was combined with beads, filigree work, and cut precious stones to make extravagant wedding wreaths, and was used in particular for delicate pins (figures for hair jewellery) and ornamental combs.

Even in the T'ang period there already existed in the imperial capital city, Changan—in the 8th century the biggest city in the world—apart from numerous private craft workshops, state manufacturers. A system introduced at this time to create forced labour (all craftsmen in the country had to work for a certain period of time with the state manufacturers), was designed to guarantee the production of luxury articles of high artistic quality such as brocades, carpets, textiles, coins, paper, and metalwork, which were produced partly to satisfy the demands of the court and partly for the lively foreign trade. There is evidence that private craftsmen have existed in the towns for at least 3,000 years. They also formed guilds, and lived in special town quarters. The craftsman who had no workshop of his own travelled round the country armed with simple tools, and displayed his skills at the edge of the road as he completed his wares, which he adapted to suit the taste of his customers.

There is proof that 27 model workshops situated around the palace grounds in Peking were re-equipped on the orders of Emperor K'ang-hsi in 1680—such workshops must have existed in every imperial capital. There were special departments for jade and ivory carving, and for laquer, bronze, glass work, and metal casting, as well as for *cloisonné* enamelling and goldsmith work.

It seems that since ancient times intricate handwork and skill have always been valued more highly in China than the pomp and splendour of more solid expensive materials. One is left with the impression of meticulous and detailed work, which is confusing to the eye, but never with the impression that something undecorative or crude has been created. The precision and skill of the Chinese craftsmen can also be seen in their wood, ivory, and horn carvings, and especially in their stone cutting—jade, amethyst, crystal, and other minerals—which are unparalleled in the world.

JAPAN

For centuries Japanese art and culture were influenced by their close relations with China and Korea, and only at the beginning of the 10th century did Japan manage to emancipate itself to a large degree from its Chinese and Korean models. Japan, however, never completely liberated itself from the influences of the mainland. As was the case in other eastern Asian countries, firmly established traditions, based in a stable feudal social order with the corresponding government machinery, could be upheld within Japan's art and culture over long periods of time. Until the Japanese Medieval Age culture and creative work were the prerogative of a small section of the court nobility who had a weakness for refined elegance and grace, and who got most of their spiritual and religious motivation from the teachings of Buddhism, which had reached Japan through China. From about the 10th century onwards strong impulses emanated from a militant section of the lower nobility.

The Japanese Medieval Age (which lasted from the end of the 12th century until the end of the 16th century) began with the Kamakura period (1185–1333), a period characterized by a government system run along feudalistic lines: a powerful military aristocracy engineered government policy, and gradually a complicated feudal order was established.

The arts and crafts of the Kamakura period are characterized on the one hand by attempts to keep up the fine work, grace, delicacy, and elegance of the traditional court craftwork, and on the other hand by visible tendencies towards a powerful, simplified style, which corresponded to the aspirations of the militant lower nobility, who were steadily increasing in strength. The most noteworthy progress was made in the field of metalwork. Not only the swords of the Kamakura period are generally thought to be unsurpassed in technical perfection and artistic quality; other articles (not only those with a functional purpose, but also those designed for decorative or representative purposes) were valued just as highly: the magnificent weapons which have survived, made from very fine iron plaquettes, gilded bronze, dyed leather, and expensive textiles resemble a composition of very detailed ornaments. A large number of skillfully executed sword guards have also survived, which, in comparison to later examples, had a relatively simple form during this period.

The craftwork of the Muromachi period (1333–1573) was determined by the taste and exclusive needs of the uppermost section of society within the feudal system. Another spell of intensified trading with China brought new influences on the decorative arts, which were not limited to Chinese ornamental motifs: the takeover of the tea cult was most decisive for Japan; this was practised, as was floral art, within the framework of Zen Buddhism.

In the field of metalwork, iron and bronze casting were mastered, and very fine sword decorations were produced for the warrior caste. These decorations included ornamental buttons (*menuki*) for sword pommels, as well as a small ornamental knife (*kozuka*) unsuitable for use, and an eel-like sword needle (*kôgai*). All of these were attached as decoration to the scabbard. They were mostly decorated in fine relief work, and were often made from pure gold. Finally the sword guard (*tsuba*), which was designed to protect one's hand from the blade of one's opponent had to be executed in as fine and elegant a form as possible. At the end of the Muromachi period skilled master craftsmen made fine weapons with pointed openwork, chase work, and gold inlay. These were often decorated with plant or landscape motifs.

In the middle of the Edo period (1615–1868) in the year 1639, Japan severed all her foreign contacts, and indeed introduced strict laws to forbid foreign contacts. Although these laws remained valid until 1854, they never succeeded in establishing the total isolation of Japan—there were always some loopholes. This period is characterized by a rapid growth of the towns, the appearance of giant commodity, and market centres, and an expansion of trade on a monetary basis. The town bourgeoisie played an increasingly greater role in cultural matters.

The craftsman, who had previously been in the service either of a feudal master, of the court, or of the Bhuddist monasteries, now began to produce his own goods. His prestige and wealth grew parallel to the rise in the level of education, and to the increasing need of the town bourgeoisie for luxury and entertainment.

Craft production in the early and middle stages of the Edo period experienced a great upsurge, and the rise, even in the provinces, of manufactures meant that a kind of mass production was introduced. The taste of the wealthy town bourgeoisie, their preference for expensive materials, and careful, technically perfect execution determined the prevailing style, now evident in several variations in the individual provinces. Chase work and metal, even enamel inlay were perfected to a high degree of refinement, especially on sword guards and sword decoration. Miniature-like representations of figures, plants, fish, birds, whole landscape and genre scenes appeared in these small objects. Sword decoration degenerated into a purely decorative

and representative affair, just as the activities of the Samurai, the warriors with the highest social standing, faded into the background during this period of peace.

Lacquer played an important role in the Japanese craftwork. The use of lacquer was developed after a brush with Chinese culture in the 4th century A.D. During this period of intense cultural exchange, Japanese craftsmen even went to China to study the use of lacquer there, and on the other hand craftsmen and lacquerware from China found their way to Japan.

The process used for mother-of-pearl inlay was also taken over from China, as was the engraved red and black lacquer in the 15th century. Lacquer sprinkled with metal (*maki-e*) was, however, a purely Japanese invention, and was developed during the Heian period (784–1192). Pulverized metal —mostly gold—was arranged in motifs and polished, usually on a background of black lacquer. Lacquer was originally used exclusively for Bhuddist cult objects, but was later also used for secular objects, for example for the decoration of ornamental combs, and for *inrô*, small cases with compartments for seals or medical pills, which had been carried exclusively by men since the 16th century, and which were attached by a silken cord to their belts. The *inrô* were also made from unlacquered wood and metal.

From the end of the 17th century onwards the Samurai in particular carried *inrô*: more as decoration than for any functional purpose. Particularly impressive boxes were decorated with lacquer, sprinkled with gold dust; others had a painted decoration of fine brightly coloured lacquer on a black background. Another piece of jewellery designed exclusively for men was the *netsuke*, which was indeed closely related to the *inrô*: it was used to attach the *inrô* or, in the case of merchants, to attach the tobacco pouch or writing box to the sash of the kimono. *Netsuke* are toggle or button-like ornaments only a few centimeters in length, and some have been found dating back to about 1700. They reached the height of their popularity, however, about 1800. They were made from boxwood, ivory, horn, stone, bamboo, porcelain, or metal. Due to their extremely fine artistic execution they became a valuable collector's item far beyond the boundaries of Japan: they were masterly shaped or carved, and given the form of small lucky deities, masks, or animals. The representations were of a realistic, yet often comical-grotesque character.

Female jewellery in Japan mostly took the form of hair ornaments, and their design was for a long time determined by Chinese influences. On woodcuts from around 1710 courtesans and actors playing female roles are wearing one or two tortoise-shell combs *(kushi)* to hold up their piled-up, arch-like hairstyles. In addition, one or more hair pins *(kôgai)* were often placed in the hair. When, about 1776, the complicated *tôrôbin* (lamp) hairstyle came onto the scene, it was accompanied by some very elaborate hair ornaments. The courtesans in particular wore many such ornaments. On the *Koryûsai* woodcuts they are often depicted wearing simultaneously three tortoise-shell combs, and several pairs of hair pins. Other representations show lacquered combs with matching pins. In the works of Utamaro one can often define through the position of the comb, and the number of hairpins the social position or even the frame of mind of the courtesan: squint hair ornaments signify frivolity or drunkenness. In the first half of the 19th century hair jewellery became rather bizarre, disjointed, and over-elaborate.

In keeping with century-long traditions, fresh flowers were still used on many occasions as hair decoration. Floral designs are also the main motifs on lacquer and metal ornaments. *Ikebana*, the art of flower arranging which grew out of the custom of offering flowers to Bhudda, upholds the three levels of the floral and plant world: crysanthemums and pine blossom (which symbolizes the unchangeable) are on the top level. They were often used to decorate ornamental combs, either worked in plastic form using silver wire, or as a pattern on lacquer. Cherry blossom, fruit, or representations of fish, which were supposed to bring luck, were also common comb motifs.

30 Signet-ring with picture. East Roman Empire, 5th century.

31 Hollow gold ring with sapphire, decorated with red, white, and green *cloisonné* work on a blue background. Probably Byzantine *c.* 1000.

32 Earring. Gold with rock-crystal. Byzantine, 2nd–3rd centuries.

33 Gold earring with representation of birds in coloured champlevé work.

34 Gold disc fibula with rounded amethysts. Frankish, 7th century.

35 Crescent-shaped gold-fibula from a Vandal Prince's grave. 4th century.

36 Five-button fibula. Silver with almandine inlay. Late period of the Great Migrations. 6th century.

37 S-shaped fibula. Germanic, A.D. 450–600.

38 Merovingian belt-buckle. Gold and *cloisonné* glass.

39 Bracelet, so-called armilla. Copper gilt, opaque
champlevé. Maas area, c. 1160.

40 *Fürspan*. Gold with gold enamelling, pearls,
precious stones—probably an engagement present.
Burgundy, c. 1430–1440.

41 *Fürspan* with pair of lovers. Gold, cast, embossed,
chased, originally mounted with precious stones.
Hungary, mid-13th century.

42 Gold-enamelled, hinged pendant in form of ivy-
leaf. Northern France or Rhineland, 1294.

43 Silver pendant. Representation of a female bust in contemporary dress. Ausgburg, c. 1530.

44 Belt pendant, pipe with toiletry articles. Silver gilt. Nuremberg, c. 1530–1540.

45 Pendant, in shape of monster's head. Gold, diamonds, rubies, mother-of-pearl, enamel. The head was cast, the console embossed. German, 2nd half of 16th century.

46 Model for a bracelet, carved from wood. German, c. 1535.

47 Pendant. Carved mother-of-pearl. Early 16th century.

48 Silver pendant, with representation of Saint Sebastian. South German, c. 1500.

49 Pendant in shape of cross, silver with rose-cut diamonds. Probably French, c. 1670.

BYZANTIUM

Constantinople, the capital of the Eastern Roman empire called by its inhabitants "the queen of cities" or "the eye of the world" was a cultural centre of international significance from the 4th century until far into the 11th century. Art schools, learning, wealth, and elegant town life were all concentrated in this town. The town's status was raised in 330 by Constantine the Great when he made the former Greek colony of Byzantium on the Thracian Bosporus into the capital of the Imperium Romanum. It also expanded towards Asia Minor across the water, became the focal point of the then still undivided Roman Eastern and Western empires and was destined to become the meeting point of the Orient and Occident, a trading centre, and a centre for arts and crafts. Gold from India, precious stones, indigo, cotton, and silk from China, expensive furs from Russia, and ivory from Africa—all these flowed into Constantinople, which, together with Cairo and Baghdad, had one of the largest precious-stone markets in the world. Constantinople was also famous for its luxury goods, and its jewellers' products were highly regarded by princes throughout the whole world. Indeed the most skilled of artists and craftsmen worked within the city walls.

Although the Byzantine Empire, which became independent in 395 after the division of the Roman Empire, employed slave-labour, especially handworkers and agricultural workers, longer than the Western empire, the beginnings of feudal relations gradually became obvious in the 7th–9th centuries. In contrast to western Europe (where the integration of state power and property ownership was coupled with the feudal dependence of peasants and small producers), the feudal relations here were not based on the power of local feudal overlords. Until the 14th century Byzantium remained a centralistic monarchy, with the emperor as its sole ruler. This did not, of course, totally exclude the creation of feudal forms of property ownership, but it did limit them.

The crisis of slave ownership, which finally led in the 5th century to the fall of the Western Roman empire, also covered the Eastern empire Byzantium, but never to the same extent, as in western Europe. Commerce and handwork retained a comparatively favourable position, since the Byzantium empire, in comparison to the Western Roman empire, could defend itself from foreign aggressors, and thus the transition from the slave-owner to the feudal society took place without any violent changes or break in cultural tradition. In areas such as Asia Minor, Syria, and Egypt production was not subjected to any interruption. There was also profitable long-distance trading, as the main east-west trading routes, especially for incense and silk, passed through Byzantium. Thus the commodity market dominated, and the big property estates did not develop into autarchic economies, as happened in the west, on the contrary, they were integrated into the world of commerce. It was also impossible for the property owner in the east to use his economic power to wield political influence, and the forces of decentralization remained weaker than in the west. Apart from this, the government's power was firmly entrenched through the existence of custom duties, state monopolies, and a strong mercenary army. Thus it was possible for the ruling class of the Byzantium Empire to stave off a crisis in the slave-owner society. The transition to a new socio-economic order did not in this case go hand in hand with the destruction of the old state power—the traditions of the antique world were preserved within the organization of the state, the bureaucracy, the town-based culture and the patronage in the towns of the arts and crafts.

The emperor's government apparatus as an economic and trading force, with its many diverse impulses, especially from the Orient; the concentration of economic and political power in the towns; the continued existence of big towns as the centres of the arts and crafts, and the exaggerated cult of imperial power, aided and abetted by a centralized state church—all these factors provide the background for the style of jewellery peculiar to the Byzantium Empire.

Under Justinian I (482–565) the use of oriental ceremony was extended within the Byzantium court: all areas of court life were subject to strict rules of etiquette, all of which actually served to glorify the "apostle-like" emperor and his spouse. The stiff, gold-studded yet colourful clothing of Byzantium rulers covered in highly stylized ornaments, as well as their jewellery, correspond to the calm ceremonial and aloof picture given of Byzantine rulers in portraits.

The imperial diadem, the sign of the ruler's dignity in the time of Constantine was then still a ring of jewels, but under Justinian, as can be seen in his portrait in the mosaics at San Vitale in Ravenna, elaborate pendants were added, which hung down on both sides of the emperor's head. His spouse, Theodora, wore a magnificent ring of precious stones and beads round her head, from which several strings of beads hung right down to her chest, resembling strands of hair which had been frozen miraculously into precious jewels. Later the Byzantine crown, such as that worn by Constantine Monomachus (1042–1054) consisted of enamel plaques, made up of eight sections decorated with portraits of the emperor, but the traditional pendants hanging down at both sides were still preserved, as is shown by the diadem worn by Nicephorus III, about 1080.

The imperial insignia also included—apart from the globe and zepter decorated with a cross—a sash which was generously covered with precious stones, and a pair of shoes studded with beads and stones. The symbolic significance of the Byzantine imperial insignia can be appreciated, if we consider that the phrase "to put on the purple shoes" was synonymous with "to ascend to the throne". Thanks to the mystical powers attributed to these insignia, one only had to have them in one's possession to command respect. In this connection the story of John Tzimisces' ascent to the throne is interesting (only one of the tales from the history of Byzantine rulers, which is riddled with intrigue and bloody struggles for power). In 969 Tzimisces, an imperial officer and nephew of Nicephorus II, murdered his uncle, in order to replace him on the throne. The old emperor's guards, however, remained loyal to his memory, and refusde to accept Tzimiskes as his successor. With much cunning Tzimisces managed to get hold of the purple shoes and the ruler's insignia: he was immediately granted all the honours worthy of an emperor, and was even allowed to rule over the empire until 976.

The jewellery of the court, just like that of the emperor, became increasingly interdependent on the splendour of the robes: the voluminous fibula corresponded to the heavy gold- embroidered cloak—the emperor's was made from purple material. The fibula—usually round, and either bordered with jewels or decorated with hanging beads—was used to fasten the cloak over the right shoulder. The tablion was a strip of material used as a sign of rank: the emperor wore it in gold, and top officials in purple. Other signs of rank were necklaces, rings with ornamental coins, or metal collar jewellery for men. The cumbersome neck- and chest ornaments, from which hung drop-pearls, precious stones, or expensive tassels, probably had a purely decorative function.

The earrings, worn only by women, were often of a considerable size. The upper part was usually shaped into a smooth ring, which then merged into a crescent shape in the lower part. They were usually decorated with delicate openwork or with enamel motifs. Sometimes an openwork shell-like part was attached to the lower edge of the gold ring. Finger-rings, of an equally extravagant character, also had precious stones set in high enamel mounts. The rules of the Byzantine state church stipulated, that the man had to wear a gold engagement or wedding ring, but that the woman, as a sign her inferior position, had to wear a silver or iron one. Since the church also stipulated that the arms should be covered, arm jewellery was only worn on the wrists, in pairs, and often in the form of expensive sleeve trimmings. Despite this, bracelets with decorative coins, a left over from ancient Rome, remained common until the 7th century. Gold filigree bracelets from the mid-Byzantine period were left behind by Hungarian princesses, and can now be seen in the National Museum in Budapest.

The ornamental and figure motifs were often a synthesis of Christian symbolism and oriental form; artistically a mixture of rich subtle ornamentation with manneristic stylization. The use of Christian symbolism as a kind of picture language meant that jewellery with Christian symbolism was considered a "bringer of blessings" or a "protection from evil"; in short, it acquired the character of an amulet, and motifs of older origins were often adapted to suit the Christian faith. The cross as the symbol for redemption, was endowed with mystical powers to fight off demons. It was used not only to decorate pendants, coins, fibulae (simple and decorative), but also towered above the emperor's crown, the imperial orb. The hand or the dove symbolized the fact that God is ever-present. The tree symbolized paradise; the peacock immortality; the deer, which according to legend was victorious over the snake, was synonymous with the victory over sin.

Round medallions with representations of scenes from the life of either Christ or Mary were used to decorate bracelets and chains; for example the baptism of Christ in the River Jordan, or the Virgin and child enthroned. Slaves wore iron chokers with the monogram of Christ. The same motif was found on numerous bone, metal, and ivory-hairpins in women's graves (tightly drawn-back hairstyles were looked on as truly Christian, loose hair-styles were considered immoral). Pendants, the so-called *enkolpien* were worn attached to a band or chain under the robe, and took the form either of a medallion with a Christian symbol, or of a capsule with a little Christian relic or Bible quote in it: an ornament which was worn only by dignitaries.

Characteristic of Byzantine goldsmith work was the preference for extremely colourful effects which were achieved by the use of cell inlay work. This technique was taken over from Persia, but probably stems originally from India. It was also already practised in Egypt. Early work done in the so-called red-enamel technique was produced mainly in the 5th and 6th centuries (the first examples of this technique actually date from before the year 300), and had inlays of Indian almandines. Later red and, less frequently, green glass was used. The gold background was pierced to form decoratively arranged openwork, which was then filled with the appropriate pieces of stone or glass. Finally the whole of the reverse side was given a covering of metal. (Germanic tribes adopted this technique, and it was thus to become typical for the jewellery of the Migration period.) For less elaborate pieces of jewellery the inlay was glued into embossed cells. Ribbed or wafer-like gold or silver foil placed underneath the inlay increased the luminosity of the stone or glass. A second, more recent version of red enamelling is the *cloisonné* technique, which, judging by the descriptions given in literature and the visual arts, was used as early as the 6th century under Justinian. It was perfected in the period between 950–1050, when red enamelling lost its significance. Coloured glass paste, which was first mixed with a binding material such as honey or resin, or even water, was poured between strips of gold, soldered onto a gold base. The exquisite designs, brilliant colours and harmonious arrangements which occupy a minimum of surface area show similarities to the best of Byzantine mosaic work.

Other popular techniques, which were usually used in conjunction with cell inlay, were filigree, niello, and damascene. Although stone cutting was practised until the 11th–12th centuries, it decreased in quality. Christian representations, such as the mother of God or Christ were predominate. Much consideration was now given to the size of precious stones, and they were only shaped into round forms. The beryls were shaped from tube-like strips of metal, and so-called shell and crab collets were also known.

Enamel ornaments, jewellery with precious stones, altar pieces, and book bindings were amongst the most highly prized Byzantine products in the Middle Ages. Strict export controls, however, meant that the export of these goods was limited. Imports on the other hand were favoured by the customs regulations, especially the import of foreign luxury goods for the court and the aristocracy. The export of valuable goods was not so much guided by the principle of expanding the market for craftwork, but the export of valuable craftwork was used rather as a political lever, to exercise some influence over the rulers of the neighbouring countries. The emperors tried to dampen the neighbouring princes' desire for power by offering them valuable gifts. These princes were nibbling away at more and more of the empire for their own lands and were thus a constant threat to wealthy Byzantium. They were appeased with diadems, gold trimmed coats with valuable shoulder clasps and silk robes with the emperor's portrait embroidered in gold.

In order either to establish friendly relations with the west or to consolidate friendly relations, some valuable objects also found their way to the west, either as presents, as a New Year's gift, or later through trading: Charlemagne's body was wrapped in a purple robe from Constantinople, which was decorated with precious stones and enamel jewellery, embroidered elephants and Greek inscriptions. It was probably Byzantine craftsmen who created a helmet-like crown of silk with ribbon-like rows of beads, trimmed with gold enamel and precious stones for the German Empress Constance, (wife of Emperor Frederick II) who died in 1223. Delicate gold chains hung down at both sides, and were reminiscent of those heavier chains once worn on the diadems of Byzantine empresses.

Handwork in Byzantium was usually carried out in a small business under the direction of one master craftsman and two assistants. They worked in a so-called *ergasterion*, a combined workshop and shop. The products of these small manufacturers were designed mainly for sale in the shop, and were made with the simplest of tools. Symeon the New Theologist (who died in 1022?), a Byzantine monk, mystic, and Christian author, held the view, which is still generally accepted, that it was the master and his skill, not his tools, which were the determining factors in production. In the imperial workshops as well as in the state-provided facilities in the provincial towns a relatively large number of handworkers was found working close together, especially jewellers and silk-weavers. This probably only amounted to simple cooperation between the workers, and they presumably continued to work independent of each other. As in the west in the last stages of the slave-owner society, the Byzantine handworkers were still organized in councils. These, however, did not attain the same stability as the later guilds. They were under state supervision, and broke up in the 12th century.

Patronage from the court, the aristocracy, and the army (in peace-time the body guards wore a uniform consisting of a gold helmet, silver armour, and expensive weapons; gold chains and bracelets were also commonly used as distinctions) meant that the craftsmen and merchants were promoted to a higher social position. The members of the council even enjoyed state protection. In spite of this, state control seems to have been resented, because those craftsmen who had become wealthy gave up their trade, providing they were financially in a position to do so, bought a title—which was their legal right—and climbed up into the class of the nonhereditary nobility. In the 10th century local feudal overlords succeeded in taking over responsibility for the civil administrative regions of the country. With the extension of feudal relations in Byzantium there was a danger that the basis of the state—the tax system—would be destroyed. Impoverishment led to disasters in the empire's foreign policy at the end of the 9th and beginning of the 10th century—Constantinople, the capital of the empire, was under threat from Bulgaria under Tsar Simeon I. In 1204 the warriors of the Fourth crusade conquered Constantinople and the European parts of the empire, and founded the Latin empire, the political and economic power of which lay in the hands of western feudal lords and Venetians. Eye witnesses' reports of the sacking of the town underline once more the wealth and splendour of the dying capital Constantinople: Geoffroy de Villehardouir (*c.* 1150–1213), a French historian and chronicler, was of the opinion, that there had never been so much plundering carried out within one town since the beginning of time. He claimed that more buildings were burned down in Constantinople than there were in the three largest cities in France, and that (after the plundering) any poor man could go to Constantinopel and make his fortune. Examples of Byzantine goldsmith work have survived as gifts from looters in the churches of Italy, France, and Germany. The spread of western European dependence forms, introduced by the new rulers, incessant feudal quarrels, and the thoughtless plundering by Venetian merchants and profiteers, all led to a steady deterioration in the position of the Byzantine people, until the Turks finally conquered Constantinople in 1453 and incorporated it into the Ottoman Empire.

CELTS

By the 6th century B.C. the Celtic tribes, first mentioned by Hecataeus of Miletus about 500 B.C., had settled round the upper reaches of the Danube. The oldest relics of this people, called by the Greeks *Keltoi* and by the Romans *Galli* were found within the area covered by the Hallstatt culture (800–450 B.C.). This early Iron Age period, which already bore clear signs of an advanced stage in the decline of the primitive society, was succeeded by the Celtic La Tène culture (named after an archaeological site in Switzerland) in the 5th–1st centuries B.C., a period of great artistic flourishing.

In the 4th and 3rd centuries B.C. the Celts carried out great expansionist wars, which brought them as far as the British Isles, Spain, the North Sea, the Black Sea, and in the 2nd century B.C. to Asia Minor.

Growing mastery of iron technology as well as extensive trading helped to accelerate economic and cultural development. The prerequisites for the development of social differentiation and features of the early class society were already present. Numerous finds have shown that there were lively trading links between the Celts and the Greek city-states and Etruria. In this way gold and silver jewellery came into the hands of the Celtic aristocracy. Apart from those influences which reached and enriched the Celtic arts and crafts in this way, the craftsmen absorbed many artistic impulses from western Asia and the eastern steppes. From the mid-5th century onwards they developed their own style, and their work was produced in large quantities, in order to meet the demands of a pretentious upper class.

The Celtic crafts reached their zenith in the 4th century B.C., when the expansionist period was also at its height. During the 3rd century B.C. the Celts were forced to withdraw from their conquered territory. Changes in the production of artistic goods took place parallel to this development: a far greater number of simple, less precious jewellery has been found dating from this period, which suggests that jewellery was now produced for a mass market.

The ornamental style of the Celts is derived from very original, abstract forms, which are without doubt symbolic, and which were later to have a strong influence on the jewellery of the Germanic tribes. Typical examples of these forms are numerous variants of masks, animals, S-shaped, spiral, wavy and other motifs; palmettes, vine tendrils, flowers and fish bladder patterns were also very common.

The Celts were well-known for their wealth of gold and for their love of pomp. Diodorus, a Roman historian who lived under Caesar and Augustus, wrote of them: "Thus they collect vast amounts of gold, which is used not only for women's jewellery, but also for men's; they wear rings round their wrists and arms, massive thick gold chains around their necks, and valuable rings on their fingers; they even wear gold armour."

Finds from a later period confirm the often impressive collection of jewellery in the possession of the Celtic aristocracy. Probably the most typical piece of Celtic jewellery, although it has only been found in the graves of warriors and wealthy ladies, was the torque, a solid, bulbous choker necklace, with an opening at the front. It was made either in one solid piece, or from several parts, and its terminals were decorated in various ways. (It was modelled on similar Persian examples.) Amongst the most outstanding examples of Celtic goldsmith work number the torques dating from the end of the 4th century, such as those found at Waldalgesheim, Hunsrück. Combinations of vine tendril, spiral, palmette, lyre, fish bladder, tongue, and mask motifs are used to form intricate decorative patterns, which in their technical and artistic mastery bear witness to a mature, highly-developed style.

Fibulae were used to fasten the robes of both women and men over the chest. Women, in particular, in the so-called princes' graves had numerous fibulae; sometimes more than twenty each. Characteristic for the La Tène style of the 5th century B.C. was the mask fibula; it does, however, not seem to have been very common, which suggests that it was only worn by those with a special rank or position. More common, thus probably designed for the masses, was the so-called wire fibula.

Arm and ankle rings were also worn by both sexes. Belts, mostly composed of bronze units in the form of plaquettes, rings, squares, often with enamel inlay, were part of the wardrobe of the propertied women. The poorer women had to content themselves with simple belts, made from cloth or leather.

The materials used for jewellery also varied according to the social position of the wearer: apart from gold, bronze, iron, amber, lignite, and glass were considered valuable.

The glass jewellery of the Celts has a particular character of its own. It was only found in the graves of the wealthy, and takes the form of beads, small ring pendants, or—in the women's graves—bracelets. The bracelets come in many forms: they are often decorated with curved sculpted lines, or with knot-like bulges. It seems, that the colour blue was a particular favourite, since it occurs most frequently in deep, full tones. Transparent pieces of glass also occur relatively frequently; they have a yellow film of opaque glass melted inside them; purple glass and, less frequently, brown and green glass were also used..

Although glass had been produced even in Egypt, for a long time it was still shrouded in mystery. The processes were passed down from father to son within the handworker families. Although up till now no evidence of Celtic glass workshops has been forthcoming, it is supposed that early glass production took place as a kind of home industry in small workshops. This would also account for the great variety of forms.

The mainland Celtic culture died out in the 1st century B.C. when it was incorporated into the Roman empire; it continued to flourish, however, on the British Isles for about another 200 years.

TEUTONS

The overall term "Germanic" was used by the Celts, and later the Romans to describe all those groups of peoples who settled to the north of the rivers Danube and Rhine, and about whose way of life and organization initially very little was known. At the end of the 2nd century B.C. Germanic tribes, the Cimbri and the Teutons, reached the northern frontiers of the Roman Republic with obviously expansionist intentions. They started the war between the Germanic tribes and the Romans, which was to last for several centuries; the struggle between the matriarchal society and the slave-owner society. The culture of the Germans, which still bore the character of that of a late primitive society, changed within a few centuries to an ever greater degree, after it had come in contact with the world of late antiquity. It did not, however, become dissolved in the culture of late antiquity, but rather used it to create something new, something original, even if all artistic expression remained limited to miniature art, such as fibulae, belt-tongues, sword hilts, necklaces, bracelets, and rings.

A deterioration in climate from the middle of the 1st millennium onwards, together with a growing population and a lower level of production forces led to the migration of whole peoples within the area between the south of Sweden and the Danube, and from the Rhine to the Oder. On top of this there were also various local factors which to a greater or lesser degree heralded the fall of the primitive society. By the time Ariovistus, the warrior-king of the Suebi crossed the Rhine to advance into Gaul, the need for expansion was no longer dictated solely by the necessity of finding new land. In order to hold on to their power, the warrior-kings were forced to organize military campaigns to prove their powers of leadership, to give their followers hope of booty and land, and to raise the prestige of the leader himself.

At this time there was already a tendency to use jewellery specifically as an award of honour from the warrior-king to his faithful and brave followers. In the later Germanic epics, which are based on old Germanic tradition, the idea of "giving" was associated with the prince, it was typical for the vassals. The throne was called *gifstôl*, the hall or castle *gifheal*. In the old English heroic epic "Beowulf", which dates from 700–900 and stems from ancient folk stories, the followers are given rich warrior jewellery, which means they are committed faithful vassals. In this connection it is worth mentioning one bracelet, a *bauge* (bouc= bent), which was used as an award of honour for men right up to the 9th century; they were also exchanged during battles, or at feasts, as a sign of friendship. Princes and princesses handed them out as rewards for outstanding service: when Siegfried in the *Nibelungenlied* announced the arrival of Gunther and his bride, he was given 24 *bauge* as a reward for his services as messenger.

The confrontation with Roman economy and culture promoted and accelerated the tendency towards class differentiation within some of the Germanic tribes. Such a development was seen above all amongst the East Goths, who had left their original home in the south of Sweden about 150 B.C., and had been on the move since then, not with the intention of finding land to cultivate, but to conquer alien tribes and to exploit them. The East Goths, whose wanderings finally took them as far as the Black Sea, later played an important role as mediator between the area covered by the Pontic culture and the Germanic areas. In particular, the jewellery from the time of the Great Migrations owes its own peculiar character to this mediating role. When the East Gothic empire was stormed by the Huns in the year A.D. 375, this triggered off a new series of migrations, the Great Migrations Period.

The first Germanic artistic products were still closely tied up with influences from the Celtic area, a primitive culture with elements of an early class society. Germanic art only began to develop along its own lines in the last decades B.C. The home industry of the primitive society where production took place within a family or group was now replaced by specialist craftsmen: the goldsmith, a much sought-after specialist, used to travel through the land as a kind of wandering craftsman, and according to demand, would complete his goods on the spot. He probably also carried finished goods with him, which he would use for trade. Growing social differentiation, the development of private property, and the increasing demand for goods for representative purposes meant that patronage could be found in the courts of the aristocracy. The rich craftwork found in the graves of the nobility and princes bears witness to the perfection of the indigenous products, but also suggests that there was a strong demand for imported luxury goods. The relatively large number of funerary gifts in the graves of the craftsmen, especially of the smiths, is a sign of their high social position: their tools were their own personal property, and accompanied them to the grave. A law in the *Lex Burgundionum* also points out the prestige enjoyed by the goldsmith; this ruled that the fine *(wergeld)* to be paid for the murder of a goldsmith was up to four times higher than that for the murder of an ordinary smith. Apart from chase-work and stamp patterns which stem from the Bronze Age, the goldsmith in the first decades A.D. also used the filigree technique, which was introduced to Germanic art by the Goths, who had taken it over from that area of southern Russia which fell under Hellenistic influences. Fibulae in particular, a favourite piece of jewellery amongst the Germanic tribes, were decorated with granulated or with plaited gold and silver wire. Granulation was also used, with grape-like or pyramid-shaped granules. In the 4th century the polychrome or multi-coloured style took over from these techniques, which usually required only one colour. This polychrome style had been developed by the Gothic smiths on the Black Sea, who worked under the influence of the highly developed mixed culture, the so-called Pontic culture. Here Hellenistic art had gone through a synthesis with the art of the Scythians and Sarmatians, and some nomadic-steppe characteristics had been added. On top of these there were also influences from the Sino-Siberian area, and the Pontic art was further enriched by elements from Persia and the Roman provinces. The polychrome technique was only completely mastered in the 5th century, but this style was from then on characteristic for the period of the great migrations and for the Merovingian art of the Germanic tribes up till the beginning of the 6th century; the Lombards continued to use it for a long time to come.

Coloured stones were also typical, especially red almandines from India, as well as carnelian and amethysts. These were originally set in low cell mounts, but were later set by glazing the cells with glass pastes in various colours, the so-called *cloisonné* technique, which produced a mosaic-like effect. The precious stones, the brilliance of which was intensified by a wafer-like gold or silver-backing, were placed between narrow strips which formed certain patterns, such as stars, rosettes, hearts, or stylized plants. A process which was related in principle to this one was the niello technique: patterns were cut into pieces of cast silver, and filled with dark molten metal. For so-called damascene work, the smith hammered threads of silver or gold onto an iron backing to form the desired pattern. This process had, however, already been practised in the Bronze Age.

Animal motifs, which were later to have a prominent place in the art of the Germanic tribes, were both taken over from other cultures and passed on by the Black Sea Goths. The eagle, which was already in Persia, perhaps even in Sumeria, the symbol of supreme power, was considered by the Greeks, Romans, and later by the Germanic tribes to be the supreme deity, and is often found as a side decoration, or in the form of a fibula. These eagle-fibulae, executed in either gold or bronze, and often with inlays of precious stones, found their way to many parts of Europe after the East Goths migrated to the west. Examples were found in Italy, the south of France, and Spain, all dating from the 5th and 6th centuries. This tradition lasted until the 11th century: two eagle fibulae, part of the jewellery collection of Empress Gisela, wife of Conrad II, are the youngest known examples of this type of jewellery.

The ornamentation of the Germanic tribes consisted primarily of simple geometric elements such as dots, lines, circles, triangles, wavy lines, and star shapes. Their great symbolic value stemmed from a strong belief in supernatural powers and in the magic held within the geometric drawings. The techniques used also corresponded to the decoration. Due respect was given to the surface of the object, and the material was shaped and decorated simply according to its form: metals were thus bent, waved, and rolled into spirals. Patterns were first used later on, under the influence of the Roman craftsmen. These were originally designed for woodwork or weaving, but they were taken over—undoubtedly due to their symbolic character—for metalwork, and used for chip carving and guilloche work.

The strong links with the traditions of the primitive society were still kept up, even when the Germanic tribes (their culture was still very much that of a primitive matriarchal society) began to be confronted with the refinement, richness, and luxury of late antiquity. There was, however, no copying: their culture was enriched in the broadest sense of the word: new, highly imaginative, ornamental variants emerged, and their techniques were extended to include the granulation technique, filigree, and stone and *cloisonné* work.

Caesar, however, looking at the Germanic clothing (including their jewellery) through the eyes of a Roman claimed that their clothing was the shabbiest he had ever come across. Tacitus noted in his *Germania* that "the Gods have denied them silver and gold—is this to be taken as a favour or an act of anger? . . . the possession and use of these metals do not wield the same power over them as over us." On the other hand, however, the tribal princes during the period of the great migrations seem to have been exceptionally desirous of gold, to have been very fond of jewellery, and to have been very willing to accept presents of gold from the Romans. There were also changes in other spheres, for example that of mythology. Odin, the father of the Gods, left the straight and narrow path which he had trodden up till now as the epitomy of the faithful husband, and following the footsteps of the fathers of the Gods in antiquity, became a sort of godlike Don Juan. When, however, he decided to try his luck with the king's daughter Rindr, and his advances were rejected in true old Germanic prudish fashion by a slap in the face, Odin became, most significantly, a goldsmith, in order to adorn his victim with beautiful metal jewellery. His victim, however, was not to be blackmailed, and his artistic efforts were rewarded with a less lady-like blow, which left him lying ignominiously on the ground. A deep sense of the need for revenge forced the father of the gods to take counter measures: he beat the beautiful woman to the point of insanity, thus managed to keep her, and she, in return, gave him a son.

Frigg, the mother of the gods, was the epitomy of female strength and virtue: she followed the father of the gods in a storm as "bride of the wind", just as the Germanic women often amazed their Roman enemies by appearing at the side of their husbands on the battlefield. Frigg held the "power of the keys" and wore veils and woven skirts. Her sacred necklace, the *brisingamen*, was not designed to give her any particular feminine charm (other qualities were, of course, far more desirable), but it burst open, when the veins of the goddess swelled up in a fit of anger. Freya, on the other hand, was probably an older version of Frigg and did not correspond in the same way to the war-like ideal of the patriarchal society, she belonged to an older generation, to the matriarchal type. She knew to use her beauty to charm, to court favour with men, and how to make women fertile. Her golden chest jewellery glistened when the evening sun went down, then it was stolen by Loki, the god of fire, who hid it in the darkness of the night, until he was forced to give it back in the morning.

Whereas Germanic art was fairly unified during the first centuries A.D., after the great migrations had begun, different styles developed amongst the Goths, the Lombards in upper Italy, the Germanic tribes in the west, the Anglo-Saxons and the North Germans. Chip carving was used from the 4th until the 7th centuries particularly in those areas which were under the greatest influence of the Roman provinces; it was used, for example, by the Franks, Alemanni, Thuringians, Bavarians, and Burgundians.

In Scandinavia and on the Anglo-Saxon territory of the British Isles the so-called animal style I began to develop in the mid-6th century out of provincial Roman traditions. Fragmented animal figures with crescent-shaped lines round their eyes, and club-like joints are typical of this style. The animal style II, which was dominant until the beginning of the 8th century, was most common in the Alemannic-Franconian area. It consisted of a fusion of abstract animal designs with guilloche patterns, which produced very imaginative compositions. One of its particular features were palmette-like animal feet. The Germanic animal style continued to enjoy great and longlasting popularity, especially in the south of Norway and in Denmark, where after the mainland animal style II and guilloche ornaments had been taken over about A.D. 600, new nordic variations on the animal style II were developed, and resulted in the animal style III. These art forms remained in use in the north for a long time, and some versions of the animal ornamentation re-appeared in Viking art, which finally broke away from the general pattern of medieval art in the 11th–12th centuries.

FRANKS

From the 5th–6th centuries onwards feudal societies began to develop out of the ruins left behind by the desintegrated Roman empire. These societies first took shape in western and Central Europe, in western Asia, and in North Africa, but the whole process lasted about five centuries.

The Frankish empire, founded in 482 in the eastern part of the Roman province of Gaul, was to become the most powerful and most stable of all the German states to emerge in the later phases of the great migrations. It provided the base for the spread of feudalism, throughout Europe until the end of the 9th century. The first steps towards feudalism were already taken under the founder of the Frankish empire King Clovis (466–511): the subjugation of Gaul, the unification of all the Frank-related tribes, and the conversion of Clovis to the Catholic faith; a step which heralded the beginning of a period in civilization which put religion and the Christian church in the service of the state.

The gradual annexation of the kingdoms and duchies of the Burgundians, Alemanni, Bavarians, and Thuringians into the Frankish empire was begun by Clovis, and successfully completed by his successors. During the Merovingian dynasty (482–751) feudal relations of production and dependence were established; a process which was more or less completed during the next dynasty, the Carolingian dynasty (751–911).

Under Charlemagne (742–814) the Frankish empire reached its greatest dimensions after the conquest of the Kingdom of Lombardy in Italy and the Saxon tribal duchies. With the imperial coronation of Charlemagne, the Frankish empire became the historical successor of the Roman empire. The early feudal state, based on feudal relations, county constitutions, imperial legislation, and the granting of fiefs in return for military service, was at its most stable under Charlemagne. After the fall of the Frankish empire in the second half of the 9th century, independent feudal kingdoms began to be established in France, Germany, and Italy.

The social system which was now formed was initially economically, socially, and culturally inferior to that of late antiquity. It was characterized by centuries of inner strife with the struggle to consolidate power, and endless defensive and offensive external wars. The social structure could be simply divided into the three main groups formed by the division of labour: the peasants, the warriors, and the priests. The peasant-agricultural economy, initially run on a very primitive basis, later became the most important material basis of society. The surplus value attained was still minimal, and—apart from covering the needs of a predominantly local barter economy—was just enough to pay for the upkeep of a relatively small section of the population: the non-working feudal warriors and priests, from whose ranks the ruling feudal class was drawn. There was also a small number of handworkers and foreign merchants, who worked for the ruling class. The achievements of antique civilization—differentiated division of labour with a large number of specialized handworkers, a high level of development in learning and in the arts, the establishment of towns as the centre for trading and for intellectual and cultural exchange—had for the most part vanished. The new units of economic and social life were the village peasant communities, mostly run on a cooperative basis, and the feudal manors. In a process of oppression which went on for centuries the feudal overlords succeeded in degrading the peasants, who in the old social system of the Germanic tribes had once been free tribal members, to a class of bonded peasants obliged to pay dues and serve in their armies. They did, however, in comparison to the slaves and colon of classical society, have the advantage of being able to work independently with their own tools. They could also maintain certain rights and freedoms within the village community.

The feudal lords who gradually emerged from the descendants of the Germanic tribal nobility, the Roman slave-owner aristocracy and from the vassals who were granted a fief (land and peasants) in return for their allegiance and services to the lords, still formed at this time a warrior class with uncouth manners. Uneducated, unable, as a rule, to read or write, the members of this class were only concerned with showing off their position, which was based purely on property and war by their swords. Members of the clergy also numbered among the ranks of the ruling class. They had more or less a monopoly over all artistic and intellectual activity, and over the education required to indulge in these activities. They were to a large degree responsible not only for the conversion of the tribes to Christianity, but also for the dissemination of ideological ideals and moral norms of behaviour, both of which were aimed at sanctifying the new forms of social dependence amongst the people. Apart from this, the monasteries and bishops' seats were the homes of many, albeit often fragmentary, relics of classical learning, art and technology. These were adapted and taken over by the Christian culture of the ruling feudal class.

Little is known about the culture of the working people. It was based on a pre-scientific magico-religious view of the world; forms of nature worship and the worship of tribal deities were upheld for a long time. The experiences, knowledge, customs, and rituals gained over the centuries simply through the battle with nature, still carried weight. In legends, myths, proverbs, magic formulae, and in the range of local art forms, these traditions were passed down orally from generation to generation, being extended only slowly and penetrated gradually by Christian ways.

With regard to jewellery making, the late Roman traditions were initially taken over and continued. In the 6th century stylistic elements stemming from Germanic forms begin to appear. The various burial finds dating from the Merovingian period—ornamental objects made from gold, silver, iron, or bronze—suggest that jewellery was very popular amongst both poor and rich. Gold jewellery from the 5th and 6th centuries, sometimes very heavy and massive, is relatively common. At this time gold mining still flourished in Gaul, and precious metals were acquired in the form of presents and tributes from the conquered territories in western Europe, and as a form of subsidy from the Eastern Roman empire. From the 7th century onwards there was obviously a shortage of gold in Central Europe; the mines in Gaul, Spain, Dacia, the Tauern and Carpathian Mountains were closed down, and groups of Arab warriors blocked the access routes to the gold countries in the south and east.

Merovingian jewellery is greatly indebted to the Germanic traditions of the period of the great migrations, both in its functional and decorative aspects. In the twin graves at Wittislingen—dating from approximately 600 A.D.—a married couple were given fairly typical gifts of jewellery, the artistic quality of which, however, towers over that of most finds from this period. The husband's grave contained the famous "buckler fibula of Uffila", named after the man, who, according to the inscription on the reverse side, had the valuable ornament made on the occasion of his wife's, Tisa's, death. Researchers found next to his mortal remains iron metal mountings with silver damascene decoration for a belt, and iron buckles from which gold threads, presumably the remains of the belt, still hung. Both the gold-leaf cross and the gold finger-ring with a relief plate depicting the bearded head of Christ, seem to prove without doubt that the owner was a Christian.

The round fibula belonging to the woman, with a covering of sheet gold and almandines on its front side reveals far more antique influences, not so much in the choice of motives—snake-shaped, crossing ribbons terminating in animal heads—as in the wealth of granulation and filigree work—the exuberance of the background. This form points to the close ties which were still kept up with the Syrian-East Roman sphere after the great migrations, and also the particularly female weakness for this "fashion". The woman's burial gifts also included bronze pins with sheet-gold or gold filigree heads, bronze pendants, buckles and metal mountings made from sheet silver, and one red and two orange-coloured glass beads.

Beads of one kind or another were threaded and used for necklaces. Glass production, introduced to the Rhineland by the Romans, flourished under the Merovingians, and provided, amongst other things, beads for the colourful necklaces which were very popular among the ladies at this time. Strings of clay beads, amethyst cylinders or amber beads were also widely used for women's necklaces, sometimes combined with each other and with metal links or pendants. The solid choker, however, retained its popularity especially in the north of Europe. Pendants, made from amber, rock crystal, or snail shells from the far-away Indian Ocean were thought to possess magic powers, and were worn as amulets.

In the 6th century jewellery forms were developed which were specifically Frankish in character, especially the different types of fibulae: bow, rhombus, quatrefoil, bird, and animal fibulae. The women obviously preferred the round and the quatrefoil fibulae, which they wore on the shoulder, and on a low belt. In the 7th century large gold disc fibulae with rich precious stone and glass inlay became popular, as did fibulae, clasps, and metal mountings made from silver or iron with silver damascene work. Bronze discs depicting horsemen were also worn as were bronze openwork discs, which the women wore on the left side—possibly as an amulet—attached to their belts by a chain or a belt. Small bronze instruments, such as toilet articles, were also worn hanging from belts.

Roman provincial traditions still dominated the decorative motifs used for fibulae: chip carving, spirals, vine tendrils, guilloche. Wafer-like leaves of sheet gold or silver were often placed under inlays of glass or stone in order to increase their brilliancy.

Ear jewellery, initially totally alien to Germanic taste first became widespread as a result of eastern influences, after the great migrations. Simple earrings were often of a considerable size and were sometimes embellished with decorative clay or glass beads, or red enamel cell work on the lower half. Magnificent examples were made using filigree work and characteristic loop decoration, either in the form of the traditional double spiral or the figure of eight shape.

Coin jewellery, probably used, as in Roman times, as a kind of award of distinction, was worn mostly in the form of pendants on necklaces, and was modelled on real Roman or Byzantine coins. Imitations, so-called pendant bracteates, with filigree and raised embossed patterns—most widespread between the years 400 and 600—became increasingly under the influence of the Nordic style: inscriptions on real coins which were not understood were transformed into runes, or animal motifs with strange fantastic figures—part griffin, part reptile, part snake, part bird. Examples from the 6th and 7th centuries have geometric guilloche ornaments intermingled with animal shapes to produce an animal style with a particular character of its own.

With the spread of Christianity the custom of giving funerary gifts died out in the 8th and 9th centuries, and with it one of the most important sources for the history of jewellery. However, sacrificial objects, such as the altar panels in Sant Ambrogio, Milan, the *Stephansbursa* of the imperial jewels, the portable altar of Emperor Arnulf, the *Codex Aureus* by St. Emeram, and the gold relief work on other contemporary book bindings—all bear witness to the high standard of the goldsmith's art at this time. Research has also been based on burial finds of Franconian origin, such as those found to the east of Franconia in Thuringian and Slavonic graves; in those areas which were converted to Christianity much later on.

From the second half of the 8th century onwards, under Charlemagne, Roman and Byzantine art forms were taken over and adapted to a far greater degree than before. A conscious return to the traditions of late antiquity, early Christianity and Byzantium, brought about the so-called period of the "Carolingian Renaissance" during Charlemagne's reign. In his residences, especially in Aachen, an independent and extremely refined art style emerged, which was also reflected in the work of the goldsmiths. Art, however, remained confined to one centre, the royal court, and only reached as far as the main monasteries and bishops' seats. On the other hand, artistic activity was widespread amongst the people: an inheritance of the pre-feudalistic traditions, with their many regional varieties at the time of the great migrations; traditions which were now continued in the empire formed by the united tribes. The split between the broad-based art of the people and the superior art of the court reflects the wide social gap between the rulers, feudal lords, and church on the one hand, and the ordinary people on the other. In the year 808 a law was passed which gave Charlemagne the right to determine the type of clothing to be worn by his subjects. Although few jewels have been preserved, the jewellery of both the ecclesiastical and secular lords was undoubtedly in keeping with their elevated position.

The precious objects made from gold, silver, beads, and precious stones in the workshop-community of a palatinate or a monastery were made in the first place for the glorification of God and the emperor, not only because of their great value, but also because of the prevailing mystical beliefs.

With the fall of antiquity and the rejection of its aesthetic values due to the Christian world's low opinion of the sensual world, a new attitude developed towards jewellery and ornaments. The belt, which in antiquity was still highly valued as a magical artistic medium of beauty and seductive powers, is a good example of this change in attitude: one of the attributes of a Christian saint is a chastity belt, which only fits the pure, and which deadens all sensuality. Saint Hieronymus (c. 347–420; he settled in Syria, and later became the head of a monastery) warns in his letters, a guide for the education of young girls up to the High Middle Ages, of the power of precious stones to dazzle and advises that children should be taught to love not precious stones, but the sacred word.

In spite of this, Charlemagne's wife and daughter liked, according to their biographies, to decorate themselves richly with jewels. Angilbert, the "Homer" of the imperial court at Aachen, praises Charlemagne's beautiful daughter, Rotrud: "her light shining hair is held by a blue ribbon, decorated with precious stones of luminous colours.

She wears a golden headband, decorated with beads and a golden clasp fastens the purple folds of her mantle." But Alcuin, from 796 abbot in Tours and adviser to Charlemagne, also tells Rotrud in one of his letters (referring to her extremely loose way of life) to decorate herself with honourable manners, compassion, and holiness, and says that she would be given more praise for the righteousness of such a transformation than for the splendour of bright shiny gold.

The little chains with diamond-studded crosses hanging from them may be taken as a kind of compromise between the feudal lords' love of finery, and their desire to be pious. According to reports these chains were particularly popular amongst women in the 8th century.

Jewellery for men (headbands, fibulae, bracelets, and rings) was used more to signify rank and distinction. Arm-rings (bauge) were, in keeping with an old custom, presented to worthy warriors, poets, and singers, and worn as a sign of bravery or favour. The treasure of the ruler, which, apart from weapons, armaments, coins, and instruments made from precious metals, also included jewellery, was as his material basis an essential prerequisite for exercising power. The treasure was added to through inheritages, payment of dues, presents, and above all through tributes gained after successful wars. The prince won friends and vassals by drawing on this store to present them with gifts of honour and recognition.

The ruler himself was expected to see that his external appearance corresponded to his social position. Whereas Charlemagne still dressed in the simple Frankish manner, and only on special occasions donned a diadem, a robe interwoven with gold, shoes studded with precious stones, and a gold clasp on his mantle, we are told in the life history of his son and successor King Louis the Pious, that he wore "clothes made from fabrics interwoven with gold, a gold tunic, a gold belt, a gold-shining sword, gold greaves (leg armour), and a mantle interwoven with gold; on his head he wore a golden diadem, and in his hand he carried a golden staff." (V. H. Elbern.)

The metal techniques were directly related to the pre-Carolingian artistic practise and the Germanic traditions, and they were developed further in accordance with the demands of the time. Most common were gold reliefs done in chase work, openwork, deep engraving, silver damascene work, and less frequently gold damascene on bronze and iron. Champlevé and *cloisonné* techniques were used as a continuation of the Alamannic-Frankish tradition, and gems were also highly valued, as products of the much admired antiquity. The stylized art of the Byzantium Empire was also not without influence. The higher level of Byzantine art was seen in the presents to the emperor and the clergy. More than anything else the technical perfection of Byzantine *cloisonné* work and gold filigree work enriched the art of the goldsmith for a long time to come.

PRE-ROMANESQUE AND ROMANESQUE STYLE

In the early 1880s pieces of jewellery suddenly turned up in the Mainz antique shops. Their high value brought them to the attention of the police, who presuming that they had been stolen, confiscated them and put them in safe-keeping until they found their real owner. However, after a year had lapsed, and their owner had still not been found, the jewellery was put up for public sale. In 1912 experts managed to bring the whole collection together making it possible both to find its place in the history of styles and to examine the individual pieces in detail.

Workers had found the pieces in a tumbled-down basement, and had then sold them. Further excavations were carried out not far from this spot in 1904, and brought similar treasures to light, namely a pair of earrings and a gold coin dating from the time of the Byzantine Emperor Romanos III Argyros (1028–1034), which gave a clue to the jewellery's age.

The individual pieces—these include a chain, a chest-pendant, one large and one small eagle fibula, two pairs of earrings, one single earring, one small and one large fili-gree ring brooch, a pair of highly arched cloak clasps, two similar single stud-clasps, two dress pins, and nine finger-rings—do not form a complete set; on the contrary they consist of several sets, some of which show signs of wear and tear, and some of which do not. They are made from fine gold and decorated with filigree, enamel, precious stones and beads, and thus number amongst the most important collections of medieval jewellery.

The types of jewellery and their delicacy suggest that they belonged to a woman, and the value and motifs on the individual pieces point to her high social position. The eagle, used as decoration for the two fibulae, was a motif used exclusively for lords' insignia, and the *lorum*, a combination of neck and chest jewellery—in this case consisting of a fine gold chain with gems, amethysts, carnelians, garnets, emeralds, and aquamarines, all of which border a crescent-shaped central pendant—clearly represents a more modest version of the ruler's insignium found in Byzantium. Apart from one ring, which without doubt stems from Byzantium, all the other pieces were probably completed in a Mainz workshop, since Mainz under Archbishop Willigis (975–1011) was one of the most important goldsmith centres. Until recently the treasure was thought to have been the property of Empress Gisela, wife of Konrad II, who was crowned in 1024 and whose beauty was praised by her contemporaries. It was thus called the "Gisela Jewellery". Recent research, however, has shown that the individual pieces probably do not stem from the same period, but from the end of the 10th century and beginning of the 11th century. This does not imply, however, that they were totally, unconnected with Empress Gisela.

In Germany a powerful early feudal empire had been founded under the dynasty of the Saxon Ottos, which lasted until the reign of Emperor Konrad II (919–1039); it was formed through the continuation of the imperial policies of the Carolingian empire, and with its conquests it managed to secure dominancy in Europe. The imperial state power initially drew its support from the ecclesiastical feudal lords and it thus prepared the way for the rise of the Roman Catholic Church, which under the leadership of the Pope waged a successful battle against the empire for dominancy in Europe. In the 12th and 13th centuries it became the strongest feudal power. With the decline in imperial power from the beginning of the 13th century onwards, the split in Germany's feudal state was complete, while in western Europe centralized kingdoms were formed and the feudal state took shape in France.

The few pieces of Ottonian jewellery which have been many include, apart from the Gisela Jewellery, the German imperial crown, which besides its decorative function is also a documentation of the close connection between state power and the Church at this time. It is thought to date from the imperial coronation of Otto the Great in 962. The octagonal shape of the crown symbolizes the "eight", the synonym for perfection, and also a representation of divine Jerusalem. On the eight gold plates decorated with precious stones, beads, and gold filigree, enamel representations are given of Christ amongst cherubs together with the inscription "per me reges regnant"; the plates also give representations of the Biblical kings David, Solomon, and Ezechias, who symbolize justice, wisdom, and longevity. According to medieval symbolism the coronation not only granted the wearer of the crown political power as Christ's representative on earth, buth through some magico-religious process the wearer was also supposed to be endowed with all the qualities of a leader, which were believed to be inherent in the crown. The big central stone, missing since 1350, was replaced by an Indian sapphire. The arch was added later, during the reign of Konrad II; the cross was added under Otto III or Heinrich II.

Feudalism, which flourished in Europe from the 11th–13th centuries, had already been fully established in Central Europe under the Ottonian emperors in the middle of the 11th century. An extensive peasant agriculture—woods were cleared, marshland was drained, the cultivation methods were improved, and new cultures introduced—meant a growing agricultural surplus, which allowed the ruling class both to increase their power and to indulge to an even greater extent their weakness for luxury. Apart from this the craftsmen and merchants also managed to split away from the agricultural workers, and to form their own independent branches of trade. Church buildings, palatinates, and fortresses, erected by the feudal lords, developed into settlements and market places for craftsmen and merchants. Thus from the 11th century onwards a growing number of town settlements were founded with their own bourgeoisie, who in the 12th century began to organize themselves into guilds, and to demand, with some success, their freedoms and rights from the feudal lords of the towns. The town bourgeoisie now became the most important progressive economic and social force within the feudal society.

Most of the surviving Ottonian jewellery was made under the patronage of the Church and was designed for monasteries or other institutions under the jurisdiction of the Church. Workshops in Trier under Archbishop Egbert (977–997), in Essen under Abbess Mathilde (937–1011), and in Mainz under the above mentioned Archbishop Willigis produced book illustrations, ivory carvings, and goldsmith work. Until the 10th–11th centuries monks and other clergymen were also skilled craftsmen, but from the 11th century onwards the work was executed predominantly by town craftsmen.

The Bernward door, Bernward candle-holder, and Bernward pillars in Hildesheim, all executed in cast bronze, are named after the Bishop of Hildesheim (993–1022), who is thought to have been their creator, and who is named by his contemporaries as the most learned and skilled man of his time. He was apparently a master of the goldsmith art as well as all other practical and artistic skills.

Roger von Helmarshausen, a Benedictine monk from Helmarshausen near Paderborn, who called himself Theophilus Presbyter, was famous for his "Handbook of the Various Arts", the most important instruction book of artistic methods to be written in the Middle Ages. It is based on theories drawn from Byzantine handbooks, on his own experience, and on the artistic activities of his contempories. It gives among other things technical instructions for metal processing: for example practical advice on how to equip a goldsmith's workshop: how one sets up working instruments, furnaces, bellows, and tools. Apart from instructions on the production of gold leaf or goldbacking for miniature paintings, the reader is also told how bells are cast, ivory dyed, beads pierced, and many other fascinating facts. Some consecrational objects, which can be traced back to him, show his knowledge of the processes and techniques used in Rhineland and Byzantium, and point to the links with the Meuse workshops.

The techniques and motifs used for the jewellery which has survived also show—apart from the influences of Germanic tradition and antiquity—the strong links to Byzantium which existed at this time. In 972 the "purple born" Princess Theophanu came to Aachen to marry Otto II (955–983). This event was to have a great influence over the development of the crafts. The incorporation of a Byzantine court-state undoubtedly made a great contribution to the refinement of the previously simple manners and taste. With regard to the goldsmith's art the perfection of *cloisonné* work, filigree work, and the mounting of precious stones is the direct result of Byzantine influence. New impulses in ornamentation and style were also felt.

The "art of painting with fire", (fire gilding), once the strictly guarded secret of Byzantium, had reached Europe at an earlier date through the the monks who had been sent to Byzantium by their abbots to learn this high art. The normal cell inlays of almandines or red glass had already fallen into disuse in the 9th century in favour of the enchanting bright enamel decoration, which like their Byzantine prototypes were translucent, and allowed the gold background to shine through. Even 11th-century Byzantine *cloisonné* work is difficult to distinguish from Rhineland work. The way in which the precious stones are cut and mounted also points to the influence of Byzantine-oriental taste: the stone was cut *en cabochon* following its natural shape—filed into a semi-circular shape with water and sand, then polished with buckskin—and mounted in a round, oval, triangular, or drop-shape form. An assortment of various-shaped stones were then arranged on the same piece of jewellery. "Capsels", thin strips of gold soldered horizontally onto the background, served as mounts. Later in the 10th and 12th centuries raised rectangular-shaped box-mounts were used. About 1000 the crab-shaped mount came into use—i.e. the gold strips were decorated with little gold leaves or with filigree loops. (See the German imperial crown and the Gisela Jewellery). Apart from producing a charming ornament this innovation also provided large stones with a more secure hold. Apart from precious stones, gems, mainly from the late Roman period, were very popular.

The goldsmith in the pre-Romanesque period used *cloisonné*, gold filigree, precious stones, beads and granulation to produce rich ornamental brightly-coloured jewellery. In the course of the 11th century a new style emerged, which was to be the transition from pre-Romanesque to Romanesque art. Stylistic innovations can already be distinguished in the work of Roger von Helmarshausen which dates from the 11th century. These new elements spread to the workshops of the Weser area and reached the Hildesheim goldsmith art. They were shown at their best in the enamel and embossed work from the Rhineland and Meuse in the 12th century: precious stones and gold enamelling became less frequent, whereas brown varnish, niello, and *opus interrasile*, relief-like patterns cut out in a metal backing, came to the fore. The bust-like figures and ornaments produced were also given engraved patterns.

In the Romanesque period (11th century to the late 12th and early 13th centuries) the goldsmith gained another patron in addition to the feudal lord: the town patrician gradually became the new patron, ordering secular objects such as jewellery and table ware. Hardly any examples of these have survived the centuries: most of them have been the victims of wars and theft: some were melted, and in times of need made into money. The lithurgical objects, however, which survived under the protection of the

Church provide us with some information about the style and technique of metalwork during this period.

In the 12th century there was a change in the artistic material and in the technical methods.

Two stylistic tendencies merged in the motifs used for the crafts: these had existed, despite their common origin, separately in their own right since the time of the Great Migrations, i.e. since late antiquity. One came from the Byzantine sphere, and the other from the Germanic. New inroads were also made with regard to technical methods.

The increasing demand for and the growing prestige of craftwork obviously contributed to the fact that solid gold was used less and less frequently, and fire-gilded copper more and more. New opportunities for artistic expression were provided by the transition from *cloisonné* to copper champlevé enamelling: the pure opaque colours produced by this method changed the pictorial and graphic effect of the finished articles. In particular the figure representations of Meuse enamel work achieved in metalwork the archaic severity and power of expression which is characteristic of the pictorial art of this period, and which reached its artistic climax at the end of the 12th century. The same was true of embossed work: the articles were also made mainly from copper and silver and the figures depicted on them became examples of medieval representation at its most powerful.

Apart from examples from both the secular and Christian spheres of feudalism, numerous bronze folk-art ornaments have survived, the motifs of which are still strongly under the influence of the Germanic tradition. Bronze experienced a new upswing in the Middle Ages after copper and zinc, previously unknown, were discovered. In the 11th century Hildesheim was the centre of bronze art, and in the 12th century Lüttich and Magdeburg became the main centres.

GOTHIC STYLE

France, under the Capetians grew to be the central power in Europe, and in the 12th century also took the lead in the field of culture: the vitality and superiority of French culture spread far over borders. The development and flourishing of the towns, which was helped along by lively trading, the growth of the handworker trades, and the transition from a barter economy to one with a monetary basis allowed the bourgeoisie to extend their influence and to become an independent class. From about the beginning of the 13th century onwards the craftwork carried out in the towns stood on equal footing with the work done in monastery workshops.

Leading goldsmith workshops were situated in Paris and Limoges, on the Rhine and Meuse, where in the 12th century a Belgian-Lorraine handworker centre acted as a mediator between France and the other European countries, and provided prototypes for jewellery forms. Jewellery of international ranking was soon being produced in Italian towns such as Siena and Florence, and later on in Venice.

Even in the 11th century the most powerful feudal lords had begun to acquire vassals (who were at first bonded) for themselves in order to be able to have total power over and to exploit the peasants. Out of these vassals there developed a lower nobility: the knights. In the 12th and 13th centuries they became the bringers of a new branch of ruling class culture which began to free itself from the Church and was expressed in certain ideals of the feudal nobility and in certain moral norms found in the minnesinger culture. The highlights of this new culture were the knightly courtly poetry of the Provence troubadours, the trouvères in the north of France, and the minnesingers; also the figure sculptures of the late Romanesque and early Gothic churchs.

In Provence trade with the Orient, an economy based on money, and a luxury and weapons industry had acted as stimulae for the rise of the secular-orientated culture of the nobility. Intellectual feeding ground was provided by oriental and antique traditions, which were given new expression due to the direct influences from the Arabian section of what was then Spain. There were also impulses from folk and minstrel songs, and the minnesinger culture made a considerable contribution to the refinement of court manners and to the establishment of a concept of "decency".

The veneration of woman and her new honoured position was reflected in all branches of culture, even in dress and jewellery. The knight wore her veil in battle, he presented her with a souvenir, a piece of jewellery placed in a carved *Minne* box before he went off into battle. She, for her part, would tear one jewel after the other from her dress and throw it to her favourite in a tournament.

"He who loves a good woman, will be ashamed of every misdeed". Thus formulated Walther von der Vogelweide the concept behind a new ethic, which advocated deeper and humaner relations between men. Jewellery gained a new imitated significance, as it was used as a sign of love and faithfulness, of as an exhortation for good Christians. Its value did not depend solely on its material cost. Both magnificent and very modest decorative objects bore, during this period, poetic or simply naive inscriptions. The ring, both in the form of a finger-ring and the ring brooch, which was used to fasten a blouse over the chest, was considered above all to be a sign of loyalty. Its misuse, however, was apparently by no means unusual: a bishop's decree from the year 1217 threatened young men in England with immediate marriage if they dared to seduce a girl by under false pretences placing a ring on her finger.

The ornaments worn in the early and high Gothic period were like the above mentioned ring brooch, mainly dress jewellery with a certain function. Ear jewellery disappeared, but was still found in the Slavonic areas and chains and bracelets, which even in the Romanesque period had been replaced by richly embroidered borders, or borders with stones sewn on them, first reappeared in the 14th century.

The tailors, who like all the other handworkers, were eager to elevate their skill into an art, now re-modelled the formerly shapeless sack-like robes into close fitting dresses which emphasized the bosom and waist. Whether the resounding praises sung about every part of the female body in the minnesingers songs was the cause or effect of the tailors skills is still a matter for discussion. Whereas the simple woman still wore handwoven and handmade dresses, the women of the 12th-century court wore robes with often exaggeratedly wide and long drooping sleeves, a full skirt, and train. The seductive sophistication, sumptuous borders and precious stone decoration of these robes awoke the fire in many a heart. About the 13th century, the classic period of medieval art, more moderation in dress and jewellery became evident. Telling with regard to the social standing of the woman is the fact that her external appearance was similar to that of her husband's. A low belt, decorated in various degrees with mounts and buckles, gathered in the folds of her dress-bodice. The semi-circular-shaped shoulder cloak, which was formerly worn only by men, was tied over the chest by a ribbon or a string of beads attached to two large identical flat or convex decorative discs, the clasps, which until well into the 13th century were decorated with filigree and granulation. It was considered a sign of *mâze*, i.e. good correct manners to place one or two fingers in the clasp ribbon. Men and virgins decorated their head and long flowing hair with a chaplet, a headband made from flowers or metal with stone inlay; married women wore it over a band tied round the forehead and chin. The knight only wore the iron armour in a tournament or in battle, and over this he wore the brightly coloured, usually very valuable tunic. During the very solemn knighting ceremony, the new knight was given among other things the right to wear the knight's strap, a often heavily ornamented belt which was also worn by kings and emperors.

Dress belts were mostly made from fabric, and had metal clasps. The clasps made from embossed gold or copper in the 13th century were popular in almost all circles. Their careful execution and imaginative motifs are proof that more value was placed on a high standard of artistic quality and handwork, than on a show of jewels. The subject matter and the techniques used to depict it show parallels to the style of figures found in Gothic cathedrals: sculpted leaf formations and floral ornaments form a light and lively framework for biblical scenes. The linear ornamentation, which was still predominant around 1200, had by the middle of the 13th century been transformed into a free realistic style with floral and leaf ornaments. The art of achieving light and shadow effects had also been mastered by this time.

Already in the 12th century copper champlevé enamelling began to take over increasingly from the exclusive gold *cloisonné* enamelling. The copper champlevé work was opaque with clearly outlined areas of colour, and was a technique which allowed colourful and expressive jewellery to be produced from inexpensive material. About 1300 it was replaced by translucent silver enamelling, thought to be the invention of Paris goldsmiths: the goldsmith pours the opaque enamel into a bas-relief carved into the silver. The silver backing shimmers when the light caught it due to the light-coloured enamel, and produces a delicate and diffused shimmer, which obviously corresponded exactly to the taste of the time, as the process spread rapidly all over Europe. Important works using this technique were produced in the Rhineland, and in Italy especially in Florence and Siena, the technique was used until the 16th century. In Hungary Gothic sacrificial objects with silver enamelling are kept to this day in church treasuries.

Pieces of jewellery with niello work also remained popular throughout the Middle Ages.

Belief in the mysticism of certain drawings and in the magical powers of precious stones is an expression of the medieval picture of the world and is only to be understood in connection with the pre-scientific outlook on nature. These beliefs were not only held amongst the ruling class, but were deeply rooted in the people.

Even the learned abbess Hildegard von Bingen (born 1098), who was interested amongst other things in the natural sciences, expressed in her book *Physica* the firm conviction even recognized by the Church, that precious stones possess magic powers, which (can) admittedly only be effective if they are reinforced by fervent prayer. About 1100 Bishop Marbod from Rennes wrote a "Stone Book", in which he revived the beliefs held in antiquity with regard to the secret powers of minerals. Albertus Magnus, a scholastic *doctor universalis* tried to connect these secret powers with astrology. Thus pulverized precious stones used as valuable medicine by medieval chemists, and the goldsmith as well had to be informed about the special therapeutic qualities of the stones, and about the secret powers of certain ornaments and decorative motifs. The engraved representation of Mercury for example was supposed to grant one good business powers; a symbol for Mars gave warriors courage, a picture of an apocalyptic rider on the front of a ring gave protection against the plague; cheap lead rings were consecrated every year by the English king and were thought to help fight cramp, merchants travelling through dangerous trading routes often wore a ring with the following inscription "Jesus walked through the midst of them" – a sort of saying to frighten off robbers.

In the 14th century the sapphire became the stone used for bishops' rings. It was thought to keep one's reason clear, one's heart free from greed, to protect one from earthly love, and to keep one's loyalty for the true love of God. The crusaders brought new motifs from the Orient, which were adapted to suit the Christian faith: the lion symbolized the strength of the Lord; the pomegranate, as a symbol for fertility became an important decorative element for young brides.

From about 1300 onwards (under the influence of mysticism) the powerful sculpted ornaments of the High Gothic style began to be replaced by graceful miniature-like forms. The so-called devotional jewellery was produced: Pendants worn on chains regained some of their popularity. It became fashionable to use areas of colour in making the pendants, and sayings written across them with quotes from the Bible point to the amuletic character of many pendants, some of which also served to held some relic or as a miniature altar which one could set up at any time to enjoy a silent moment of prayer.

The pendants and rings speak above all of a warmth and depth of feeling, and often show in symbolic form the intimate relation of the wearer to the one who gave it: the initials of a beloved one—priests usually wore M for the Mother of God—were worn as clasps or brooches; the heart, rose, and key were also popular symbols. For "love rings" intertwined hands formed the ring shape itself and either the inscription "You mine, I yours" or a hand taking an oath were engraved on the plate. Apart from these, usually personal symbols, heraldry also began to appear in the jewellery of the High Gothic Style. In 14th-century France the fleur-de-lis was used for the first time as an emblem. The turn to individual jewellery, which emphasized personal feelings was already—as was the mysticism—a sign of the growing influence of the town bourgeoisie who were asserting themselves more and more against the dying culture of the nobility and knights.

The popularity of jewellery grew steadily from the beginning of the 14th century onwards. Ornaments, which already had a function in themselves, were decorated with additional ornaments: pendants were complemented by numerous lockets, which were metal mounts cast or punched from sheet metal. They were round or rosette-shaped, often additionally decorated with niello or enamel work, and were sewn onto the appropriate garment. A particularly large number of such ornaments have been found on the Baltic coast, in the area under the influence of the rich Hanse League towns.

The citizens of the towns, less familiar with the rules of *mâze*, but on the other hand wealthier than the impoverished nobility, began in the 14th century to have more say in matters of fashion and taste. The amount of money which the citizen could afford to pay for precious fabrics and jewellery meant that he began to present real competition to the court circles who tried to protect their privileges through laws on clothes and luxury goods. Such a regulation is known to have existed in France as early as 1180, and Pope Gregory X tried in 1274 to dampen the desire for finery in Italy by forbidding luxury goods. In Germany, where the bourgeoisie developed at a later date, laws of this type were first passed in the 14th century. In Florence, so the story goes, the counsellors demanded a considerable

fine from the fathers or husbands of women citizens who were dressed too ostentatiously, and who spent more money on their finery than was allowed by law. Apparently the men paid up, and the women did what they wanted.

LATE MIDDLE AGES

Although the 14th and 15th centuries saw the flourishing of the medieval urban communes and an advanced stage in handworker specialization, this period still bore the marks of a fully developed feudal society. However, the first rifts and contradictions within the social system began to make themselves obvious, and in the field of culture took the form of decline and decadence. Characteristic for this period was the increased use of mechanical production aids such as forges, paper mills and the like. The invention of the printing press around 1445 was also to be of great significance as was the appearance of mills for cutting and polishing precious stones and an upswing in mining, which helped countries like Saxony and Bohemia, both of which had rich silver deposits in the Erzgebirge mountains, to achieve prosperity and an economic upswing. Long distance trading became more extensive and more consequent, especially with regard to the Hanse League towns on the Baltic and North Sea. In the 14th century the League included approximately 200 towns. Large sums of capital were amassed by merchants and profiteers and the banking system developed. In a few regions of Europe the first forms of capitalist production developed under particularly favourable conditions in, for example, upper Italy, Flanders, and in a few French and German towns, such as Nuremberg and Augsburg. Rich citizens often invested their capital in property and in putting their life style almost on a par with that of the lower feudal nobility.

The intellectual leadership of the Church was curbed to a certain degree: a bourgeois school system was developed. Thus the rise of the natural sciences and bourgeois art became possible, and anti-Church, heretic and reformist teachings were widespread. In Italy the development of the bourgeois renaissance and humanism began in the 15th century.

The payments in kind which had been the usual method of remunerating labour and production until now, were gradually replaced by monetary payments, the old personal relationship between the feudal lord and peasant was replaced by a purely financial relationship, which made the exploitation of the peasant all the crasser. This led to peasant revolts, which flamed up especially in France, England, and Germany. Feudal state power was extended in an attempt to combat growing social contradictions. This meant that in France, England, and Spain centralized feudal monarchies were set up, and in Germany and Italy feudal territorial powers began to deprive the towns of their freedom in order to profit from the financial power of the bourgeoisie. The contradictions inherent in the late Middle Ages, the conflict between old and new, between the pomp of the parasitic feudal nobility and the simple naturalism of bourgeois art were all reflected in dress and jewellery which came in delicately simple, extremely sophisticated or even absolutely bizarre styles. It was also by no means unusual for representatives of the bourgeoisie to fall back on outdated ideologies; indeed the wealthy bourgeois circle showed a tendency to orientate their life-style towards that of the feudal upper class.

For the first time in history the quantity and the variety of forms of folk jewellery was greater than those of the precious jewels found in court society. A kind of midway position between those two poles was taken by the jewellery of the wealthy bourgeoisie: they preserved some folk-art characteristics, but were also at pains to emulate the splendour of the court—not always with much success.

After the invention of the printing press the wood-cut technique became increasingly widespread from 1460 onwards and enjoyed great popularity in the first decades of the 16th century. The motifs used for jewellery also became well-known over a large area since they were used for wood-cuts. Pendants were made in greater numbers, and attached to belts, chokers or rosaries.

The subjects used for motifs in jewellery point to a stronger, more intense adherence in the Christian faith, which at this time shaped the consciousness of the people. The popular motifs were almost exclusively biblical representations, now predominantly from the New Testament: the birth of Christ, the Virgin Mary, or depictions from the life of the saints. There are numerous cast-silver talisman pendants which have been preserved with figure representations of the patron saints of a profession or of some other category. The most popular was Saint George, the dragon slayer, patron saint of warriors and peasants, travellers, and hospitals, the protector of the merchant trade. From the 10th–19th centuries he was the subject of innumerable artistic representations. Saint Christopher was thought to carry responsibility for travellers on land and at sea, and his likeness was supposed to protect one from sudden death. Saint Sebastian, patron saint of huntsmen, also helped to keep away the plague, whereas Saint Michael enjoyed the veneration of numerous fencing societies. Motifs of saints also occurred on rings.

The simple Christian felt protected when wearing pilgrim badges which were cast in tin or lead and sold on the pilgrimages (on the occasion of the consecration feast in 1466 the impressive sum of 130,000 such badges were apparently sold to the people at 2 Pfennigs each in the monastery at Einsiedeln). The same protection was guaranteed by carrying a reliquary in the form of a pendant or a ring.

From the 14th century onwards—as a result of an expansion of sea trading, the first European mother-of-pearl work worth mentioning was produced—the front sides of reliquaries were often mounted with mother-of-pearl reliefs done in the outer shell of the seapearl or of the giant sea butterfly (*strombus gigas*). Pendants and medallions, ring brooches, lockets, and hat brooches were also made from these shells. Mother-of-pearl carving, which is relatively easy to learn, flourished mainly in the 15th century in the workshops of Germany and Flanders, and was a cheap substitue for onyx cameos, which were particularly popular in Italy. It was soon to replace ivory carving completely, as ivory became rarer and rarer. The favourite motifs were the same Christian subjects as used in metalwork.

In the 15th century it was no longer unusual to see men or women of the bourgeois class wearing four, five, or more rings, the forms of which were, in comparison to the delicate examples of the 14th century, greater in size and value. One's own emblem, which even the bourgeoisie and peasants now had, was often worked into the plaque of a signet ring. Belts, usually made from cloth, had little silver or gold plaques as decoration or small loop rings, which had delicate objects such as toilet articles, talismans, or other small instruments attached to them.

The accounts of a goldsmith in Constance by the name of Stephan Maignov, with entries from the years 1480–1500 give some quite illuminating facts about the jewellery worn by the bourgeoisie and by the lower nobility at this time: orders for finger-rings were by far the most frequent, then came chain necklaces, women's belts, crosses, hearts, silver bells (bells worn on coat tails, collars, caps, and shoes were very fashionable in the 15th century, especially in Germany). Expensive chains, probably chains of office, are priced in the accounts at about 100 Guilders each. Master Maignov apparently accepted old gold as payment or for re-use, he did repairs, did re-gilding at very reasonable prices, accepted payment in installments and gave loyal customers credit (from Bassermann-Jordan).

The newly elevated bourgeoisie also took over the ring brooch, decorated with enamelled figure designs, and the bridal crown, which was obviously a derivation from the chaplet, the woman's headdress worn by the nobility in the High Middle Ages. Precious bridal crowns were often in the possession of the church or parish, and were lent out for weddings. The possession of a round perforated scent box, often richly decorated and called a pomander was a sign of great wealth. Inside was a container for the most expensive scents at that time: musk or amber, the smell of which was supposed to protect one from the plague. The first descriptions of pomanders, in the shape of pomegranates, rosary beads, betel nuts, pendants, or ring attach-

ments, stem from inventories of the 14th century. Those with lids had pictures of religious scenes inside them, and also served as a devotional prayer treasure. Towards the end of the 16th century, pomanders fell into disuse and were replaced by phials.

Within the dying feudal culture the life-style of the Duke of Burgundy's court is a typical example of how the economic strength and handworker skills of the bourgeoisie were exploited by the feudal nobility, so that they could enjoy a reactionary and parasitical way of life. In the 14th and 15th centuries the Dukes of Burgundy (originally part of France) had either bought up or won in battle territory in the Netherlands and in present day Belgium, in countries which at this time were economically amongst the most progressive in Europe. The Burgundy culture, however, remained that of the knights court, whereas in Italy the way was already being prepared, in the bigger towns, for early capitalism, and art was largely in the hands of the bourgeoisie. In Burgundy most of the income of the towns flowed into the treasury of the Duke's court, where the love of pomp, purchase of luxury jewels, extravagant way of life, fashion, and the strictly regulated manners were all taken as a model for the whole of Europe—albeit a model which could not always be emulated. In the end the central power, which with its absolutist methods was becoming more and more powerful, destroyed its own life-source. The towns lost their rights, their independence, and their wealth. With their decline, the Duchy of Burgundy also fell, and its provinces came into the hands of France and Germany.

The comfortable bourgeois fashions which were still worn at the beginning of the 15th century were replaced under Burgundian influence in the mid-15th century by a somewhat bizarre court fashion—the higher one's social position, the more pointed one's shoes, the longer one's trains, and the taller one's hats. These fashions also led to the introduction of a new tailoring technique with an erotic element, the décolleté, which was initially slight, but eventually reached as for as the highly-corsetted waist, and was filled with all sorts of precious, mostly tiny, bodices decorated with brooches. The low cleavage set off necklaces and pendants as well, and these became once more the centre of attention (In Germany the simple choker had long been considered an incredible luxury.). The prince wore a diadem round his long felt hat (which was rather like a top hat) as a sign of his rank, otherwise hat badges or brooches —in the Burgundian Court these took the form of golden feather ornaments—were the favourite ornaments usually worn by men on tall hats, by women of the nobility on their steeple headdresses or on the wide two-part horned bonnets. Belt mountings made from precious metal, expensive lockets, clasps, buttons, and ring brooches were commonly worn on colourful brocades, velvets and silks, with trimmings of embroidery or precious stones.

A new tendency in jewellery began to make itself obvious: in the late Middle Ages the court fashion turned away from the more functionally orientated jewellery with high symbolic value in favour of the ornament used purely for representative purposes, for a show of pomp. This tendency is seen clearly firstly in the way which clothing was laden with jewels (an addiction, in which all strata of society indulged, in so far as they were in a position to do so), and secondly in the profanation of religious motifs: on clasps we find pretty little pictures of Mary and cute representations of Jesus as a boy, holding a spoon or bowl, as well as friendly animal faces which laugh at us from behind floral scrolls.

The Dukes of Burgundy are thought to have been amongst the first collectors, although their collections, like those of their contemporaries, were still no more than an indiscriminate accumulation of curiosities, worthless trinkets, and on the other hand precious carpets, miniatures, jewels and other examples of miniature art. According to legends, John of Burgundy (1371–1419) kept foreign envoys waiting because he had been told that jewel merchants had arrived. When Charles the Bold (1433–1477) met the German emperor near Trier in the year 1473, his cloak alone with its trimmings of gold and diamonds was estimated to be worth 100,000 Rhine Guilders. This prompted Propst Arnold of Belain in Brugge to make the following comment "It takes so much poverty to dress one person! One must be filled with an almost immeasurable and insatiable greed in order to squander so much on such a simple matter."

On journeys, even in war campaigns the Dukes of Burgundy were accompanied by much luxury and splendour: the heralds rode with them dressed in expensive tunics bearing the Duke's coat of arms and the members of the court in cloaks made from gold fabric and wearing gold chain necklaces. When Charles the Bold, who was always laden with jewels, together with his splendid army of knights was defeated in battle in 1476, near Grandson and Murten (Switzerland) in the so-called gold battle, a legendary wealth fell into the hands of the victors, a Swiss army composed of members of the peasent and bourgeois classes. 30 years later the Basle councillor got into financial difficulties and offered the Fugger family a *federlin*, a hat brooch called the "white rose" (a jewel with a large spinel) for 40,200 Guilders, and the "three brothers" jewel (three 70 carat rubies grouped round a diamond), both of which had once belonged to Charles the Bold. Jacob Fugger wrote about this transaction "The simple common-or-garden Swiss people, who know more about cows than jewels, sell the valuable precious stones for a pittance." Today the jewels have disappeared, they have probably been long since re-modelled.

Further evidence of the courtly love of pomp in the late Middle Ages are the extremely valuable decorations which were often awarded by a ruler for the slightest service. The distribution of such awards was aimed at re-enforcing the exclusive privileges of the feudal knights, and was also a means of keeping members of the lower nobility in the service of the court and state power. In Hungary there was a "Dragon Award" in Denmark an "Elephant Award", in Austria a "Pigtail Award", in Brandenburg a "Swan Knight Award". Amongst the most famous are the "Golden Fleece Award" presented by Philip the Good,

Duke of Burgundy on the occasion of his birthday, and the English "Knight of the Garter" award. This was apparently granted by Edward III, when during a banquet his lover, the Countess of Salisbury, lost her skyblue garter, and the king picked it up. "*Honi soit, qui mal y pense*" he exclaimed. (Dishonourable, he who thinks bad of this!) He then had this wise saying embroidered in the blue award, which (like the garter) was worn on a ribbon below the knee. The award was first worn on a ribbon round the neck in the 16th century. This new award was obviously dedicated to the "Honour of God", the Holy Virgin and Saint George.

Christian dignitaries were not far behind their pecular counterparts with regard to their show of pomp: whereas on the one hand the Italian Johann Capistranus (1451) took up the fight in Saxony and Silesia against the "tools of the devil", and the penitent Christians sacrificed not only their board games and die, but also their jewellery to him, Pope Eugen IV had a tiara made for himself by Ghiberti in Florence, which required five-and-a-half pounds of pearls, rubies, sapphires, and emeralds, estimated by contemporaries to be worth 20,00 Francs.

It was characteristic of this period to use busts for ornaments. The gold enamelling technique *en ronde bosse* developed by Paris goldsmiths in the late 14th century was well suited to the tendency towards very effective rich and brightly coloured ornaments: various colours of glass flux were melted over a gold core, and combined with beads and precious stones, pale-red rubies and watery-blue sapphires being the most popular. In the mid-15th century painted enamelling began to be practised. This was an adaption of the Dutch art of illumination: a molten mass was painted onto gold or silver foil with a brush. In Hungary, which from the 13th to 15th century was the European country richest in gold, wire enamelling was taken over from Italy, reaching an artistic climax: twisted gold wire formed the contours of the design and the hollows were filled with an opaque molten mass. Hungarian wire enamelling came to be highly regarded in many parts of Europe.

In the 14th century stone cutting had already progressed from the *en cobochon* method to the production of the table diamond. In the 15th century a forerunner of the diamond faced cutting was practised. The Dutchman Louis de Berken, was the first to discover in Brussels that a diamond could be polished with pulverized diamond moistened with oil. In 1476 he succeeded in applying facet cutting, which had previously been used for rock crystal, to the diamond. Charles the Bold emplayed de Berken at his court. By 1465 the guild of *Diamantsliper* had already been founded in Brugge.

In the big Italian towns—Venice, Genoa, Milan, and particularly Florence, a centre of the merchant oligarchy—the first features of early capitalism appeared as early as the 15th century. These were based on the large-scale manufacture of cloth and silk, the activities of financiers and profiteers and extensive, highly organized trade. The upper bourgeoisie not only controlled the comprehensive guild organizations, but from 1400 onwards also had in fact, (represented in Florence, for example, by the Medici family of bankers), economical and political power in their hands. The wealthy bourgeoisie were great patrons of art and science in the towns, gave big orders to the craftsmen, and filled their palaces with paintings and luxury objects, which in number and in value often surpassed those of the nobility.

The 15th-century fashion and jewellery in Italy, bear witness to a kind of transitional style: the emphasis on the horizontal, a feature of Renaissance fashion, was not yet common. Dresses with long cleavages were worn reaching down to the waist, as was the practice in Burgundy, and had been copied all over Europe. Belts were worn in a matching colour to that of the still narrow-cut dress. The Italian women, however, wore as a sign of their own style, a crown-like brooch attached to a hair-ribbon and placed over their shaved, artificially raised foreheads.

The preference for the type of ornaments which were to become typical for the Renaissance could already be seen in the demand for metal chains, in the form of neck, chest,

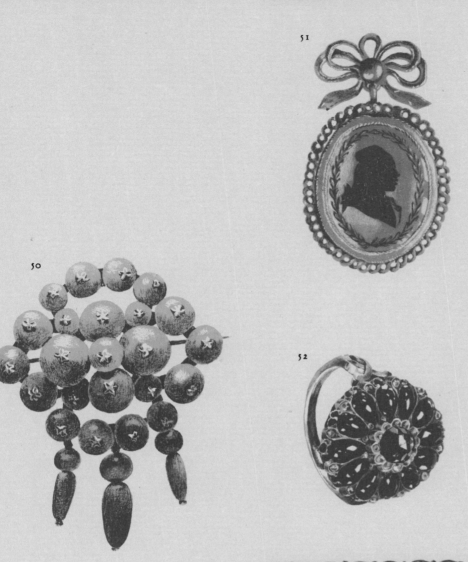

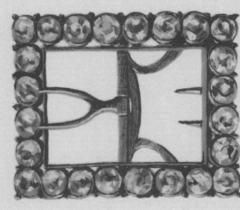

50   Brooch, made of gold and coral. Probably Italian,
c. 1850.

51   Silhouette pendant, mounted in silver frame.
Late 18th century.

52   Gold ring with rosette of garnets. Bohemia,
c. 1830.

53   Silver earrings with stone mounting and hanging
pearls, supposed to be the work of J. M. Dinglinger.
Late 17th century.

54   Shoe buckle, silver, crystal. 18th century.

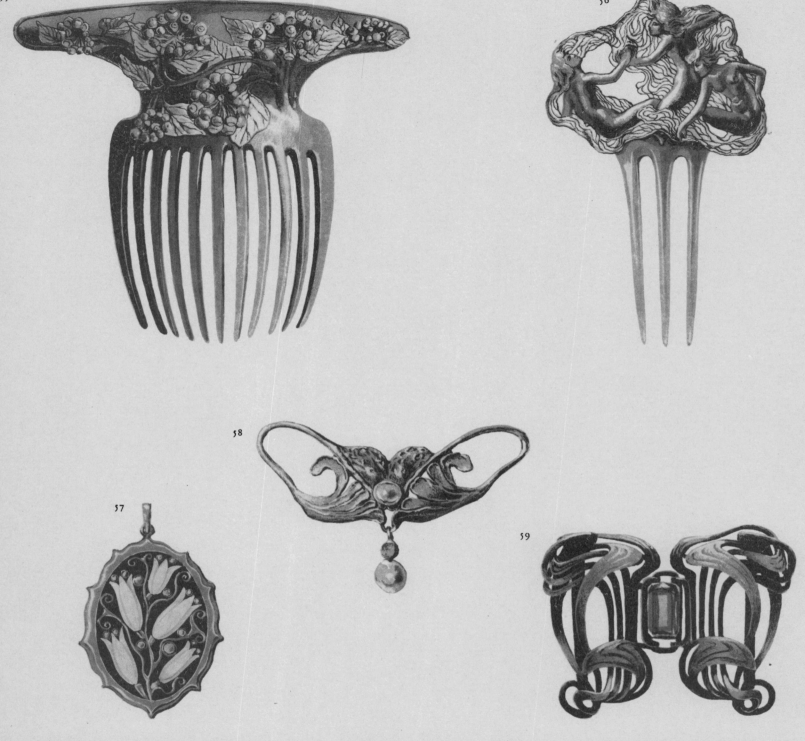

55 Decorative comb with ivy branch made from horn and gold enamel. René Lalique, Paris, c. 1900.
56 Decorative comb with female figures. Horn, gold enamel. c. 1900.

57 Gold pendant, with coral and ivory mounting. Design by E. I. Margold, who worked in the Vienna workshops from 1909–1911.

58 Brooch. Gold, silver, and pearls. Paris, 1906.
59 Belt clasp. Silver with amethyst. Design by Henri van de Velde, c. 1900.

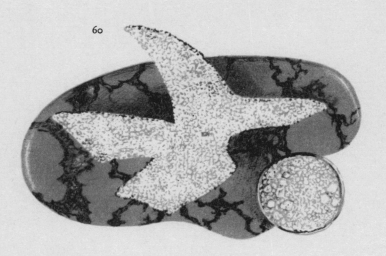

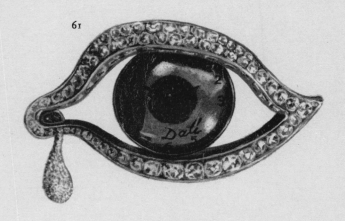

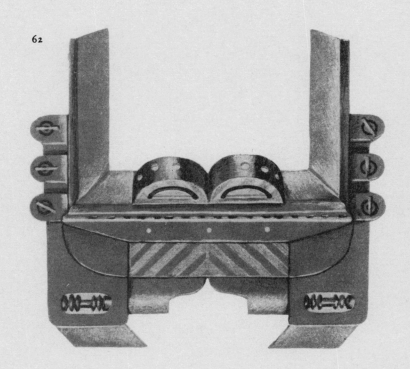

60 Brooch, turquoise, diamonds, gold. Design by Georges Braque (1882–1963).

61 So-called eye of the time. Watch, designed as brooch. Diamonds, ruby, mounted in white gold. Design by Salvador Dali.

62 Pin-on jewellery, yellow and white gold. Claus Bury, Hanau, Federal Republic of Germany, 1973.

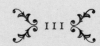

63 Bracelet. Silver, industrially produced. Design by Gübelin, Lucerne, 1973.

64 Choker with pendant. Silver, glass, piacryl. Monika Winkler, Leipzig, 1972.

65 Finger-ring, gold, moonstone, ruby. Elisabeth Kodré-Defner, Vienna, 1973.

and belt jewellery, and for beads, which were used mainly for women's jewellery. Towards the end of the century artificial plaits were worn, which, intertwined with strings of beads, were wound round the back of the head in various fantastic arrangements.

Long thin chain necklaces were often weighed down by heavy oversize pendants, sometimes with pictures of saints or in the shape of small hinged altars, (the latter could also be worn on a belt). Other types of neck jewellery consisted of colourful glass beads, often alternating with semi-precious stones mounted in metal. Bracelets, which only at the beginning of the 16th century regained popularity in the rest of Europe, had been worn faithfully by Italian women since ancient times.

The variety of styles in the individual towns meant that a bright mixture of mainly colourful jewellery was to be found. Venice the "mistress of the Mediterranean" and the centre for the pearl and precious stone trade was, for example, more open to oriental influences than the other towns, especially with regard to material and ornamentation. The impulses were handed on not only to the rest of Italy but also to northern and western Europe (the trade routes went via Venice, Augsburg, Nuremberg, to the Netherlands and right up to England.). New elements also reached the art of ornamentation via Venice: the arabesque, a tendril-like ornament known even in the late Gothic period; the grotesque, often used together with animal or human representations; mythical creatures such as mermaids, dragons, dolphins, lions—motifs, which had already been found in the art of antiquity, and which inspired Dürer to create enchanting designs for jewellery after his trip to Italy.

RENAISSANCE

The end of the 15th century in Europe saw the start of a new epoch in world history: a transitional phase marking the decline of feudal society and the gradual development towards a capitalist society. Characteristic for this period, which lasted until the French Revolution in 1789, was the spread of manufacturing capitalism to almost all European countries. This form of capitalism, unlike industrial capitalism, was perfectly compatible with the continued existence of feudalism. The first bourgeois-capitalist nations, such as the Netherlands, Great Britain and North America now came into being after successful bourgeois revolutions.

In the first decades of the 16th century—earlier in Italy—the goals and ideals of the new bourgeois-capitalist era found their expression in the art and culture of the Renaissance, in Humanism and in the Reformation. The main element was a drastically different way of looking at the world: an awareness and utilization of Nature; a liberation of the individual from the social and religious fetters of feudalism; a move towards a more worldly, though not antireligious view of life; a new consciousness of and orientation towards national communities. In the humanistic *Weltanschauung*, in the natural sciences, in technology and in the arts, an anti-feudal, this-worldly view of Man and his environment was formulated which owed much to the classical world.

For a certain length of time the cultural forms of feudalism continued to exist parallel to these progressive currents. This can, for example, be seen in the reactionary revival of knightly values and customs as ocurred under Emperor Maximilian I (1459–1519), or in the adoption of Renaissance elements, both in their art and their *Weltanschauung*, by princes who then used these for the glorification of their own persons and of feudal power in general.

A process thus becomes clear which is typical for the whole period: the ruling feudal classes adapt to the new social and cultural circumstances, taking over bourgeois elements in order to maintain and strenghten the feudal order of society. Thus the first beginnings of a bourgeois culture in the 14th century developed into an increasingly strong current of progressive, anti-feudal bourgeois or folk culture as a rival to the culture of the ruling feudal aristocracy. There was, however, considerable intermingling and mutual influencing of the two cultures.

This modernizing and adaptation of feudalism to the changing pattern of power meant, above all, an increasing centralization of the feudal state and an extension of its power in the form of absolutism. The growing economic strength of the bourgeoisie was tapped for this purpose by the imposition of taxes, customs duties and the distribution of economic privileges. Towns lost their medieval economic independence and the life-style of the feudal aristocracy took on an increasingly parasitical character as attempts were made to maintain social distinctions by a show of pomp and splendour; eccentric extravagance and formalistic ceremonial found their expression in all areas of art.

Renaissance art and culture with their links to antiquity, were adopted not only by the feudal aristocracy but also by their strongest ally, the feudal papal church. The themes of this art and culture—elements of classical education, styles derived from antiquity, and idealized relationship to Nature—continued to be used and re-interpreted even during the period of the Counter-Reformation from the mid-16th century right up to the baroque era.

With the start of the classical period of bourgeois art, the High Renaissance at the beginning of the 16th century jewellery gained a new importance which derived from antiquity but, which took antique ideas much further. Jewellery became assigned to the natural grace of the human body—a sign of an increasing sophistication of taste and a triumph of the mind over medieval-courtly ceremonial. This, of course, presupposed a certain level of spiritual and artistic refinement and therefore remained essentially a privilege of the aristocracy and upper bourgeoisie.

Italian portrait painting in the early 16th century, as represented by the works of Raphael (1483–1520) Giorgione (c. 1478–1510), Titian (c. 1477–1576) and many others, is a typical expression of the discovery of the individual, a revelling in the physical, in human beauty in general. Jewellery is shown as a clever means of underlining female beauty, of contrasting pearls, cool metal, or sparkling stones with naked female shoulders, shimmering velvet and fur trimmings. The male equivalent, firmly embedded in the bulky attire of contemporary fashion, was relatively sparsely decorated. On a cap, worn at an angle, a brooch gleams (such caps with brooches were also worn by women after the disappearance of the bonnet), occasionally a ring was worn on the hand. It was typical for a citizen, who had a particular position of responsibility, to wear round his neck a chain of office with a medallion.

The medallion and the portrait-cameo are classic examples of the way in which the new Renaissance attitude towards Man and the world was given expression: the rich citizen's self-confidence, individualism and awareness of social position is expressed, just as is the prince's need for fame both during his lifetime and in posterity. Enamelled miniatures, profiles cut out of stone or cheap mother-of-pearl were set in metal and provided with clasps, and were worn on caps or berets and as pendants on belts or neck-chains.

The so-called *medaglie* (Italian metaglia = medal), cast in metal and engraved with a chisel, was used almost exclusively in Italy. The most brilliant master of this art was Antonio Pisanello (1395–1455). At the beginning of the 16th century the first medals, minted like coins, appeared, and later became very common. At the same time the technique of casting and engraving asserted itself. The best-known masters were Francesco-Francia (c. 1450–1517), Benvenuto Cellini (1500–1571) and Carodosso (died c. 1524). The latter worked for the court at Milan and also for several Popes. During the 16th century the fashion for medallions spread across Europe and became popular in the Netherlands and Germany.

In Germany, casting and engraving in bronze, silver and lead—i.e. also in cheap materials for all levels of society—was common, using wax, wood or soapstone models. Apart from portraits—Dürer created a number of medallions with a portrait of his wife and himself—it was customary to record important family events on a medallion. Thus there were, for example, wedding and baptism medallions.

As early as the beginning of the 16th century, as the importance of craftsmen grew, chains of honour for officers and deserving members of the guilds began to appear. Later, these became increasingly elaborate, as they began to be used as visible means of denoting and underlining differences of position in feudal society. Among the town bourgeoisie cross-bow shooting was a popular sport and the champion archer would proudly display a silver chain, usually in the form of a *Hobelspankette*, sometimes with a pendant in the shape of a bird, or the figure of Saint Sebastian. It was only in Germany that the wife of a burgher would wear, as a sign of her "Authority", a bunch of keys on her belt, or indeed a piece of cutlery—the fork was the latest aquisition—and various objects such as ear-scrapers, nail polishers, hooks to draw in the lace on one's dress, small diaries, etc. Men also made use of such practical belt-decorations. It was a common custom to distribute *Gnadenketten* as well as the *Gnadenpfennig* and the *Schaupfennig*. A *Gnadenpfennig* was a richly ornamented medallion which, right up until the 18th century, used to be presented by the ruling lord or his lady to subordinates who had been particularly faithful or had won particular favour (a small sack of such medallions would often be carried when a journey was undertaken). This sort of medallion could indeed be said to be the predecessor of the orders commonly bestowed in the 19th century on individuals of particular merit.

The *Schaupfennig* was exchanged by princely families in order to initiate or continue friendly relations—a personal visit would have cost time and effort.

As more importance became attached to active, creative work so, too, the prestige of the artistic craftsman grew (art and craftsmanship were still regarded as one) in proportion to the role he played in satisfying the needs of the wealthy for symbols of the impressive luxury they lived in. Famous masters of the plastic arts were proud to point to their origins as goldsmiths—for example the sculptor Lorenzo Ghiberti (1378–1455), the painter and sculptor Andrea del Verrochio (1436–1488), and the painter Sandro

Botticelli (1445–1510). Regrettably, however, there are no pieces of jewellery extant which can be definitively traced to any of these masters. In Germany, the most important name is Albrecht Dürer (1471–1528), who began in his father's goldsmith workshop and even later in life continued to design pieces of jewellery. During his employment as court painter to Henry VIII of England, Hans Holbein the Younger (1497/8–1543) made designs for jewellery of considerable elegance and beauty, whose form much enrichened the art of English jewellery. The writings of Heinrich Aldegrevers (1502–1555) and the *New Kunstbüchlein* of Hans Brosamer (*c*. 1500–1554) provided Germany with guidelines and gave the craftsmen information and ideas. Aldegrevers, Brosamer and a most of other artists in 16th-century Germany, France, and the Netherlands were among the so-called miniature masters, whose graphic work—mainly copper engravings—were carried out on a particularly small, often minute scale. These miniature graphics conveyed ideas and forms derived directly from the Italian Renaissance, and included, among other things, sketches of jewellery and ornamentation which could be bought by a wide circle of people and served as a basis for the work of many craftsmen. Thus it was that many countries were introduced to themes—motifs from antiquity or of a mythological or allegorical nature—and typical ornaments of the Italian Renaissance—grotesque, mauresque, arabesque, scrollwork, loopwork etc.

In Germany, which in the first half of the 16th century was the centre for European silver-mining, which housed important humanists such as Ulrich von Hutten, Philipp Melanchthon and others, and where, from the rich town of Augsburg, the Fuggers and Welsers pulled the strings of the trading, mining, and banking worlds, and were, indeed, the very personification of bourgeois power, the booming economic and cultural life brought the art of fine metal-working to a high level of sophistication, though not quite to the heights that had been reached in Italy.

Life in 16th-century Germany, if one ignores the interest in rich jewellery, was of a much more sober nature. In the first decades fashions—particularly for women—and jewellery were much closer to Gothic traditions. The bonnet remained; attempts were made to make the narrow gowns more substantial by adding naughty padding, slits or wide breeches. The old naive pleasure in decoration can still be seen in the use of heavy ornamentation. Heavy chains, rings, hat badges and medallions were used in large numbers. The so-called *Hobelspanketten* made of massive rings, in England and France almost exclusively worn by men, were used in Germany (on more or less tender female necks) often in large numbers, forming a wide collar. If they were made of gold, then the individual links were used as a means of payment if the need arose while the wearer was on a journey. Pendants in the form of letters of the alphabet or richly ornate religious symbols were adopted from the late Gothic period. The lansquenets *(Landsknecht)*, who anyhow drew the disapproval of some citizens, especially those of the clergy, on account of their "unseemly, undignified" clothing, wore enormous wooden rings, held together by a silver band, on their thumbs.

The aesthetic values of the Italian Renaissance were matched in particular by niello decorations with their clear, straightforward lines; these even temporarily eclipsed enamel work in the first half of the 16th century. Silver relief work for ecclesiastical decorations were produced up till the early 16th century in Upper Italy. In well-to-do Venice old oriental techniques, such as damascening and filigree work survived. Filigree work spread after the 16th century from here across many parts of Europe and survived until recent times, particularly in folk-art.

In the production of such jewellery—particularly where figures were represented—use was often made of cast work, which was afterwards decorated in a variety of ways. Limoges, the medieval enamel centre in the heart of France, held an important position in the manufure of objects and jewellery with painted enamel decoration from late 15th to early 17th century. It was typical to decorate also the reverse side, the contreemail, not just for aesthetic reasons, but to prevent distortion of the copper base during firing.

Stone-cutting was an important art-form during the Renaissance, particularly in Italy. Here, thanks to finds of antique cameos, which. according to Giorgio Vasari (1511–1574), were made almost daily among Roman ruins, the cameo became popular among princely collectors. Contemporary cameos made in Milan in the second half of the 16th century show a high level of workmanship. The favourite motifs were either portraits or scenes from ancient mythology.

Another significant characteristic of this period is the perfection of stone-cutting and polishing techniques. Since the late Middle Ages semi-precious stones, especially quartzes, had been polished on large sandstone wheels which rotated vertically. At the end of the 15th century the old *en cabochon* cut was replaced by the facet cut. Most jewels in the 16th century had polished tablet-shaped translucent stones which were often set on coloured foil in order to increase their brightness.

Even in the second half of the 16th century the technical achievements and artistic forms of the Renaissance continued to exercise an influence. However, as the Renaissance lost its antifeudal, bourgeois character, the cultural ideas of the ruling feudal aristocracy began to predominate. Above all, the great feudal monarchies exercised an influence and, of these, Spain was the most important.

The style of the second half of the 16th century is given the controversial name of Mannerism, and was, in its content, an art of the Counter-Reformation. Typical for this style is the development—often in distortion—of Renaissance art towards the fantastic, the ornate, the over-pompous, which involved a technical perfection of craftsmanship verging on virtuosity, and produced works of high quality and great variety.

The continued expansion of world trade, furthered by geographical discoveries and the acquisition of colonies but also by an increasing supraregional division of labour, was used to strengthen the power of the feudal state. This development made possible the spread of international cultural currents and forms over great distances and across national boundaries. Thus it was Spanish dress fashions which spread across most of Europe in the second half on the 16th century. In the field of jewellery, too, there developed for the first time a sort of aristocratic standard type with identical or similar characteristics whichever country it was produced in.

Spain, which had been a strong seafaring power since the 14th century now became the richest country in the Old World, thanks to Columbus' voyages of discovery, the conquest of Central and South America during the first half of the 16th century, and the flow of precious metals which followed. As a unified national state it had initially offered good conditions for a flourishing of its towns, but had later destroyed their independence and introduced reactionary absolutist rule. Since 1480 Spain had possessed the Inquisition, a state church organization whose function of persecuting religious non-conformists was also used against craftsmen, peasants and merchants. The results weakened the bourgeoisie of the country. Later, Spain proved to be one of the main supports of the Counter-Reformation—the attempts made by the Catholic church in the second half of the 16th century, with the help of re-organization, to regain some of the ground it lost as a result of the split in the Christian church.

Typical above all for the strict etiquette at court was the courtly dress, which contrasted strongly with the comfortable clothing of the normal citizens in the Renaissance: the stiff, starched ruff, which separated the head from the rest of the body, was, for women, the upper part of a dress which, with the help of a corset (a popular tool of female coquetry) made of wooden and leaden plates, gave the upper body a triangular shape. With this was worn a stiffened, cone-shaped crinoline, nicknamed a "guardian of virtue". The men's clothing was no less uncomfortable than that of the ladies and was, if anything, even more gimmicky. This so-called "international Spanish style" spread through all the courts of Europe and only showed slight national variations. In England and France bright colours were worn in addition to the black popular in Spain; the Italian ladies rejected the tight corsets and liked to display their often ample charms in large decolletés. But common to all these fashions was a preference for many pieces of jewellery.

The full exploitation of the precious raw materials from the colonies, combined with the economic progress achieved by manufacturing capitalism meant that society's riches could grow steadily and relatively rapidly. The feudal lords were able to use these riches in a parasitical fashion to increase the luxury and magnificence of their life-style. Contemporary reports and inventories point to the existence of veritable fairy-tale treasures, especially towards the end of the 16th century, when, in addition to removable jewellery, clothing was also sewn with pearls and stones. On her death, in 1603, Elizabeth of England apparently left 3,000 robes decorated with jewels. It is reported of Gabrielle d'Estrée, Henry IV's mistress, that she appeared at a party in 1594 in a black atlas robe so heavy with pearls and precious stones that she was incapable of standing upright without support.

The most popular form of removable jewellery was the pendant. Often virtually a miniature, highly decorated piece of sculpture, it was worn not just on a neck-chain but also, in different sizes, in the hair, on a hat or as a clasp on a metal-mounted leather belt or a chain-belt made of ornamented metal sections. Depicted were mythological scenes such as the judgement of Paris, figures of gods, Christian motifs and, later, profane subjects such as pairs of lovers, animals (cocks, doves, pelicans); from Venice came ship and gondola motifs. Great numbers of neck-chains with a variety of ornamentation were worn round ladies' necks, often like a wide collar, and bracelets, usually in pairs, were worn above long sleeves. The coiffure was combed up and held in place by a precious comb or a diadem made of gold filigree and pearls.

An important element in the men's "Spanish grandezza" was a hat with a band set with precious stones and, from 1580 onwards the "hairpin", made of jewels, often in the form of a bunch of feathers. Ear jewellery, which in England, the Netherlands and Germany, was rare until the 17th century, began to regain popularity in the Romance countries as early as the 16th century. A source of information about this is provided by a remark made by the Venetian ambassador to the French court, Morosini, in a letter to his wife in 1573. Describing Henry III he says: "...any remaining dignity is removed from him by his ears, which have been pierced like a woman's—incidentally a fashion here in France—but he doesn't make do with just one ring in each ear—he has two, with long pearl pendants and precious gems."

In Germany, where the art of the goldsmith was at its height, but fashion was largely provincial, due to the divisions within the nation and the lack of any models, rings were worn in large numbers by both men and women, often on various joints of the finger, except on the middle finger. The stones, often cut to high, pointed shapes, were framed by richly ornamented settings. Their large size made it possible to wear them over gloves, which were now a necessary part of every man and woman's wardrobe. Ever since the Middle Ages favourite decorations for love-rings had been intertwined hands, hearts, or sayings. A novelty was introduced in the form of twin-rings which were separate during the engagement period and were then put together to form one ring on the wedding day. Technical progress even made possible the production of rings and pendants which contained watches or tiny mathematical-astronomical instruments. A watch which could be carried on the person, although first produced by the Peter Henlein of Nuremberg in 1511, was still a rare luxury in the 16th century. In these times clocks were regarded as a reminder of transitoriness and death, and decorations such as a small cross or a death's head expressed this clearly.

Nuremberg and Augsburg were the chief centres for goldsmiths in Germany. Further manufacture was carried out in the traditional Italian centres, such as Florence. Milan, which was the centre for stone-cutting, also produced imitation material and jewellery: false rubies and emeralds made of crystal glass and set in silver not only met the needs of the poor city-inhabitants and peasants but also provided useful material for frauds. In the 16th century new cultural ecntres such as Vienna, Munich, Dresden and Stuttgart grew in importance and were developed as cours and princely residences by the ruling feudal classes. In order to satisfy the ensuing increased need for luxury goods, particularly skilled masters were often called to these courts and often remained there for some time.

From the middle of the 16th century cultural exchanges between countries intensified. German masters worked in England, Scandinavia and Spain, French, Dutch and German ones in Florence. Italian goldsmiths worked in France—for example Benvenuto Cellini who, after working in Rome (for two popes, among others) worked from 1540–1545 at the court of Franz I in Paris as an architect, sculptor and goldsmith. (The only extant work is a magnificent salt-cellar produced for Franz I).

These masters took with them their casts, technical processes and ornament models, which contributed to the development of a supra-regional style. Even in Spain, with its endless supplies of gold, Juan de Arphe, the "Spanish Cellini" complained, in 1587, that his fellow goldsmiths nearly all worked to ornamentation models produced by relatively minor French and German masters. The strict bigot Philip II, when he took over power at the Spanish court, forbade in his *Pragmatica* all cavaliers to wear any gold or silver, and only allowed the ladies a small amount of jewellery. Nevertheless, the court jewellers were kept busy. In particular, Italian craftsmen dominated the scene. Thus Spanish decorations also bove an unmistakably "European" stamp. Certain religious groups were the only sources of any sort of local folk-style: four-cornered copper pendants decorated with blue, black and white champlevé work originated from Barcelona. Other work displays a characteristic preference for bold enamel colours. The most precious objects—crosses, Mary-monograms and other Christian symbols—used emeralds.

In the second half of the 16th century a new function emerged for jewellery in addition to its use for personal decoration: the aristocracy began to include jewellery in their collections of art objects for display purposes. Pieces commissioned were expected not only to have a pleasing form but also motifs which would be appreciated by people of a certain cultural sophistication: scenes from mythology or symbolical motifs had to be explained or their significance guessed by the owner's guests (this was also a popular society game at this period). The fantastic forms of contemporary miniature sculpture were used—goblets made of ostrich eggs or coconuts, curved beakers and dishes. Also, bizarre natural products such as misshapen pearls or shells were decorated with gold, enamel and precious stones to form human heads, animals, gondolas or fabulous creatures and made elegant or unusual pendants.

The strikingly large number of pearls which were used in the 16th century not just for sumptuous decorations on clothes but also for laces and buttons can be explained by the large number of freshwater pearls which were available in those days. From as early as the 15th century until the 16th and 17th centuries freshwater pearl-fishing flourished under the protection of the law in mountain streams in Saxony, Bohemia and Bavaria.

The need for a show of colour and sumptuousness was satisfied particularly well by the *émail en ronde bosse* technique; whose range of colours, now greater and subtler than in the 15th century, was supplemented by precious stones, cameos and pearls. Copper champlevé work, which was carried out in all parts of Europe, was produced in particularly delicate, translucent colours by the craftsmen in Augsburg. Cellinis *Trattati dell'oreficeria*, the most important contemporary handbook for goldsmiths, reveals that the craftsmen were also skilled in niello, filigree work, the setting of precious stones and the preparation of gold- and silver-leaf. With a certain satisfaction Cellini mentions the striking effect of an idea he developed—that of backing a ruby with red silk. His written works also show him to have been an expert in the art of embossing. His own descriptions (for example of how he produced a golden pluvial clasp for Pope Clement VII) reveal that he used to create the decoration directly on the worn metal, without using the customary wax or bronze model.

Cellini was an important co-founder of the Fontainebleau school, and during his stay in France contributed significantly to the production of a new catalogue of ornamentation which had a seminal influence throughout Europe. Sculpted scroll-work, enturnied grotesque and mauresque, combined with medallions and many other artistic and highly complex creations provided a strong contrast to the classical simplicity of Renaissance ornamentation. The French artist, René Boyen (*c.* 1525 – end of 16th century), a contemporary of Cellini, produced a book *Livre de Bijouterie* in the style of the Fontainebleau school.

Worthy of a place alongside Cellini's work is that of Wenzel and Albrecht Jamnitzer. The former was called "the German Cellini". Both moved from Vienna to Nuremberg, in 1534. Wenzel Jamnitzer was later to serve as goldsmith to four Emperors in succession. Work by him is now in the hands of museums in dozens of European cities, from Leningrad to Paris, Vienna to Stockholm.

BAROQUE

The term "baroque" is probably a derivation from the word *barucca*, the word used by Portuguese jewellers for an irregular, disproportionate pearl. This term, which was already in use about 1570, was wrongly used in classicist art theory to denote the exceptional or the strange. In the second half of the 19th century it was introduced as a term denoting a particular style, and up till this day it is commonly used for the art of the period from approximately 1580 to 1750. The baroque style began in Italy, and only spread to the rest of Europe about 1620–1630 (it reached Germany even later because of the Thirty Years' War), and then developed into the rococo style from 1730 to 1750.

This period in the development of art and civilization was set against the background of the feudal-absolutist society and the Counter-Reformation. It represents a particular form of attack (in world outlook and artistic ideas) on the considerable power of the European manufacturing bourgeoisie who were increasingly making their presence felt in the economic, social, and cultural world. The bourgeoisie had stabilized their position especially after the successful bourgeois revolutions in the Netherlands at the beginning of the 17th century and in England (1642–1649). In 17th century France and in Germany after the Thirty Years' War the bourgeoisie also became more powerful. Within Europe there was an invisible boundary between the bourgeois and feudal states. The reaction of the feudal class took the form of a concentration of feudal state power, and the absolutist state with an even stricter caste-like division between the social classes and a clear social hierarchy. These developments found their expression in a new artistic tendency—the baroque style.

The baroque style was actually a conscous attempt to produce art mass appeal, and it thus made use of a very secular and comprehensible language. It is often sensual to the point of the ecstatic, and hints at the social subordination and dividing up of the different parts of society within the whole, the dividing up of the people under their heroic and glorified rulers as well as the dogma of the Church. This social function was emphasized in the huge buildings erected at this time, the representative way of life, and the pomp. Art and culture, however, did exploit the characteristics of the bourgeois culture to their advantage: the heritage of the Renaissance was kept alive; the realism of bourgeois art from the Netherlands, and elements of folk-art were adopted.

There is a clear boundary between the jewellery produced in the baroque style of the bourgeoisie in the Netherlands, and the feudal baroque style of the absolutist states, although they did exercise a certain influence over each other. The technical innovations in the craftsmanship usually came from the side of the bourgeoisie, whereas the feudal nobility supplied influential and financially powerful patrons, who served progress by promoting, for example, the development of stone-cutting and polishing techniques.

There was a notable decrease in the amount of jewellery worn by the bourgeoisie, especially in the Netherlands, but also by the anti-feudal bourgeoisie in some other countries. The intellectual and historical reason behind this lies mainly in the attitudes of the calvinistic or puritanical bourgeoisie in Holland, England, and France, who showed tendencies towards capital-saving, thrift to the point of miserliness, and whose way of life and way of thinking was permeated with self-sufficiency. They thus tried to detach themselves from the life-style of the nobility through their new attitudes. Therefore, when the Puritan Oliver Cromwell (1599–1658) destroyed the crown jewels after the English King Charles I had been beheaded, and consequently had the stones sold, his action was more than just symbolic.

After the revolution in the Netherlands artistic and cultural influences with strong bourgeois elements gradually spread over large parts of Europe. These were also incorporated into the culture of the feudal nobility, but only after they had been suitably adapted.

The Netherlands also became the initiator of a growing preference for floral and leafy ornamental forms. New flowers, which had previously been unheard of, were now brought by the new trading partners in Asia Minor, India, and China. Representatives of all social classes became fans of the tulip and of horticulture in general. Even well-to-do ladies did not shrink from ordering flower beds to be dug behind their houses, and to be filled with everything which was fashionable and which the climatic conditions permitted. Bunches of flowers were a popular room decoration not only in Holland, but also in the neighbouring countries; in the Netherlands' art the naturalistic flower still-life became common and was done in exact botanical detail; bunches of flowers made from precious metals and stones and shaped into brooches were worn either on hats or on the chest; finally, floral and leaf-ornamentation became typical for the style of the 17th century.

The severe dresses became looser—as in the Renaissance —first in bourgeois Holland, then elsewhere; they became wider, more comfortable, and colourful. Dress soon had the function of expressing sensuality through its clinging material, and cheerful contrasts of colour and shape.

In the first half of the century stunning decorations, such as bows, lace, ribbons, shining pearls next to the skin, were the most popular forms of jewellery. Pearls were sometimes attached to the wrist by a ribbon, sometimes hung in several rows round the neck, or were worn as a drop-shaped pendant on a velvet ribbon. They were also used for ear-jewellery.

The rich metal jewellery disappeared and, as can be seen in the account of the Duchess Elisabeth of Saxony's dowry (1614), even the chain belt was no longer worn. Metal rings remained in use, but their forms were adapted to produce wide openwork wreaths or flowers, or rings covered with enamel ornaments. The simple wedding ring came into general use, and was often worn on the thumb.

The numerous emblems of various political, literary or secret societies, and especially "memorial jewellery" came under the category of jewellery produced under the auspices of the bourgeoisie. Their jewellery reflects to a far greater degree than the schematized jewellery of the court a conscious participation in contemporary life, and also reflects to a greater degree individual sentiment. Pendants or rings containing miniature pictures or inscriptions were especially widespread in England, and were supposed to help cherish the memory of a close deceased person. They often gave a clue to the political opinion of the owner—after the death of Gustav II Adolf of Sweden (1594–1632), pendants with the king's profile shown in relief were commonly worn. After Charles I of England was beheaded, rings or lockets were worn containing a picture of the deathly-pale king with an expression of great suffering on his face. These then kept his memory alive amongst the Royalists. In Germany the harrowing experience of the Thirty Years' War gave the skull a new symbolic meaning—a heart-shaped pendant with a skull bears the following inscription: "Nothing but mortality is dear to me." Death symbols combined with a cupid on engagement or love jewellery meant "love till death us does part".

With the rise of France as the leading feudal absolutist power in the second half of the 17th century, the fashions favoured by the French nobility once more became the model for all court dress. Goldsmiths and jewellers had, in fact, already been employed under Louis XIII to work in the workshops of the Louvre, but with the founding of the "Manufacture Royale des Meubles de la Couronne" in 1662 by Finance Minister, Colbert (1619–1683), the Parisian arts and crafts grew in significance. Skilled craftsmen from all over Europe poured into the city, and Parisian ornamental engravings were copied in some form or other by other countries. One of the most fecund artists at Louis XIV's court was Gilles Legaré (born *c.* 1610), jeweller and enameller. He brought out a book with ornamental engravings in 1663, *Livre des ouvrages d'orfèvrerie*, and specialized in transforming loop motifs into jewellery designs.

Up till the 1680s Louis XIV had dressed relatively simply but then, after his regular army had been organized, and his finances taken in hand by Colbert, he began to make notable changes in his appearance. The "allonge" wig also became the fashion of the day: the "lion's mane", worn by the ruler as a halo symbolizing greatness and dignity. The *justeaucorps* (right next to the body), a men's jacket, was derived from the soldiers' uniform, and was made from silk, velvet, or brocade. On festive occasions it was embroidered through and through with gold and silver, and sometimes studded with diamonds. This impressive show of gold was on the one hand a sign of absolutist self-aggrandissement, and on the other a sign of the return to stiff ceremonial behaviour at the court of Versailles, the "nobleman's casern" of France. The women wore corsets and crinolines, not however, as in the Spanish period, to practically kill the female shape at birth but to draw attention to their figures by means of low décolletés, coquettish frills, bows, and headdresses. The women—or rather the mistresses—were the focal point of the court. It was not unusual for them to pull strings in politics, and they knew how to combine the demands of court etiquette with an elegant and attractive appearance and manner.

Court jewellery, which from the end of the 17th century onwards was worn to a far greater degree by women than by men, now began, amongst other things, to degrade itself by dabbling in a refined form of erotic seduction; a tendency which was to have interesting consequences in the 18th century. (The morals were left in the hands of the lady). One example is the invention of "ribbon language" (the ribbons were made from silk, or often from jewels). The initiated could tell by this language what the object of his desire thought of him: the so-called "murder" ribbon was worn round the neck; a ribbon round the forehead meant "rascal"; over her heart, "loved one", round the waist, "joker", and a ribbon nestled in the deepest point of her cleavage meant "touch me".

The introduction of the *parure* represented a certain refinement in taste. This was a set of jewellery composed of individual pieces of a similar form and ornamentation. On the other hand this fashion also served to unify jewellery to a greater degree than ever before and it also represents the practical implementation of one principle of baroque art, namely the subordination of different parts into the whole. The women's *parure* was usually made up of ear pendants —girandoles—which since the middle of the 17th century had taken the form of delicate but excessively large metal loops mounted with precious stones which almost hung down to the shoulder. These were complemented by loop-shaped Sévigné brooches, named after the Marquise Marie de Sévigné (1626–1696), who at that time was the centre of a Parisian literary society, and the composer of very intellectual letters containing criticism of contemporary life. The aigrette, a delicate piece of hair jewellery, often in the form of a stylized feather or of a flower, completed the set. Neck, arm, and finger jewellery became less and less common.

Male jewellery was almost entirely restricted to buttons and shoe buckles of varying value. Less valuable, yet very picturesque buttons were decorated with enamel flowers (the reverse sides of precious jewellery were also decorated in a similar way). A great luxury at court were diamond buttons: it has been claimed that in 1686 Louis XIV paid 360,000 Francs for a waistcoat, the buttons were made of 816 coloured precious stones and 1,824 diamonds. It is also reported that for state receptions he adorned himself with diamond jewellery worth from 15 Million Francs upwards —this consisted of buttons, shoe buckles, daggers with precious stone inlay and garters. In 1690 and 1710, when the politics of conquest had proved to be a particularly heavy financial burden, almost everything was made into coins: Louis XIV even found it necessary from time to time to forbid the wearing of jewellery at court.

The diamond was admirably suited to the artistic *raison d'être* of baroque jewellery, i.e. to provide the feudal rulers and nobility with an aura of glittering splendour and wealthy exclusivity thus separating them off as a social entity. The diamond was the most precious stone from the mid-17th century onwards. Precious metalwork and ornamental framework began to play a secondary role, and the art of the jeweller became more important than that of the goldsmith. New diamond deposits had been discovered in India, in Golcanda and Hyderabad. Diamond cutting was probably developed in Amsterdam and Antwerp about the middle of the century. The rose-cut was preferred in the 17th century. The so-called Holland Rose had 18 horizontal facets and 6 star facets. In the mid-17th century, Cardinal Mazarin, a passionate collector and lover of diamonds, founded the diamond-cutting industry in Paris. Finally, at the end of the 17th century, Peruzzi, a Venetian, invented the brilliant-cut with 32 facets. This cut further increased the possibilities of attaining the best optical effects from the diamond, and through a very skilled cutting technique gave the diamond great powers of refraction and reflection, making it sparkle and glitter to maximum effect.

Germany's villages and settlements were left devastated after the Thirty Years' War. The continuous process of artistic development had been interrupted by the war, and Germany thus lost its leading position in goldsmith work. Although German artists did manage to follow up the baroque movement after the Treaty of Westphalia in 1648, the rules of the guilds had now become a fetter to the development of bourgeois craftmanship. The territorial princes came out of the Peace of Westphalia stronger than ever. By scrupulously exploiting the bourgeoisie and the ordinary people, they were able to imitate with varying degrees of success the example set by Versailles. In the prevailing conditions of the small state these attempts at imitation could only result in caricature. However, towns such as Munich, Dresden, and Berlin, where princes had their seats of residence, became centres of court art. The craftsmen employed at the courts stood outside the jurisdiction of the guilds, and they also had the opportunity of keeping up to date with all technical and artistic innovations by working together with leading architects and painters, who were summoned to the courts from Italy and France. Through their so-called ressettlement policy, which was supposed to draw members of the bourgeoisie and peasant class back to the land to make up for the losses of the Thirty Years' War, the Prussian rulers tried to attract foreign labour in order to fill up the state coffers, which had been heavily drained by the cost of the war and the luxurious life of the nobility. Thus the protestant Prussian court, because of France's misfortunes under the Huguenots after the lifting of the Nantes Edict in 1685, landed in the lucky position of being able to offer the most skilled craftsmen of Europe a new home. This "compassionate" deed meant that the finest jewellery came into the possession of Berlin's nobility, and made them independent from imports of expensive luxury goods from Paris. In 1740 the import of French goods to Berlin was finally forbidden by Friedrich Wilhelm I.

Towards the end of the 17th century Augsburg managed once more to establish a certain name for itself as the centre of German baroque goldsmith work. Johann Melchior Dinglinger (1664–1731) probably acquired his skills both here and in Paris. In 1692 he came to Dresden and from 1698 onwards worked as court goldsmith under Augustus II, also called Augustus the Strong. One of the first pieces, which he completed for Augustus II in about 1700 was a set of sapphire jewellery; later he completed several pieces for a set

of carnelian jewellery as well as numerous representative pieces designed for display. (The sets consisted, as a rule, of hat badges, shoulder bands, knee and shoe clasps, decorative awards, daggers, hunting knives, walking sticks, riding whips, tobacco tins, pocket watches and buttons).

One of the numerous guests who came to Dresden to see the royal treasury "The Green Vaults" was the Russian Tsar Peter I (1672–1725) who, although a room was prepared for him in the royal residence, preferred to spend the night in the house of the court jeweller, Dinglinger, in the Frauengasse, "next to the wooden bread benches". In the daytime he soujourned in the workshop and laboured over a gold goblet in an attempt to find out the secret of the goldsmith's skill. Later he insisted on allowing initially only German goldsmiths to settle in St. Petersburg.

Medieval feudal Russia followed the traditions of the Greek-Orthodox Byzantine culture in its intellectual, cultural, and artistic life. In ornamental art and jewellery it held onto Byzantine forms for a lot longer than western Europe, albeit in a style which had a very distinct character of its own, enriched with Asiatic elements. Russia first came into contact with the rest of Europe after its liberation from the rule of the Mongolian Tartars. Moscow, the capital since 1328, was also the centre of a prestigious jewellers' trade, which in the 15th century produced particularly beautiful filigree work. In the 16th century the niello and enamelling techniques flourished in simple, yet very expressive forms and ornamentation. These remained relatively constant and traditional until the 17th century; they were linked to folk-art and hardly affected by changing fashions.

After Peter I's reforms and his conscious turn to western and southern Europe, these areas influenced the styles and fashions in Russia to a greater degree than before, and there, combined with the heritage of Russian national culture, they contributed to the development of the Russian baroque and rococo styles. In keeping with the artistic taste of the nobility, the ruling class, brightly coloured enamel work and coloured precious stones remained characteristic for the work of the Russian jewellers.

ROCOCO

In the first half of the 18th century the traditions of court jewellery were continued after the death of Louis XIV (1715) in France and with the introduction of the 18th-century rococo style the most delicate and precious of jewels were made.

The flight from the "noblemen's casern" led to the retreat of the nobility to their Parisian town palaces: to intimacy. The lady of the house held her own little court; *la femme* ruled supreme. Typical for the first half of the century was its open sensuality; a sensuality which was already inherent in the baroque style but which was now exaggerate to the point of frivolity. It can be seen in the ambiguity and visual intellectual punning in the pictures of Nattiers (1685–1766) and Boucher (1703–1770) with their representations of women, who, although covered sophisticatedly with layers of dress material, have a very graceful seductive quality. Jewellery became more than ever an artistic medium of coquetry, of whimsical moods, and playful extravagance. The social classes were differentiated not by the amount of jewellery they displayed, but rather by the degree of taste shown in the choice of jewellery and the way it matched one's garment. We have records of small sparkling diamond buttons which were worn on delicately coloured silk gowns and button holes surrounded by tiny diamonds. The sole decoration worn in the daytime with the casually sophisticated dress of the Regency period (1715–1723), the *contouche*, was a silk ribbon tied around the neck, and flowers in one's hair or bosom. Artificial flowers, which had previously been used exclusively by the Church and produced in Italian convents, became fashionable, and in the 18th century were produced in France. After the 1830s when Louis XV came into power and there was a turn to the court fashions of earlier times, ruffs became more common, especially high lace collar ruffs with tiny diamonds sparkling in the folds. The garter became the playful and frivolous guardian of secrets: it was camouflaged as a piece of jewellery and covered with precious stones and ribbons, but in its centre it had a medallion with a hidden fastening which was concealed from the eyes of one's spouse, but which contained a miniature portrait of one's lover. The rosette worn on the elegant high-heeled shoes drew one's attention to a dainty foot. Later the shoe buckle took over this function, and embroidery and precious stones were not unusual. *Venez-y-voir* (look at me!) was, for example, the message conveyed by tiny emeralds on the stitching of the heel; one of the many passing fashions worn in the second half of the century.

The *parure*—choker, aigrette, Sévigné brooch or dress brooch and earrings—was kept for special occasions, and still retained its basic baroque style, but in a more refined, elegant, and delicate form. The jeweller achieved a graceful mobility in the individual pieces by placing a large number of tiny diamonds (up to 150 diamonds per carat) in rows, tightly packed in thin silver mountings on silver wire, then arranging them to form removable aigrettes or Sévigné brooches in the shape of feathers, star-shaped rosettes, or butterflies. These glinted and fluttered attractively in the candlelight and in mirrors. A new brooch began to replace the Sévigné at the beginning of the century. This was a triangular-shaped piece of chest jewellery, which was attached to the dress and was made from diamonds or crystal, decorated with beads. Diamond ear-pendants, drop, loop, or star-shaped, often had an additional *pendeloque*, a second small drop or star, hanging from them.

The elegant *giardinetto* ring with a plate in the shape of a gently curved assymmetrical branch of blossom, replaced the wide baroque ring with its generous floral decoration. About the middle of the century the marquise ring appeared on the scene: a cluster of small diamonds, ("rosettes") round a large four-cornered or oval coloured stone. The general taste in cut precious stones was shared, among others, by Madame de Pompadour (1721–1764), the beautiful and influential friend of Louis XV: she etched a series of 63 leaves after sketches by the Parisian stone-cutter Guay, and worked with her own hands an agatonyx which can still be seen in the Louvre.

The discovery of diamonds in Brazil, in 1725, contributed to this stone retaining its popularity. It was not until the last three decades of the century that topazes, sapphires, emeralds and garnets came into fashion, or, as in daytime jewellery, turquoises cut *en cabochon*.

Male decoration still consisted largely of shoe and belt buckles and precious buttons "... they have dozens, nay hundreds of waistcoats", wrote a nobleman who came to Paris from the provinces, "wonderfully embroidered with buttons as big as six-livre pieces decorated with valuable miniature pictures", (from Gleichen-Rußwurm). Many an artist who later became well-known, such as Isabey (1767–1855) earned a living in his youth by painting buttons. In Dresden buttons made of Saxon precious stones, set in gold or silver by the court jeweller Neubert in the years 1786–1795, were much in demand: a dozen made of chalcedony exchanged hands for 26 Reichsthaler.

There was also a *parure* for men—it consisted of buckles for shoes and knee breeches, buttons and brooches, often with miniature portraits. Apart from their decorative awards, the *châtelaine* was an essential element in a cavalier's dress: this was a watch chain decorated to a greater or lesser extent with tinkling charms (watch-key, seals, toiletry objects, decorative discs); the watch itself was also an object of decoration and hung freely from the belt. The centre-piece of the *châtelaine* had chinoiseries or subjects taken from pastoral idylls—necking doves, scantily dressed lovers in a meadow, landscapes with towers, temples or defiant-looking castles.

Female jewellery of this period consisted also largely of such pictures on metal or porcelain, made into brooches, pendants, crosses, ear-pendants, or buttons. In the 1770s when courtly fashion developed bizarre extravagances and excesses, and the ladies' coiffure hit bombastic heights, it became not uncommon for the hair to be decorated not just with a sailing ship or a basket of fruit or a wet-nurse, but also with locks of hair of the lady's father or her lover and with miniature portraits of loved ones—children, friends, bullfinches, lap-dogs. When later on, the bourgeois hat was adopted by court-fashion, such hair decoration was used for the ladies' hats as well.

The young and vain Marie-Antoinette of France (1755–1793) appeared at a court function in 1772, so the story goes, with a coiffure which, with its ostrich feather ornamentation, reached a total height of approximately one and a half metres and the left side of which was decorated with a pink ribbon with a ruby set in gold. "All reports agreed", wrote her mother, Maria Theresia of Austria (1717–1780) in a letter of September 2nd, 1766, "that you had bought bracelets for 250,000 Francs, ruined your finances and incurred debts. In order to cover the latter you had sold off your diamonds very cheaply. But it is also suspected that you are leading the king into more and more unnecessary expense, which is dragging the state into financial ruin ... This French frivolity and exaggerated frippery! The thought that you should become like this is quite unbearable." (Schaller) The cost of such Versailles extravagances only served to increase the people's hatred of the feudal regime. The picture of soft-living and extravagance which emerged from court society was completed by the scandal of the "necklace trial" in which Marie Antoinette, although this time innocent, became involved in 1785. The circumstances surrounding the mysterious purchase of jewels by a trickster dressed as a queen may not have been fully explained, but what did emerge was the circumstances at court, the extravagance and moral unscrupulousness, and the publicity given to this helped to fire the dissatisfaction of the people and prepare for the revolution.

Living beyond one's means seems to have been an infectious disease among the aristocracy of many parts of Europe at this period. Prince Potemkin (1739–1791) a favourite of Catherine II of Russia, had crystal dishes filled with diamonds, and spoons with which to serve them, presented as the dessert for one of his dinners. Reichsgraf von Brühl (1700–1763) the Prime Minister of Augustus II of Saxony, changed his suits daily, as well as his jewel-studded tobacco jars and matching sticks of which he possessed hundreds. There were countless more examples.

In Prussia only thrift was practised. The "soldier king" Friedrich Wilhelm I (1688–1740), according to reports of his courtiers, used to take individual pieces from the considerable treasury he had inherited and sell them in order to have money to build up his army. His wife, who did not dare wear her many diamond jewels in his presence, had once put all her finery and gone to the gaming table, when the king's unexpected return was announced. According to a lady of the court, the queen in front of everybody hastily began to take off the jewellery and hide it...

The British bourgeoisie had emancipated themselves from the affected court fashion immediately after the bourgeois revolution in the 17th century, and had developed their own more moderate style of dressing, more suited to the life of a working man. Due to the prevailing conditions in Great Britain (which were particularly favourable for the free development of the capitalist mode of production) and to its vast colonial territory Great Britain grew to become the richest and most powerful country in Europe. London now stood on a equal footing with Paris as the centre of the jewellers' trade.

Since capitalist relations of production were developed at an early date in England and were soon firmly entrenched, England became the inspiration for a steady flow of bourgeois forms of jewellery. Once the industrial revolution was underway in the second half of the century England was finally in a position to cater for the growing demand for cheaper jewellery by putting its large-scale, factory-based production into use. Another truly revolutionary achievement in the history of jewellery was the production of new materials, such as steel, and stone imitations produced through chemical processes. All jewellery was still, of course, modelled on the extremely refined court art— on the other hand the nobility were, more than ever before, dependent on bourgeois discoveries in the field of imitations: court ceremony demanded that on certain festive occasions men and women should don rich pieces of jewellery, and it was by no means unusual for the nobility

to wear jewellery which was either an imitation or had been borrowed from someone else.

The growing demand for decorative, yet cheap ornaments was covered by the imitation industry in Bristol where crystal jewellery was produced for the first time and in Birmingham, where the "Metal Company" had had a monopoly over the mass production of steel buckles since 1778 and now exported them all over the world. "Diamonds" made from cut and polished crystal and coloured "precious stones" made from glass were produced in vast quantities. Steel, usually used for shoe buckles was given polished facets, and its sparkle vied with that of diamonds. Imitation jewellery was also produced in Paris, but still on a handworker basis: In 1767 the guild of the *joailliers faussetiers* had 314 members.

The innovations made by the London watch-maker Christopher Pinchbeck (died in 1732), and the Austrian Joseph Strasser were to be extremely important for the future development of jewellery. Pinchbeck was the first to produce an alloy of copper and tin which was very similar to gold, and which was generously employed in the production of buttons and *châtelaines*. In 1758 Strasser, who like many of his contemporaries, carried out many alchemic experiments, succeeded in producing a colourless glass mass by mixing and melting green flint, "iron-oxide", argillaceous earth, chalk, and sodium. This mass was strong and hard enough to be cut and polished, and the final product was very similar to a real diamond. Strasser had hoped, with some justification, that this invention (which is still used today) would bring him financial succes. He was, however, disappointed, because Maria Theresia declared that it was impossible to give anybody and everybody opportunity to wear the same jewellery as the nobility, and consequently proceeded to forbid the production of artificial diamonds. Only much later on did the *pièrres de Strass* spread from Paris all over Europe.

Silver filigree ornaments made by hand had been part of folk jewellery since the late Middle Ages and had always, with regional variations, more or less modelled on the courtly prototypes, or they had been inspired by folk art traditions. They were always, however, far behind in the fashion world.

The turn to antiquity, which had been latent since the Renaissance but which had been intensified since 1760—about the same time as the industrial revolution started in England—was a purely bourgeois attempt to free themselves from court art and to find their own style forms. The turn to antiquity "was unavoidable in the unfettering and the establishment of the modern bourgeois society—and its gladiators found in the severe classic traditions of the Roman Republic their ideals, and the art forms, the self-deceptions, which they required in order to hide from themselves, the limited bourgeois substance of their struggle . . ." (Marx).

The influence of classicism on the Louis-seize style of the aristocratic court art also shows the growing influence of the bourgeois opposition culture and art on the nobility in the period before 1789. Some of the French nobility were already tuned into the atheistic ideas (of the bourgeois opposition even) before the great revolution. Many of the nobility's salons also liked to play around with some elements of bourgeois and folk-art. Some examples of this are the pastoral plays, the use of rural decoration in the rococo style such as ploughing tools, bee hives, idyllic landscapes, and the adoption of a rural intimate way of life. Apart from these symptoms, which show their inability to produce something of their own, the effect of the rationalism of the bourgeois enlightenment was also reflected in the culture of the nobility.

This attitude is expressed in the jewellery produced in the two decades before the French revolution: on the one hand in the luxurious jewellery with its greater compositional strength and concentration of forms, and on the other hand in the preference for antiquity motifs used in the miniature paintings worn as jewellery—these were used first in folk-art ornaments, then also by the court. Of greater significance, especially for the motifs in jewellery making, was the originally bourgeois cry, which was by now also current in salons, sparked off by Rousseau's (1712–1778) works, and did not lose its influence until well into the 19th century.

DIRECTOIRE AND EMPIRE STYLE

The international effect of the French revolution was reflected in all aspects of culture. The social conditions had been shaken at their foundations, and thus the ideological significance formerly placed on jewellery traditions was also shaken. This situation was seen at its clearest in France where the feudal past was in comparison to other countries, radically swept away. The "Constitutional National Assembly"—which was formed by the representatives of the Third Estate on June 17th, 1789—not only proclaimed "Liberty, Equality, and Fraternity"—the bourgeois revolutionary illusions which were upheld long after their time and spread far beyond the French borders—but they also announced the abolishment of the class-biased, law-making powers. Theoretically then, the "dethroning" of class jewellery took place before the actual fall of the monarchy: jewellery was deprived of its function of acting as a sign of class privilege. However, in practical terms, due to the continuing social injustice, only the wealthy bourgeois gained from the abolishment of the former class jewellery.

As a result of the French revolution in 1789 and the ensuing wars, which were to pitch bourgeois France under Napoleon I (1769–1821) against the rest of feudal Europe until 1815, the bourgeois revolution got underway in most of the other European countries. However, the victory of the capitalist system and the gradual disappearance of the feudal society, which took place in the first decades of the 19th century, was not a smooth process. It was spurred on by the bourgeois revolutions in 1830/31 and 1848/49, but then interrupted by periodic set-backs. The process came to an end in the 1860s, when Tsarist Russia embarked on the road to capitalism after the abolishment of serfdom

(1861) and the introduction of bourgeois reforms. This period is also marked by the onward march of the industrial revolution which had been underway in England since the last decades of the 18th century. Now not only a large part of Europe was affected by it; it had also reached North America and Japan. The machine replaced handwork, and the factory replaced small manufacturers. Steam engines, railways, and steamships began their victorious march.

England, where the industrial revolution was over by about 1830, became economically the most advanced country in the world, and a model for the other developing bourgeois-capitalist nations. In Germany and France the industrial revolution was completed by about 1870, but initially it affected only a few branches of production such as the textile and metal industries. Jewellery production remained largely in the hands of craftsmen and small manufacturers.

In their confrontation with nobility the bourgeoisie grew to be the richest and the ruling class, while the former feudal nobility became more bourgeois and merged increasingly into the new class. The new money-aristocracy made a show of their wealth and claim to social recognition in front of the normal people—just as the nobility had done before them—but they also put on the show to prove themselves in front of the former ruling class: property and valuable ostentation possessions were put on show.

A second line of tradition in the history of jewellery was tied up with the middle class and petit-bourgeoisie and with the peasant workers, who had just been freed from the fetters of feudalism. The small independent producers grew out of these social strata—the small producers who were more or less at the mercy of the capitalist market and the pressure of competition. Last but not least another new social class—the proletariat, came into being. At this time, i.e. during the industrial revolution, the proletariat was still living in the most miserable of conditions, so that it was hardly in a position to own or wear jewellery. We also do not know today exactly what individual, well-off members of the working class could have worn in the way of jewellery.

At the end of the 18th century the prototype was still republican simplicity which the pre-revolution bourgeoisie had already seen realized in antiquity. This prototype gained in strength after the excavations of Herculanum and Pompeii, and the publication of Winkelmann's (1717–1768) writings on art theory. People began to collect antiques, and pictures of the ruins of antiquity—for example the series of graphic works by Piranesis (1720–1778)—were in great demand amongst admirers and specialists as were the ornamental patterns done in antique style by Pergolesi.

France and England held the lead in the cultural world during the 18th century right up to the middle of the 19th century. In France the bourgeoisie in the form of the Directoire (1795–1799) took over power after deposing the revolutionary Jacobins. "The graces and the deities of joy, which had been driven away by the terror, have returned to Paris. Our pretty women ... are worthy of adoration the concerts—wonderful", so ran an article in a bourgeois periodical of this period (Köller/Töpfer). The life of the upper bourgeoisie was again one of pleasure and fashion, although consisting of new freer dress-forms, was again demanding. The inspiration for the fashions came from antiquity and obviously, due to the gaps in people's knowledge, meant that a certain amount of fantasy had to be employed. The women thought it wise to appear covered in "Greekness" rather than following the principle of "noble simplicity—quiet greatness". The colourless, transparent dresses with daring décolletés encouraged them to cover their bare arms, neck, bosom and ears with all sorts of jewellery. Thin chains, filigree earrings, up to three bracelets on each wrist, diadems, gold belts, brooches on dresses slit up to the knee, rings with cameos on the fingers and even on the toes, when sandals were worn—all this was still thought to be modelled on antiquity. Madame Tallien, the beautiful friend of Count Barra, the most powerful man in the Directoire, appeared at the Paris opera house in 1795 dressed in a sleeveless, transparent tunic, slit up to the knees, worn over a skin coloured slip; even the numerous gold rings she wore on her arms, fingers, ankles and toes could only partly cover her nakedness, and Talleyrand, who witnessed her appearance, noted: "One could not reveal oneself in a more pompous manner."

With the establishment of the bourgeois-monarchistic regime under Napoleon—he was crowned emperor on December 2nd, 1804—France, having been republican since 1789, was again given a hereditary monarchy which did not miss a chance of showing off its exclusive position through a show of pomp and splendour. Napoleon's support of capitalist production, trade and industry consolidated the social rise of the bourgeoisie, and made France a serious competitor to English capitalism, since England was now set on becoming the factory of the world.

The military campaigns of General Napoleon Bonaparte against the coalition of counter-revolutionary feudal monarchies, apart from winning victories for the cause of the revolution also brought in a considerable amount of booty (polished precious stones from collections of the Roman nobility!); large amounts were gathered, mainly from Italy. The repeated successes of the Napoleonic wars made France territorial lord over most of Europe. The conquered territories supplied France with huge amounts of grain, and taxes. Marshals, ministers, and the new service nobility created by Napoleon received fabulous gifts for their services.

The return to the monarchic system with its magnificent feasts, receptions, and victory celebrations meant the return of the jewel, of the *parure*, of the absolutist period. They were, however, much more bitty, more ostentatious than before. Original pieces of old rococo jewellery were often worked into new pieces, and classicist parts were added.

The cold representative pomp of the "antique-orientated" empire shows more talent for creating theatrical effects than for elegance; this, of course, was in keeping with the taste of the rising bourgeoisie, the nouveaux-riches.

The relatively simple forms used by the Directoire style changed in the Empire period. The classicist elements were retained but given greater ornamental variety.

The antique-based ornamentation, however became a little artificial and clumsy thus making the precious jewellery often seem somewhat pompous and pathetic.

Cut stones had since the beginning of the 19th century been collected once more to a greater degree. When Napoleon had himself crowned king of Italy in 1805 his own crown was actually decorated with glass paste and not with precious stones, but for his first wife Josephine he had a *parure* made from 82 antique cameos, taken from the state collections, and many pearls. The *parure* consisted of a diadem, comb, collier, earrings, two bracelets and turned out to be so heavy that Josephine could never wear it.

A contemporary noted in 1812 that "the Queen of Naples (Napoleon's youngest sister—author's note) appeared today in jewellery made from stones excavated at Herculaneum and Pompeii—her head, arms, and chest were covered in them. A three-strand belt with straps under the arms and antique relics running down the front of the dress, set in mounts shaped as crowns. The earth had been wrenched carefully between the stones and the mounts" (Biehn). Antique stones with antique earth—an innovation in the history of jewellery!

In 1810 Napolean presented his second wife, Marie Louise von Habsburg, with a wedding present consisting of no less than five precious stone *parures* made from diamonds, pearls, sapphires, emeralds, and rubies worth a total of half a million Francs.

Growing demand meant that stone-cutting skills were improved. The Italian stone-cutter family, Pichler, from the Tyrol were amongst the most famous. They were active from the beginning of the 18th century until the mid-19th century. Napoleon himself founded a special school for stone-cutters.

The so-called ceramic biscuit-reliefs made by the English manufacturer Josiah Wedgwood (1730–1795) were reasonably priced yet very attractive ornamental pieces. Wedgwood introduced them into the European market in the second half of the 18th century. In Naples cameos were cut from the lava of Vesuvius, and became increasingly popular with the tourists—(tourism was just at its beginning stages). The cheap shell cameo (from time to time large-sized ones were produced and decorated with profiles crowned by leaves) almost eclipsed cut precious stones in the course of the century.

ROMANTICISM AND BIEDERMEIER STYLE

The bourgeois revolution after 1789 had also gradually liberated the petit bourgeoisie and the peasant workers from the feudal class conditions which had been prevalent up till now. In the last decades of the 19th century the proletariat, the new class, began to organize itself step by step within the social, political and ideological spheres, and from then on also numbered amongst these who wore jewellery.

The better-off peasants, petit bourgeoisie, and representatives of the middle classes and intelligentsia now became the patrons of a development in the history of jewellery which was more or less independent—romanticism and Biedermeier. Peasant jewellery is a chapter for itself. From the same social strata were to become the last decades of the 19th century onwards to an ever greater degree the consumers of the industrially produced jewellery.

The liberation of the individual from class-biased ties, which was begun in 1789, also meant that one was freed from social inferiority and became—to all outward appearances at least—a free individual owner of goods, and producer, who had to develop a new attitude towards their environment and come to terms with various social relations. The emotional involvement in clubs or in ideological, political, or simply social groups and the more intense emotionally-tinged turn towards the family or towards one specific person corresponded to the desire for personal development, the devolopment of new needs and the cultivation of social contacts. Thus jewellery became a means to aid the formation of the personality: it served to emphasize individuality, even amongst peasants, the petit-bourgeoisie and the better-off members of the working class, even although capitalism in principle laid down barriers for the working class. Jewellery, in any case, lost its old function as a class representation.

This breakthrough to individual ornamentation, used to enhance one's personality, represents the beginning of a development which has a direct link with today's attitude to jewellery, and which is to be evaluated as a decisive and progressive step in the history of civilization. Even the openly sentimental elements of romanticism do in fact represent a step towards jewellery's new function; a function which is closely tied up with bourgeois subjectivity.

In particular, the Biedermeier and the peasant jewellery with their often relatively simple, sometimes naturalistic and sometimes moderately classicist range of forms is still completely acceptable from an aesthetic point of view to the modern observer; many individual pieces are even considered extremely attractive.

The bourgeois jewellery from this period (the motifs of which were also used for the daytime jewellery of the upper class), from the cheap imitation jewellery to the valuable pieces with precious-stone inlay, reflects the new emphasis put on feelings: friendship rings were decorated with bunches of flowers made from coloured stones, fervent inscriptions, or with pictures of one's lover. Rings with representations of burial urns, weeping willows, broken pillars, or mourning widows were worn by the relatives of a prematurely deceased, especially in England. The miniature portrait or the shadow portrait, the silhouette of a close friend or relative, of one's child, for example, were now set in brooches, pendants, medallions or bracelets. This was a long-lasting fashion which only gradually fell from favour with the spread of photography in the second half of the century. In England, where so-called sentimental jewellery was very popular, especially in Victorian times, Queen Victoria had a bracelet made from the milk-teeth of her nine children.

After Bonaparte's abdication and the reinstatement of the pre-revolution monarchy, the believers in the deep-rooted Napoleon myth owned technically ingenious trick rings, which would open up when a special button was pressed and a little Napoleon in uniform made from wood or metal would pop out of a miniature coffin. Shortly after Napoleon's fall Napoleonic souvenir jewellery was forbidden, however: soldiers wearing uniforms with buttons showing the Napoleonic eagle were sent to the galleys. Jewellers who made jewellery with pictures of Napoleon on it ran the risk of being sentenced to three months imprisonment.

Ornaments made from the so-called base materials such as the iron jewellery in the first decades of the 19th century were closely tied up with the jewellery traditions of the middle and petit-bourgeoisie. The general poverty which reigned after the Napoleonic Wars was a contributing factor to the great development of fine cast-iron. Already in 1789 cast iron jewellery was known in France, and there was a saying which went, "I gave gold for iron." In Germany as well, when gold was sacrified for the fatherland during the anti-Napoleonic liberation struggle, iron jewellery became very popular, and it retained its popularity in later and better times. The delicate filigree-like ornaments were produced in particular in Berlin foundries which specialized in this work—their artistic peak was reached between 1813 and 1840—and the ornaments were bought throughout Europe and in North America. The individual parts were cast, soldered together and covered with a black varnish made from soot and linseed oil. A report from the year 1830 claims that the fineness of the forms and the cast was due to the use of very fine moulding sand which came from the Altmark near Seehausen and Rathenow (Potsdam District).

This kind of jewellery was produced by the Berlin jewellers Geiß and Davaranne and the goldsmith, Hossauer, all of whom sent models to the royal iron foundries. The formal charm of iron jewellery was given competent encouragement by the building-master Karl Friedrich Schinkel (1781–1841), who in his books "Models for manufacturers and handworkers" (1821) and "Patterns for Gold- and Silverwork" (1837) had considerable influence over the German late-classicist ornamental art.

The life of the middle classes still ran, in general, along very unromantic, limited lines, and they had no chance to build up large amounts of capital. Moderation, thrift, and self-satisfaction were the qualities which ran through the German Biedermeier period, and through its equivalents in the other European countries. The female members of the family showed a preference for either large flat ornaments or ones with small delicate sections, both of which were demure and intimate. The increasing cost of such ornaments bears witness to the growing prosperity. Apart from a tie pin, buttons and a pocket-watch, men hardly wore any jewellery; women, however, made up for them. The *ferronnière* consisted of a small metal chain tied round one's head with a pearl or precious stone hanging over the forehead—this was undoubtedly borrowed from the 16th century. Medallions often as big as side-plates were worn as chokers, and the earrings were of a considerably length and many-sectioned pendants. Brooches and bracelets, often in the form of a bow, were amongst the most popular pieces of jewellery in this century. They had little capsules (this was also true of love and friendship rings) which served as containers for locks of hair belonging to one's lover, or to a dear deceased person. In the 1830s and 40s whole "armbands of feeling" were woven from the hair of one's nearest and dearest: sometimes even ear jewellery or chokers were made from hair. Decorative belt clasps, diadems and ornamental combs were also part of the many-sided repertoire of jewellery. In the 1860s the pendant-cross began to be worn; a fashion which was adhered to, especially by the women of the demi-monde.

In Italy, where excavations throughout the 19th century were a continual source of inspiration for antique-orientated jewellery, particularly charming pieces of jewellery made from semi-precious stones or glass mosaic were produced, which were obviously inspired by the Pompeian mosaics. There were specialists in Rome, Florence, and Venice for mosaic work done in semi-precious stones depicting butterflies, bunches of flowers or landscapes with ruins. Glass mosaics were done in Naples. Coral, which was industrially used in Naples to make jewellery, also became more and more popular. Coral, like amber, rock crystal, Venetian glass beads, bright enamel work and hair-work, was worn not only by the middle classes, but also by the nobility and the financial aristocracy as daytime jewellery.

Parallel to the development of the jewellery forms pertaining to the middle and petit-bourgeois, the rural folk jewellery went through a period of blossoming during the first half of the 19th century. While the feudal dress stipulations had imposed strict limitations on the development of peasant jewellery right up to the mid-18th century (up till then predominately natural materials such as fruit, seeds, animal teeth, amber and coral were used), from the second half of the 18th century onwards peasant metal jewellery became more and more common. Not everywhere, but in some areas with favourable economic conditions such as northern and southern Germany, there was a prosperous self-confident peasant class, which showed its own class consciousness through its gene rousdisplay of jewellery.

In spite of the often great stylistic differences between the different regions in European countries, the peasant jewellery did have some common features: silver was the most popular material, and gold was only used in a few areas (Frisia and parts of Silesia). Wealthy peasants and their families were obviously in a position to wear jewellery of this kind. The poorer peasant population had to content themselves with gold-plated silver, and silver-plated copper and brass alloys. Colour was introduced by using mainly red stones such as rubies, garnets and glass fluids which are usually red, green or blue. The most highly developed technique was filigree work, although this was formed and worked in very different ways from region to region. Whereas, for example, in North Germany the ornamentation tended to be flat and divided into clear parts, the South German filigree work was characterized by generous, sculpted ornamentation with tendrils, spirals, multi-layered lattice work, and artistic knots.

The range of motifs used for peasant jewellery corresponded to its highest function, i.e. an engagement or wedding gift, or a means of social representation. The range included coins, religious symbols such as crosses, but also love tokens such as necking doves, intertwining hands, and burning hearts. There were many different forms used for women's hairpins, combs, headbands, frontlets, bridal crowns, temple and ear-jewellery and the chest pendants, chain clasps and ornamental buttons which were usually attached to the dress. Men adorned themselves with hat badges, belts, hanging watch chains, decorative buttons and clasps, and in some areas earrings were also quite commonly worn by men.

Peasant jewellery made from metal was usually made by town-based craftsmen and traded at the town markets. Only in a few particularly prosperous areas such as North Germany were there village gold or silversmiths. During the second half of the 19th century industrially produced goods began to eclipse handmade jewellery.

HISTORICISM

The eclectic imitation of style traditions from past centuries reached its climax in the field of jewellery making—as in all other fields of the arts and crafts—in the second half of the 19th century. The seeds had been sown, however, in the first half of the century. In France particularly, where after the fall of Napoleon I the feudal reactionaries in the form of the Bourbon Dynasty came back to power, style elements from the 18th century from the rococo period were taken over, and the classicist empire style was banished from the face of the earth. After the 1830 July revolution in France a pompous neo-Renaissance style swept through Europe and became the style preferred by the climbing bourgeois financial aristocracy, who were at this time striving towards power. Their preference for this style lasted until the 1860–70s. "The Renaissance is now the fashion in Paris", noted Heinrich Heine as early as 1836; "everything is furnished and dressed in the style of this time ... as far as the decoration of the Rothschild Palace is concerned, everything which is reminiscent of the spirit of the 16th century and which the money of the 19th century can pay for, has been gathered here." The nobility and the courts also adapted themselves to the preference for the high-Renaissance style, the style of the upper-bourgeoisie and princes. The neo-rococo style did in fact, still exist in the 1830s and '40s, but it re-appeared in full force only during the restoration period in the 1850s. In the 1880s and '90s there was a turn to the neo-baroque style which was an expression of the nationalistic, imperialistic struggle for internal and external power—clear evidence of the bourgeois desire to show off their wealth, and of the social barriers between them and the classes below them.

These ever-changing preferences for various historical styles shown by the nobility, courts, and the climbing upper bourgeois in the 19th century was to a large extent the expression given to an idealistic, deeply romantic self-complacent attitude, which penetrated all social and cultural life. The main reasons for the development of historism, which had a very bourgeois character, was the need for social representation before the nobility and the rest of the population; besides, this art was seen as a purely formal matter, which was independent and separate from any functional purpose and the materials used. As a style, as an ornament, art actually had a functional character in that it was expected to act as a disguise and to point to a higher, ideal reality, which could keep the cruel everyday banality and ugliness of reality at bay. The cruel aspects of life in the capitalist society such as competition, desire for personal property, greed for capital were not ideologically acceptable to the bourgeoisie as worthy of culture, (only in the 20th century did ideological forms expressing cultural approval of the capitalist reality come into being). The upper bourgeoisie disguised the situation by adopting romantic illusionary cultural ideals from past times: the average member of the bourgeoisie thought of himself as some sort of Renaissance personality, as a "prince of capital", a "railway king", and in this way tried to glorify his everyday life.

After the unsuccessful revolution of 1848 when the impossibility of realizing the democratic aims of this revolution became clear, the way was clear for the establishment of the second empire under Napoleon III (1808–1873). "The ideal breeding ground for unfettered capitalism" (Köller/Töpfer), offered profiteers and speculants, adventurers and fortune-hunters greater opportunities than ever before to make their fortune. Even ministers and members of the court did not shrink from choosing an adventurous way to make their fortune—or to lose it. The economic upswing in the 1850s and '60s provided the upper class with the opportunity of leading a life of luxury and pleasure. At grand balls, for example, lotteries were held for the amusement of the ladies, and some hosts spent up to 30,000–50,000 Francs on one ball. Helmut Graf von Moltke marvelled at Lady Westminster's diamonds in 1856; in size and cut they vied with the crystal of the chandeliers. Edmond de Goncourt when he expressed his wonder at Madam Payva's huge emeralds, received the following reply: "Yes, they are so expensive, that a whole family could live for a long time off them."

Empress Eugénie, with her excellent figure, the perfect model of function and good taste, called her numerous jewel-studded toiletries a "political" matter, with the not altogether unfounded justification that their production helped promote French industry. In 1887 when her crown diamonds were auctioned, a piece of jewellery in the form of vine-leaves with garlands, made by the jeweller Bapst, attracted particular attention. It contained more than 3,000 diamonds and was beautifully executed in the contemporary naturalistic style. The same was true of a comb containing 208 diamonds, and a belt with pearls, sapphires, rubies, emeralds, and 2,400 diamonds. One could go on giving endless lists of this princely love of pomp using examples from the ruling houses of Austria, Russia, and Prussia.

From the 1850s onwards historicism received various new impulses: the London World Exhibition in 1851 acted as an assembly place for the whole width and breadth of industrial and hand-manufactured products from almost all the European countries. Here contemporaries were clearly shown on the one hand England's industrial superiority, and on the other the shockingly low level of aesthetic quality displayed in the handworkers' products in almost all branches of trade.

The abolishment of the guilds, free enterprise and free trade—in Germany the lifting of the customs barriers—were all to have a decisive influence on the art industry. A greater number of handworkers, who had previously been the elite of the working class, became the wandering proletariat. The "masters" of the trades now stood in tough competition, in particular with the newly established "firms", which later became industrial enterprises. The old masters not only had to readapt themselves to cater for the demands of a broader more folk-orientated sprectrum of buyers; they also had to adapt to a much more rapid changing of fashions, which were dictated by industry. In order to survive they had to make their products attractive. Now the customer did not, as previously, come to the master's workshop, but rather went to the "shops" which, with their windows brimming over with goods, enticed the customer to buy.

Despite the fall in aesthetic quality, the technical quality of the handmade crafts remained the same in the 19th century; in fact, in the second half of the century it reached a particularly high standard. In the 1850s and '60s, at England's initiative, greater attempts began to be made to raise the level of taste in general. However, apart from these attempts, which were often a desire to do something for the common good, the competitive struggle amongst the bourgeois nations was taking place on the capitalist market, which was becoming more and more concentrated.

Thus after 1851 a number of art schools, art museums, clubs and societies were founded in England to help promote trade and industry.

By publishing comprehensive works with models for handworkers and manufacturers, holding exhibitions and opening libraries, it was hoped that the nation's taste would be improved and that in this way new impulses would be imported for the creation of stylistically suitable products using the art styles of historicism. In 1864 a corresponding institution, the Museum for Art and Industry was founded. Out of its 24 sections one was dedicated to gold and silversmith work, and a second to costume jewellery. In 1867 Berlin followed suite with the founding of the Berlin Museum of Arts and Crafts which was connected with a school of industry. Similar institutions were set up in many other towns.

The result of these actions was a spread and expansion of historicism throughout all branches of the arts and crafts. In the later World Exhibitions, which were held at regular intervals, the European nations competed in their interpretation of more and more historical styles: Renaissance, rococo, oriental, eastern Asian, and regional folk-art traditions.

Even the masters of the crafts followed the trend of using historical motifs for their creative work. Although numerous examples of the products from this period are totally alien to today's taste, some charming and imaginative pieces were produced: figure representations borrowed from the Middle Ages or the Renaissance, have heroic or touchingly sincere faces. Renaissance scroll work for example, was intermingled with neo-Roman ornamental elements in the 1840s and supplemented by new self-thought-out elements. It was also popular to mix neo-Roman, Egyptian, and baroque elements—especially towards the end of the century—to revel in the joy of a new discovery. One was not only well acquainted with all the styles (a collection of ornamental patterns put together by Eugène Julienne in 1844 was named to this effect) from the past, but also with the technical processes used in the past.

Many handworkers became research workers: gold enamelling was re-discovered. After a long search the jeweller and merchant Fortunato Pio Castellani (1803–1865) managed to track down the secret of the Etruscan granulation technique: an achievement which was exploited throughout Europe. In the 1860s Castellani also encouraged the revival of old folk art techniques and forms, and brought filigree back into fashion. Inspired by rococo the *monture illusion* became popular in the 1860s. This was an almost invisible mounting for precious stones which was made with the new metal, platinum, and used mainly for diamond mountings.

Diamond cutting based on scientific methods reached for the first time an extremely high degree of perfection. The discovery of large precious stone deposits in Brazil and the diamond fields in South Africa in the 1870s and '80s meant that the jeweller had a vast reservoir of material at his disposal.

The increasing show of pomp in the 1870s–'90s was a sign of the wealth now accumulated by the bourgeoisie and was characteristic of the bourgeois struggle for social and national recognition. The value and splendour of the jewellery was openly displayed, often in a parvenu-like manner. The bright splendour of coloured precious stones and enamel work began to overshadow diamonds. The naturalistic representations of animals, flowers and plants were, from the 1880s onwards replaced by the overwhelming ornamentation of the neo-baroque and later the neo-rococo style.

The industrial production of certain individual pieces of jewellery, some even made from precious metals, had already been intensive in the first half of the 19th century. In the 1870s industry had in its possession rolling mills, punches, cutting-out machines, coining stamps, guilloching tools and many other machines which it could use even to produce gold and silver jewellery. It was discovered how to use chemical means to give alloyed gold the colour of pure gold, to boil silver white and colour it with acids, and how to give precious metals a polished or matt finish. Industrially produced jewellery, however, began to concentrate more and more on cheap mass ornaments, which was what was needed to satisfy the demands of the less well-off customers, the petit and middle-bourgeoisie and the better-off members of the working class. The materials used were mainly imitations or cheap alloys of precious metals. German silver, so-called argentan, and alloy made from copper, zinc, and nickel was already known in the mid-18th century. From the 1830s onwards it was used in fairly large quantities to make utensils and jewellery. Some articles were even given a silver coating by using galvanism. Gold imitations were produced by using the reddy-yellow tombac or the so-called similor, both of which were made from a mixture of copper and zinc. The term talmi or talmi gold came to be used synonymously, in a negative sense, for anything which was fake. This was a yellow copper alloy which, when plated with gold, was used in sheet or wire form for making jewellery. The best talmi with a gold content of 1% was produced in the 1880s by the Paris firm, "Tallois". Glass, rock crystal, paste stones, and strass were all used to produce cheap stones or imitations of precious stones.

The jewellery forms, keeping in line with the trend towards historicism, represent attempts to produce convincing imitations of precious jewels. This jewellery symbolizes a progressive step in social history: even the working people now had the chance and the means to develop their own personalities. The lack of aesthetic education which often came to light was embedded in the contradictory nature of the capitalist society.

Jewellery made from cheap materials came under attack from all sorts of fighters for "aesthetic" ideals, and was also dismissed as trash or kitsch by contemporary collectors and museum directors. For this reason only a small number of examples of this type of jewellery has survived, and we also have hardly any illustrations of it.

ART NOUVEAU

About the turn of the century, to be more exact between 1895 and 1905, an international art movement known in general as Art Nouveau developed. In France it was known as "Art nouveau", in Germany as "Jugendstil" and in Austria as the "Secessionist style". The arts and crafts blossomed, and also reached a turning point: next to their high aesthetic quality, unmistakable signs of decay in the late bourgeois era became obvious. The turn away from historicism was ideologically inspired and given artistic and formal inspiration by English social reformers such as John Ruskin (1819–1900), who proclaimed the social function of introducing the idea of beauty into the shaping of the environment; and by William Morris (1834–1896) who worked for the revival of good old solid handworker traditions. They both not only postulated the turn away from historicism, but also the search for material justice, and the rise of a new, highly-stylized ornamentation. The striving for social aims in art was a new revolutionary phenomenon.

At the turn of the century man's environment also went through certain decisive changes: electricity was used to a greater degree; the cinema, photography, and the car were invented; the steadily growing world trade meant that all kinds of articles, both functional and luxury, could be brought without any difficulty from every possible country; the means of communication, even the fashion magazines grew in number and size and their lay-out and information-content had been considerably improved since the mid-19th century. In the age of imperialism, industry and colonies seemed guarantees one could depend on for economic growth in the industrialized countries, and for security and property within the bourgeois system.

However, under this smooth surface the social contradictions were becoming more and more intensified. The powerful rise of industrialization in Germany from the 1870s onwards resulted in social re-groupings: a ruling class made up of the nobility and the bourgeoisie which then developed into the monopoly bourgeoisie and which proclaimed growing imperialistic aims was diametrically opposed to the working class, who were becoming increasingly trade-unionized. In between there were the groups of the middle and petit-bourgeoisie, within whose ranks the bulk of an opposition movement was to be found, which, with its idealistic, social-reformist aims, was of great significance for the arts and crafts. Any success it had, however, was essentially limited to the field of art forms.

Characteristic for this period, in keeping with the call for a new, more beautiful environment, was the search for new artistic forms in the fields of town planning, external and interior decoration, design, and applied art, including machine-made products.

Apart from doing interior decoration painters and architects also designed vases, carpets, book illustrations, even clothes and jewellery. However, in contradiction to the social aims laid down in their theoretical programmes their creations remained as a rule exclusive, and machine production was still technically not in a position to keep pace with the new demand, and neither were the majority of entrepreneurs willing to cater for it. One of the best-known personalities of this movement was the Belgian, Henri van de Velde, (1863–1957), architect, designer, and art theoretician, who worked in Weimar, Germany, when his influence was at his greatest. He argued passionately for machine production as "adaption to the demands of today" and claimed that the machine would "with its powerful iron arm ... produce beauty, as soon as beauty fed it". Later he gave in, in the face of the "greedy self-interest of the industrialists", and retired to concentrate on private orders only.

Van de Velde's work had a great influence on art, especially between 1896 and 1902. The jewellery made by him —belt discs, pendants—are excellent examples of his examplary art theory which put new emphasis on the expressive power of the line, colour, ornamental and plain surface, light and shadow effects. The autonomy of the materials was seen in a new light, and their processing and various combinations were revolutionized, knowledge and ex-

perience were gained, the rational content of which is still valid today.

During the 1890s applied art was still largely restricted to the stylized floral field: elegant plant-like curvilinear natural forms such as lilies, water-lilies, and curved leaves next to purely abstract patterns were dominant. Animal representations, such as peacocks, swans, and even female heads were depicted in the form of opulent blossoming plants —a poetic and exquisite flat style designed for people of taste. At the beginning of the 20th century this romanticizing phase was replaced by soberer forms which were, however, still fairly complicated. This development was due to a greater awareness of the new technical and industrial conditions, and it was a development which found its best expression in the form of functional realism adopted in the 1920s *(Neue Sachlichkeit)*.

In France, the traditional source of luxury goods, there appeared towards the end of the 19th century the most elegant and sophisticated of ornaments, which were to prove seminal for the jewellery of the next ten years, if not longer. The name of René Lalique is the one which towers above the other famous names of this period: Tiffany, Vever, Masriera, Jensen, Wolfers, etc. Lalique (1860–1945), whose work attracted much attention in the "Paris Salon" as early as 1894, was jeweller, silversmith, glassmaker and designer. In 1897 he was appointed "Knight of the Honorary Legion". His greatest success was secured at the Paris World Exhibition in 1900. Like many of his contemporaries, Lalique was promoted by an industrialist—by Gulbenkain—yet despite the use of machinery his work still gave the impression of being handmade individually.

The general trend towards "rediscovering the inherent qualities of the material used", towards "the Animation of the Material as a Principle of Beauty" (title of an essay by van de Velde) was also reflected in Lalique's work. In a very imaginative, unconventional yet highly sophisticated manner he managed to combine old traditional materials in a new way: apart from gold enamelling with delicate colour shading he used mainly horn, ivory, amber, mother-of-pearl, silver, and pearls for his work, and managed to combine the most costly of materials with the cheapest. His favourite motifs were leaves, stalks and flowers with softly-flowing contures or thistle-like shapes arranged in rhythmic "prickly" ornaments; anemones, violets, iridescent dragon-flies, orchids, fairies or mermaid-women with long flowing hair decorated with flowers—a very refined romanticized range of forms, which when coupled with the now technically perfect execution, corresponded exactly to the taste of the bourgeoisie, who had been educated in aesthetics, and were wealthy and sophisticated to the point of being decadent. During his lifetime Lalique's jewellery creations also sold well (he opened his own shop in 1905), since soberer, more abstract ornaments were also beginning to catch on in Germany and Austria. In later years he concentrated more and more on glasswork, but his practice of using completely new combinations of materials—arranged exclusively according to their aesthetic value—has been continued up till today although the materials and forms have been changed radically.

As opposed to the jewellery of the French Art Nouveau with its beautifully temperate colours, metal jewellery, mostly silver, was produced in other countries. In Denmark a new style variant emerged from the workshops of Georg Jensen, E. Magnussen, and M. Ballin. Their style, however, was almost devoid of colour, and concentrated mainly on silver embossed work, similar to that produced by van de Velde and Peter Behrens in Germany.

Apart from Weimar, further centres of the German arts and crafts were situated in Berlin, Munich, and Darmstadt. Influence was exercised, in particular, by the Austrian designers of the Vienna Secessionist group. In their work they used flat, geometric forms such as circles, triangles, rectangulars, etc., and they prepared the way for a new, more functional form of jewellery.

In general, metal dominated the scene at the beginning of the century: gold (which now came in various shades due to the use of alloys), silver (which was artificially given a grey or black colour), and in particular copper, brass, nickel, and steel supplemented by shiny pearls, enamel inlay or round cut and polished decorative stones.

Amongst the most popular pieces of jewellery at this time were ornamental combs, hat pins, pendants worn on long chains, and above all brooches, which were worn on the high necks of dresses, stiffened with fish-bones, and were often used to hold a small lace frill (jabot). There were also numerous variations of belt clasps, which were often worn coquetishly at the back of the dress.

Whereas women were, as ever, covered in rich jewels, especially on festive occasions, men had almost only practical jewellery: the buttons on their waistcoats and cuffs were made of gold, glass stones, of gold or silver plated material. The one exception was the decorative award. The higher the social position, the greater the desire seemed to be, amongst the more ambitious, for a "decoration". The huge number of awards with their various forms and colours often made it seem as if a "plumber's shop" were hanging for display on the front of a dress-coat. From 1890 onwards there was an outbreak of decorative award fever, even in England where the bourgeois gentlemen had been dressed for the longest period of time in inconspicuous functional grey and black suits, men paraded around with often excessively big shiny awards.

ART TRENDS UP TO THE PRESENT

Whereas magnificent pieces of jewellery were still executed individually for the thin top layer of society by a few chosen jewellers, the industrial production of both precious metal and imitation jewellery grew steadily in importance.

In 1904 the French chemist, Verneuil, succeeded in producing for the first time synthetic rubies, and in 1909 synthetic sapphires. The prices for the real stones began to fall, but rose again suddenly when it was discovered that the synthetic stones had little microscopic bubbles in them. Later corundum and spinel were made using similar modern methods, and both aquamarine and turmaline shades could in turn be produced from them.

More recently synthetic emeralds have been produced in the U.S.A.—Chatham-created-emeralds—and in Austria—the sygmerald.

In 1913 the Japanese, Mikimoto, discovered how to create culture pearls (little balls of mother-of-pearl are laid within the outer coat of a shell and, over a growth period of five to eight years, cover themselves with layers of mother-of-pearl), and this meant that larger numbers of less wealthy women could wear pearl jewellery.

Traditional centres of the jewellery industry which to this day have an international reputation are Birmingham, Valencia near Milan, Pforzheim, Schwäbisch Gmund, Hanau, and Jablonec in Czechoslovakia for glass and gems. The use of machines for metal processing was extended and improved. Although machine punches and presses had been used in the 19th century, every individual piece was still made by hand and given subsequent treatment. In the 20th century a machine was created which could punch, cast, and cut independently. The preparation of the metals —preparing either sheet or wire—had formerly been done by the goldsmith himself, but now machines took over. The various parts can be obtained ready for use at special cutting shops. The guilloching tool which was invented more than 100 years previously and which is used to cut fine linear patterns in the metal, has now been perfected, so that today patterns can be produced at a greater speed and with more variation. Since 1950 machines have been used which work simultaneously not with one but with several needles. The granular or shaded patterns produce a fine silky gleam which makes polishing unnecessary. More recently numerous other means of working the metal surface have been brought into use.

The die-casting process introduced after 1945 makes it possible to produce many copies of one model while retaining a greater exactness of detail. It could also produce a bark-like or relief-like pattern. (For imitation jewellery made from metal with a low melting point a simpler variation of this process is used.) The gold plating methods— the first attempts at the *doublé* method were made over 150 years ago, and the galvanizing method (gold and silver plating done in galvanic baths using electrolysis) has been practised since 1840—were likewise improved.

The further development of the chain-making machine after 1945 meant that it was no longer necessary to go through the long process of soldering each individual chain-link together. By the way, so-called chainmakers employed by the Pforzheim jewellery industry in 1903–1905 earned an average 4.04 Marks per day, and women earned 2.49 Marks for the same work. Gem workers numbered amongst the better paid of the labour force. Today when the chain links are put together a conveyor-belt takes them slowly through a soldering-oven. Only particularly expensive jewellery still has to be completed by hand from start to finish.

As a rule, the handworker also buys individual parts such as needles and hinges for brooches, clips for earrings, and stone mountings in various sizes ready-made. These few examples should give some idea of the rapid technical developments within the jewellery trade.

With regard to art forms in the 20th century, the work of the 1920s has proved especially fertile and seminal. Only then could the theories of functionalism, the necessity of which had already been recognized by the progressive forces by 1900, be put into practice, since only then was industrial production in a position to permit, or even to promote "functional" forms. The activities of the Bauhaus in Weimar and Dessau (1919–1932) were to have international resonance. In 1927 Georg Muche wrote in the magazine "Bauhaus": "the industrial form as opposed to the art form is 'supra individual'—as a result of its objective attitude to a problem. The arguments for purposeful forms and for technical, economical, and organizational profitability produce ideas for forms which represent in their own way a new conception of beauty." The art forms of the new functional realism *(Neue Sachlichkeit)* which developed out of these theories were a denial of the ornament which has no function, of the scrolls and aesthetic design: the new forms were aimed at creating unity of function and form.

The jewellery made in accordance with the principles of the Bauhaus, is mainly silver and has an exceptionally clear and simple form which makes use of simple geometric shapes and smooth or curved metal strips, the finely hammered surface of which are often the sole ornamentation.

In contrast to these usually hard-wearing and sound-looking ornaments was the work of the French jewellers, who were still considered to be leading in their field. Both types of work were, of course, geared towards different groups of buyers: one towards a broad spectrum of less wealthy citizens (to support the aims of the Bauhaus was a political move), the other towards a small elite group of buyers with a taste for luxury.

Apart from those jewellers whose work consisted largely of variations on traditional forms there were other outstanding names such as Georges Fouquet (1862–1957), who produced completely new work, and who in their choice of forms orientated themselves towards the contemporary art movements such as cubism and expressionism. They also showed a preference for unconventional combinations of material. Even well-known painters and sculptors made pieces of jewellery, or at least designed some jewellery, sometimes for other institutions, and sometimes to give as presents to friends and relatives, or sometimes just as a break from some other big work or as a kind of sketch for a big work. Georges Braque (1882–1963) at the age of 79 designed 133 pieces of jewellery, from which the Musée des Arts Decoratifs bought ten. Jean Arp (1887–1966), one of the initiators of the Dada-movement and from 1925 onwards associated with surrealism, made numerous characterful pin-on ornaments as presents to his friends. In the '50s Giorgio de Chirico (born 1888), who is considered to be the forerunner of surrealism, presented his wife with a small number of jewellery pieces made by himself from metal and plastic. Salvador Dali (born 1904), since 1928 the main representative of surrealism, endowed his peculiar jewellery creations with a striking character drawn from an absurd dream world. Some of them are horrific: one heart designed by him is made from precious rubies and has a small mechanism built in it which enables the jewel to beat like a living heart. He liked to give his jewellery creations, which were always mounted with precious stones, the form of a human organ such as the mouth, eye, or hand. Pablo Picasso, Jean Cocteau, Max Ernst, Emil Nolde, Ernst Kirchner, Karl Schmidt-Rottluff, Erich Heckel, Arnaldo Pomodoro, Jean Lurcat and many others also designed jewellery.

In present-day jewellery-making a noteworthy progressive movement has developed between the two extremes: jewellery of the traditional kind (now using modern technology for stone and metal processing), which is often looked upon as a kind of investment, and fashion jewellery (the form and type of cheap material used vary greatly). This new movement is an attempt to draw jewellery into the fields of plastic and graphic art, and often sees a piece of jewellery as a small piece of sculpture or a miniature picture. The best works of this kind are those which are obviously designed to enhance physical beauty and individuality. Many representatives of this trend, who work as designers and thus design and make their "miniature works of art" themselves, reject the idea of jewellery as an investment, or of jewellery being a slave to short-lived fashions. The formal mark of "real" of "fake" is no longer put on jewellery. Gold, silver, and enamel are treated in the same way as stainless steel, bronze, copper, aluminium, synthetic material, or a rare wood. Some particularly suitable variants of the synthetic material which has been developed over the past thirty years, such as acrylic glass, is used to make highly artistic brooches and pendants, as well as simple designs for mass production. Precious metals, especially silver, are extremely well-suited for modern designs, as has been shown in particular by Scandinavian artists, who make jewellery with clear strict linear designs, and sometimes use combinations of stones, such as *Rauchquarz*, rock crystal, rose-quartz or amethysts.

The new results and experiments in form and technical design have enriched, to a certain degree, the range of forms used in jewellers' work and in fashion jewellery.

Fashion jewellery has only really become presentable since the 1920s. The successor of the old imitation jewellery, well-designed cheaper jewellery became a necessity as a result of the relative democratization of fashion and the growing significance of the ready-made clothes industry. Paris fashion houses saw they had to exploit this trend in order to survive, and they thus began to accept ready-made clothes and jewellery. Coco Chanel, who claims to be the initiator of the short haircut and the short skirt (a sensation in the '20s!), was one of these fashion-house owners. According to contemporary reports she always wore, with a certain nonchalance, piles of jewellery. Copies of her own jewels made from glass and gemstones brought her the financial success she hoped for. Later a lucrative design-office for fashion jewellery geared for mass production, and this office succeeded in transforming the contemporary clear style of new functional realism *(Neue Sachlichkeit)* into extremely refined pieces of jewellery.

Elsa Schiaparelli's fashion house in Rome caused a stir in the 1930s up till the beginning of the Second World War because of its striking jewellery creations: at one point the circus served as inspiration, then the Chinese, and then folklore. However, the first fashion salon to take the leap into big business was Christian Dior in Paris: it produced new fashion jewellery every saison to go with the new fashions!

The ornaments propagated by well-known Paris houses, despite the less expensive material now used, still have expensive prices. The producers of the cheap mass article, of the attractive and fasionable "seven-day wonder", are the real kings of fashion jewellery. There is almost no limit to the materials and forms used—bright plastic, wood, metal, enamel, leather, and fabric cord. A large number of buyers get great pleasure out of attractive new toys, and after they have had enough of it lay it aside, and buy another.

The socialist countries do not have this quick charge of fashion associated with the comparatively strict dictation of available designs, caused by competition and the subtle pressures put on the customers to buy. The range of forms for fashion jewellery changes less hectically, is not so wide, especially in the Slavonic areas, influenced to a large degree by folk-art.

However, in all industrial countries jewellery seems in general to be accepted as having a purely decorative function, and, ideally, fulfilling its specific task of reflecting the contribution made by a country to cultural progress, the main aim of which must be to promote the development and perfection of man and his personality within society.

Plates

1   Comb. Bone, Gotland, Sweden, *c.* 2000 B.C.

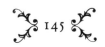

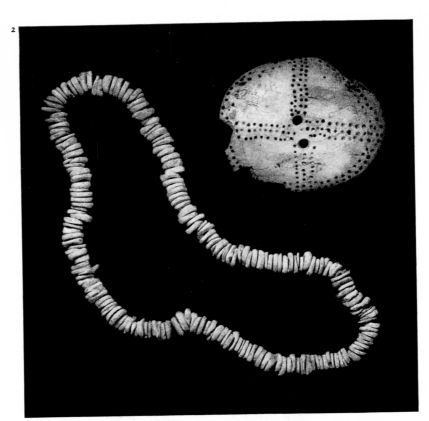

2   Shell disc with crossed rows of dots and chain of shell discs. Thuringia, German Democratic Republic, 2400–1800 B.C.

3   Two chains. Shell discs and dogs' teeth. Thuringia, German Democratic Republic, 2400–1800 B.C.

4   Torque. Hammered gold ribbon. Hook-terminals
end in knob-finials. Ireland, *c.* 1500 B.C.

5   Headdress. Bronze with engraved ornaments.

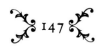

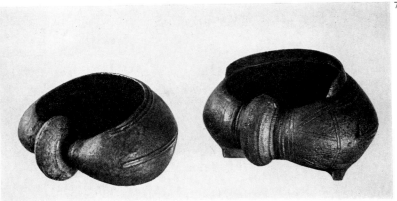

6   Armlet. Bronze with spiral discs. Halle county, German Democratic Republic, 1500–1000 B.C.

7   Kidney-shaped bronze bracelet with knobs. Magdeburg county, German Democratic Republic.

8   Belt-plaque. Cast bronze with punched spiral ornaments. Sealand, Denmark, 1300–1100 B.C.

9   Collar. Knit coco fibre cord with white snail segments. New Britain, Melanesia.

10   Forehead ornament. Kangaroo teeth glued with resin onto plant fibres. Australia.

11 Neck ornament. White and orange snail shells. Marquesas, Polynesia.

12 Neck ornament. Pearls and teeth. Cameroon.

13 Neck ornament of a Papuan. Part of a rhinoceros bird's beak, boar tusks, seeds of Job's-tears, and nassa snails; wig of human hair, decorated with pieces of kangaroo skin and tiny human faces made from bark chips. Papua New Guinea.

14 Papuan in festive ornament: Kingfisher's body attached with parrot feathers to wig of human hair, on the left and right pieces of kangaroo skin, cockatoo and parrot feathers; earrings with fruit pips and shells, nose ornament, bamboo. Papua New Guinea.

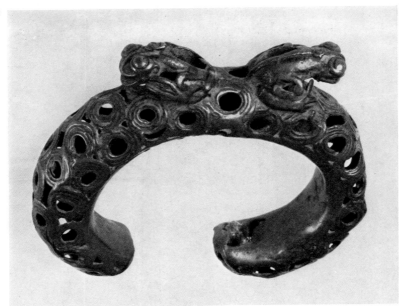

15 Copper armlet with the representation of two toads. Lost-wax casting. Cameroon.

16 Chieftain's brass ornament from the Bamum. Cameroon.

17 Gold neck ornament from the Ashanti. Ghana.

18 Wealthy Masai woman with colourful neck and ear ornaments. Glass beads. East Africa.

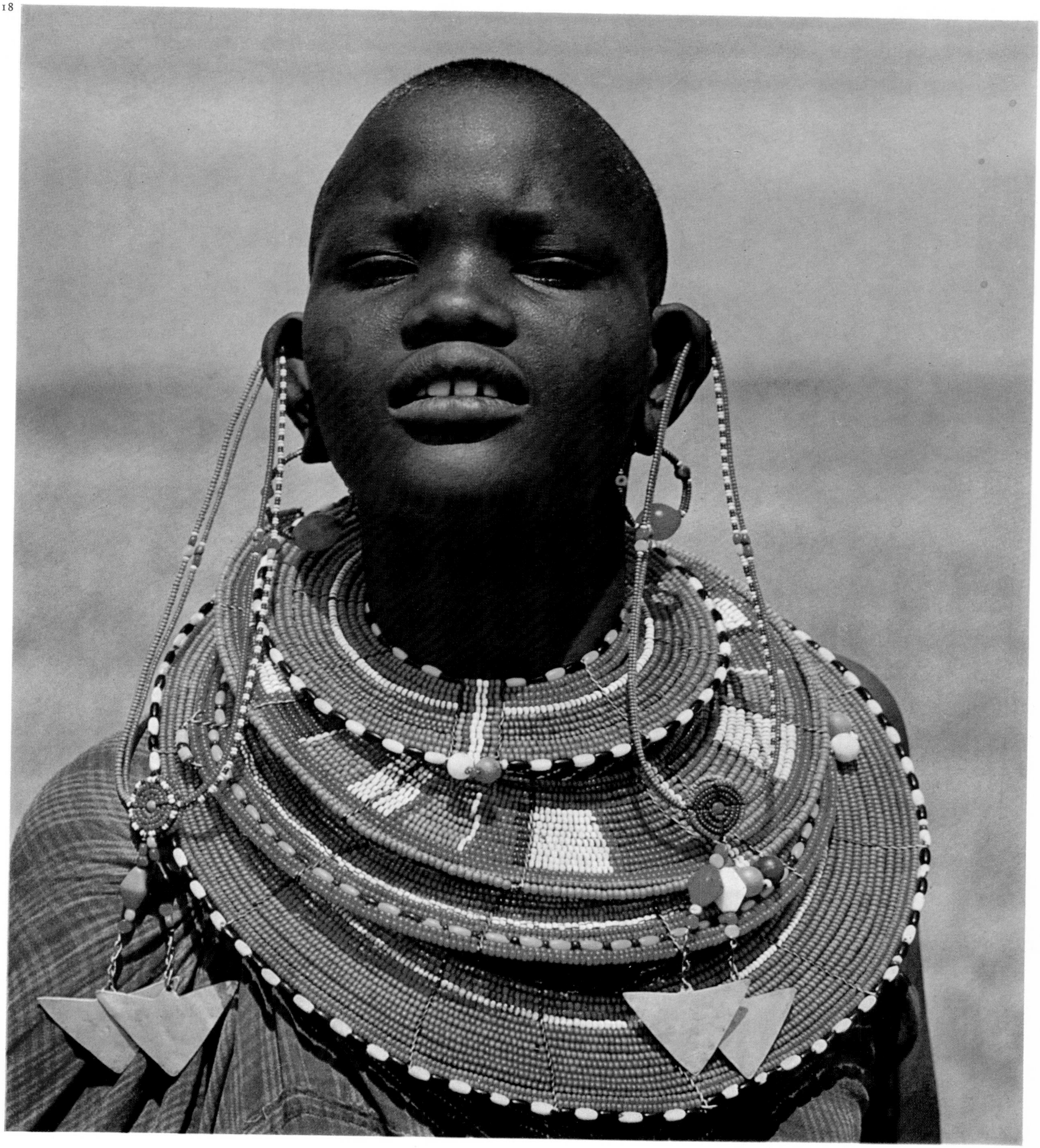

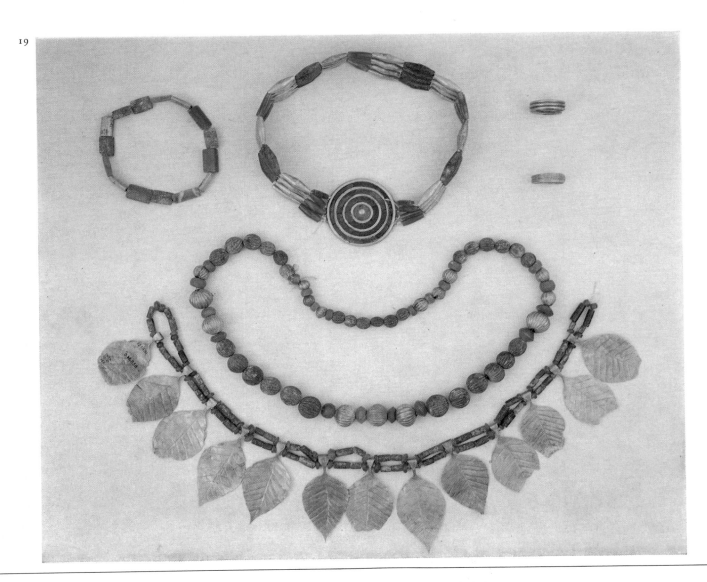

19 Parts of the jewellery of Sumerian Queen Shubad
(2685–2654 B.C.). Gold leaves, gold beads and stones.

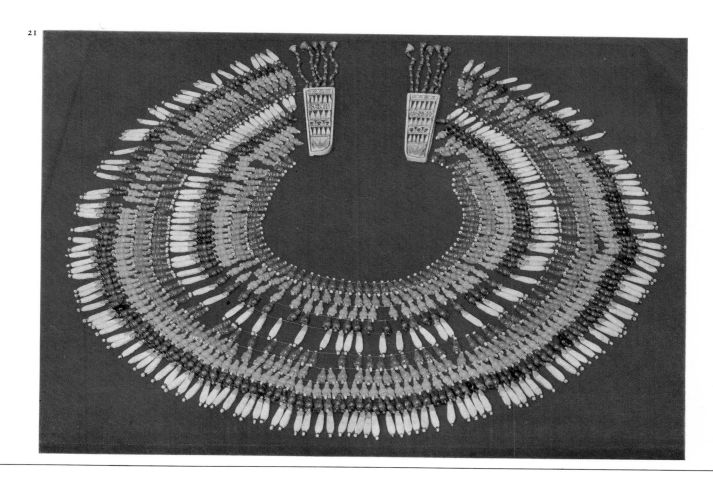

20 Wreath of fine gold leaves, found in a Sumerian
grave. Uruk, early dynastic time, 2600–2340 B.C.

21 Collar of cylinder beads, from the grave of the
Egyptian Pharaoh Tut-ankh-amun, 18th Dynasty.

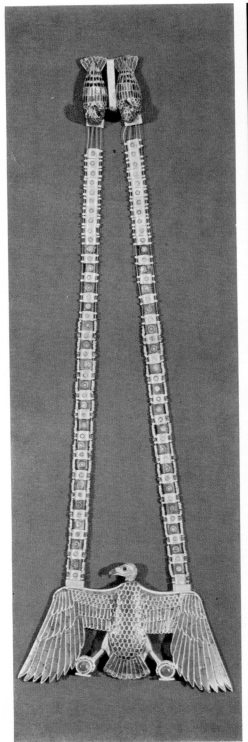

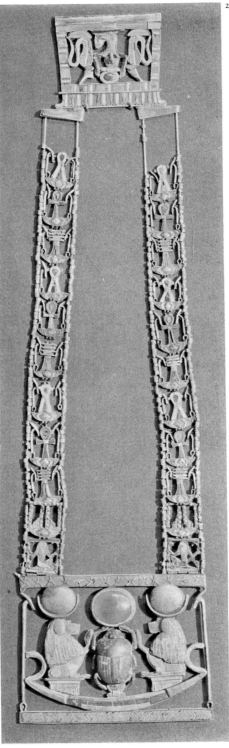

22 Gold pectoral, belonging to Tut-ankh-amun, in shape of a vulture, symbol of the Egyptian death goddess Nechbet.

23, 24 Ear ornament of Tut-ankh-amun. Gold with stone inlay.

25 Large collier of Tut-ankh-amun. The scarab, carrying the symbol of the sun, is represented in the pectoral.

26   Two necklaces and bracelets. Jade. Maya.

27   Double chain of elongated and round stone beads with pendant in form of human head. Maya.

28   Link of a spondylous-shell chain. Central Peruvian coast, 10th–12th centuries.

29 Bracelet. Sheet gold with upset edges. The figures, two fishermen on bunches of rush, were cast in the round and soldered onto the sheet. Chimú, Peru, c. 1300.

30 Headdress. Gold and platinum alloy with representation of stylized feather-snakes. Ecuador, c. 100–500.

31 Gold helmet with embossed décor. The holes on top were evidently used to put in feathers. Colombia.

32   Head-dress. Sheet gold, llama hair and feathers.
Inca culture. South Peru, 1000–1470.

33

34
35

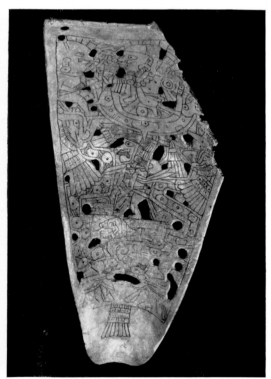

36

33   Chain. Cast gold beads. Mixtec style. Mexico, *c*. 1200–1500.

34   Finger-ring. Copper in form of a decorated skull. Mixtec style. Mexico, *c*. 1200–1500.

35   Pendant. Pierced through its length. Greenstone with brown veins, in shape of a skull. Mixtec style. Mexico, *c*. 1200–1500.

36   Breast ornament. Incised shell. Huaxtec. Mexico, 14th–15th centuries.

37 Part of Mycenaean court diadem. Sheet gold.
Probably attached to cloth ribbons, worn round the
head. Similar pieces were found on Cyprus, in Syria
and Egypt. 1500–1100. B.C

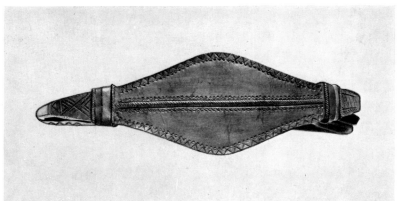

38

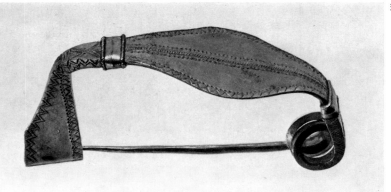

39

40

41

38, 39 Bird's view and side view of a gold fibula with geometric ornaments. Attica, 850–820 B.C.

40 Gold earrings with stylized figures of bulls' heads. Cypro-Mycenaean, *c.* 12th century B.C.

41 Finger-ring. Gold with incised religious scene 'Goddess and Worshipper'. Minoan, *c.* 1500 B.C.

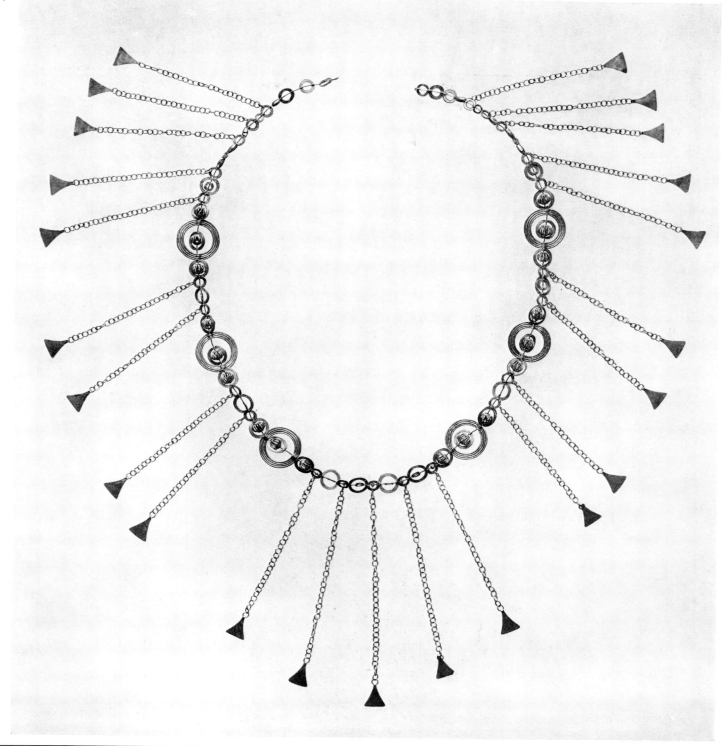

42 Parts of gold necklace re-arranged according to
the supposed original form, from a treasure in the
Thyreatis. Gold beads, wire rings of different sizes,
chain with axe-shaped pendants of sheet gold. Early
Hellenistic, *c.* 2000 B.C.

43

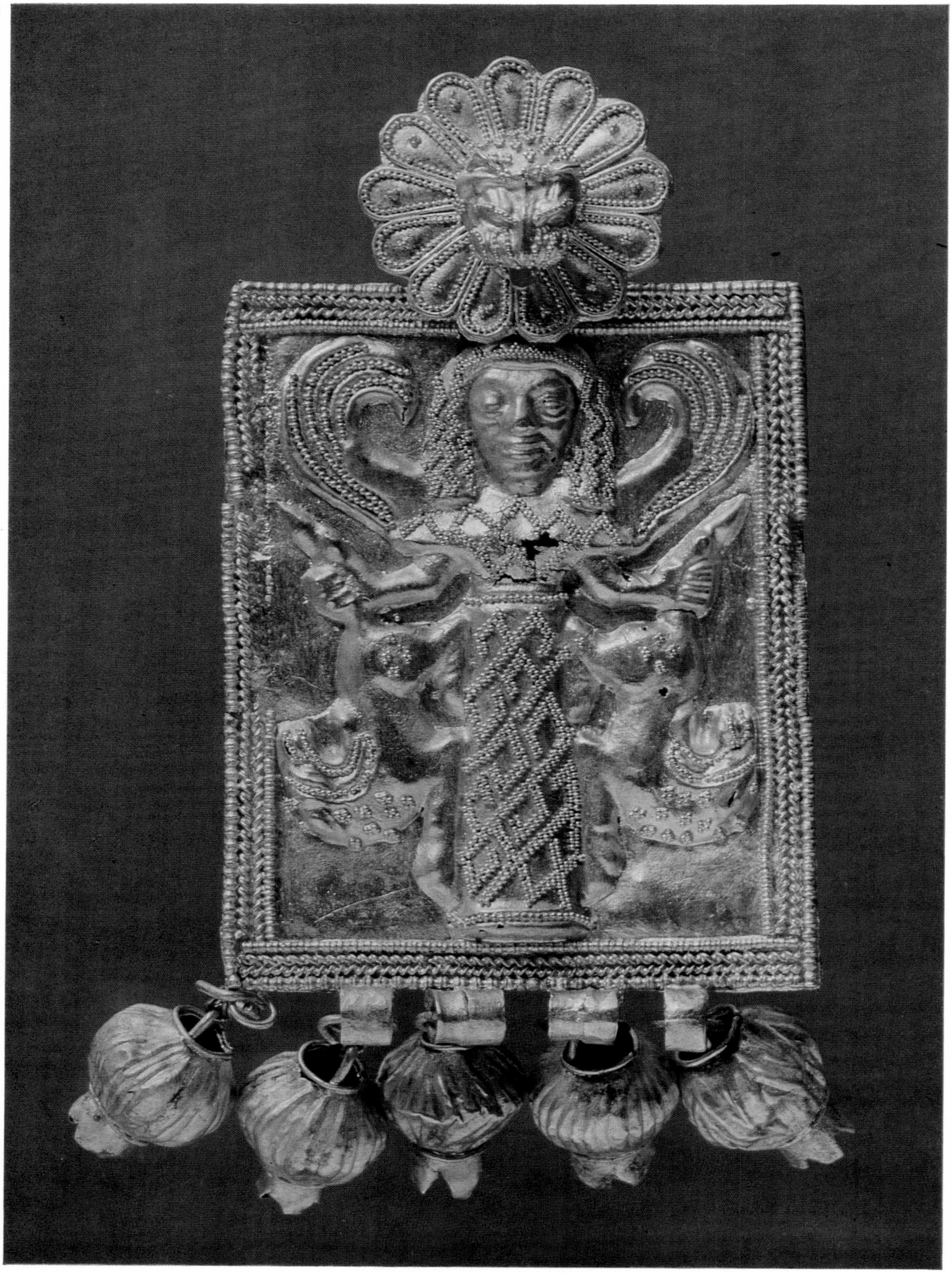

44

45

43 Decorative piece of sheet gold with representation of 'Mistress of Animals'. Lower edge with pendants in shape of small pomegranates. Rhodes, mid-7th century.

44 Spiral earring with women's heads. Gold. Greek, 4th century B.C.

45 Gold filigree ear-disc with woman's head and two strings of gold beads. Hellenistic, 3rd century B.C.

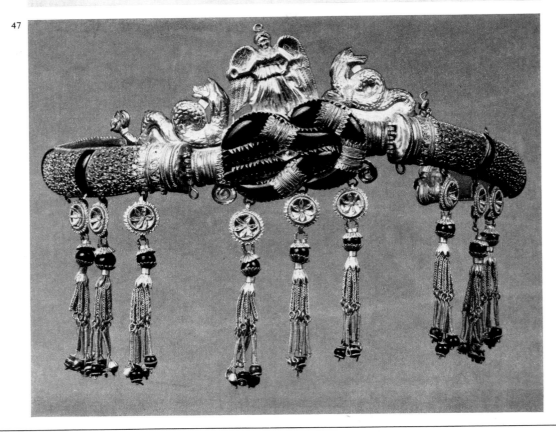

46 Gold ear ornament with pendants in form of
cones, erotic figures and female idols. Aeolis, Hellenistic, 2nd century B.C.

47 Gold diadem, with garnet-mounted 'Hercule's
knot' in centre. Found in a grave in the south of present-day U.S.S.R. Graeco-Macedonian, 4th/3rd centuries B.C.

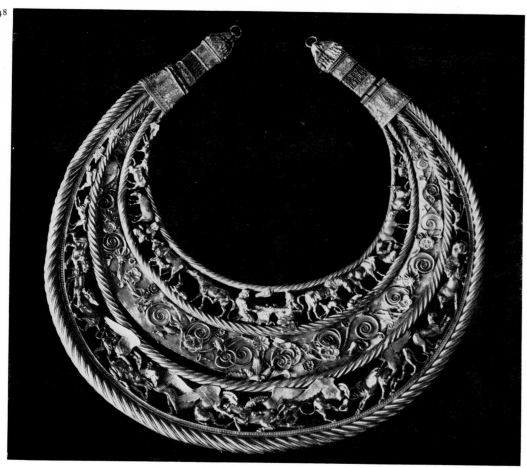

48 Gold pectoral with typical scenes from a Scythian cattle-breeder's everyday life. Kurgan Towsti, Ukrainian Socialist Soviet Republic, 4th century B.C.

49 Bronze belt-buckle. 2nd century B.C.–3rd century A.D. East of the Black Sea, in present-day Georgian SSR, representations of characteristic animals were developed rather early. Motifs such as stag, horse or fantastic creatures can be traced back as far as Hellenistic times, and they, too, had an influence on Scythian art.

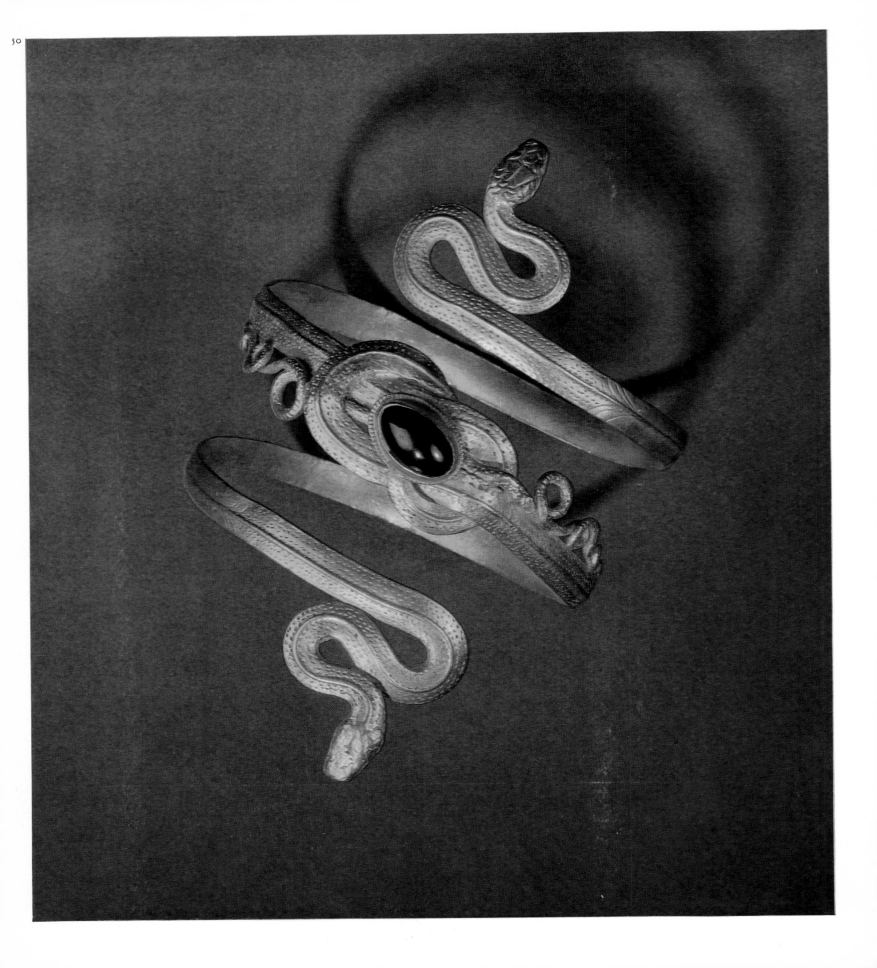

50 Gold armlet. Two snakes form a 'Hercule's knot' with a garnet cabochon in the centre. Hellenistic, *c.* 300 B.C.

51 Central part of decorative gold ribbon with mounted garnets. Delicate gold strings hold garnet pendants. Part of a Thracian find. Hellenistic, early 2nd century B.C.

52 Phoenician bracelet. Gold with embossed and granulated decoration. Tharros, Sardinia, 7th century B.C. The granulation technique may have come down to Etruria via the Phoenicians.

53   Gold bracelet, in two parts. Top with fine granulation in strict geometric pattern. Etruria.

54   Two gold neck ornaments, lower one with Acheloos-mask. Etruria.

55   Lavishly ornamented fibula, probably sign of imperial dignity. Etruria.

56 Three Etruscan pendants. Embossed sheet gold in form of a *bulla*, the amuletic capsule later on taken over by the Romans.

57 Capsule-shaped pendant. Sheet gold, decorated on either side. Necklace and ear ornament. Gold and beryls. Central Italy, 9th century B.C. and 6th century B.C.

58 Bust of a wealthy Roman woman of the imperial age from a grave door in Palmyra, 2nd century. Head and upper part of body richly decorated with chains and medallions. On left shoulder a fibula with decorative pendants.

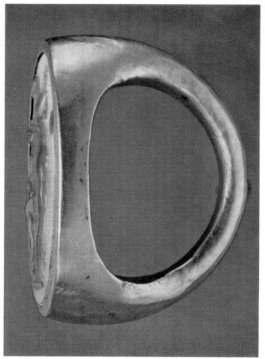

59, 60   Bird's view and side view of a gold finger-ring. Onyx carnelian cameo with representation of a satyr and a nymph. Part of a treasure from Petescia, Sabiner mountains, 1st century.

61   Amber ring. Amber was thought to have magic powers, and was often found in graves. Roman, c. 100.

62 Indian miniature 'Lovers by the Window'. Both
woman and man wear jewellery rich in pearls and
precious stones. Early 18th century.

63 Ring and gold necklace with enamel work. An instance of the original Indian variations on Hellenistic style. Found in Taxila, North India.

64 Medallion. Gold-mounted, cut agate: Moghul emperor Slaying a lion. India, 17th century (?).

65 Ear ornament with half-moon motifs and stylized
fish; pearl strings, gold filigree and precious stones.
India, 19th century.

66   Two necklaces. Gold, lower one set with rubies. Sri Lanka and South India.

67, 68   Obverse and reverse of two pendants. Gold enamel with religious scenes. Jaipur, 17th/18th centuries.

69   Gold filigree ear ornaments. India, 17th/18th centuries.

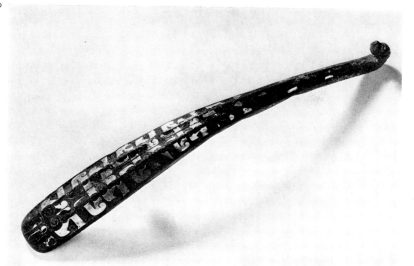

70 Bronze agraffe with inlays of sheet gold and silver. Terminal is a stylized dragon's head. Ordos type, 400 B.C. – 100 A.D.

71 Plaque of pierced sheet gold. Representation of female deer with young. Ordos type, 400 B.C. – 100 A.D.

72 Decorative plaque. Gold with stone inlays: dragons with five talons, the sign of imperial dignity, among cloud-ornaments. Single piece of a pair to be attached to front and back of the emperor's robe. Ming Dynasty, China, early 15th century.

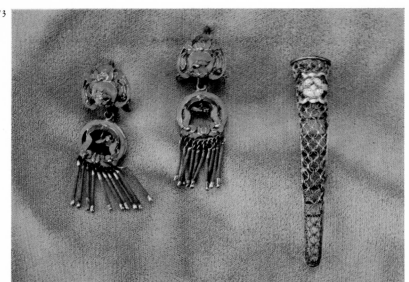

73 Ear ornament. Brass-mounted kingfisher's feathers and brass finger-nail guard. China, 2nd half of 19th century (?).

74 Three hair-pins with charms, brass-mounted kingfisher's feathers. China, 2nd half of 19th century (?).

75 Enamelled decorative comb with charms. China, 2nd half of 19th century (?).

76 Bridal crown. Brass-mounted kingfisher's feathers, with glass stones, jewels and pearl pendants. China, 2nd half of 19th century (?).

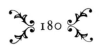

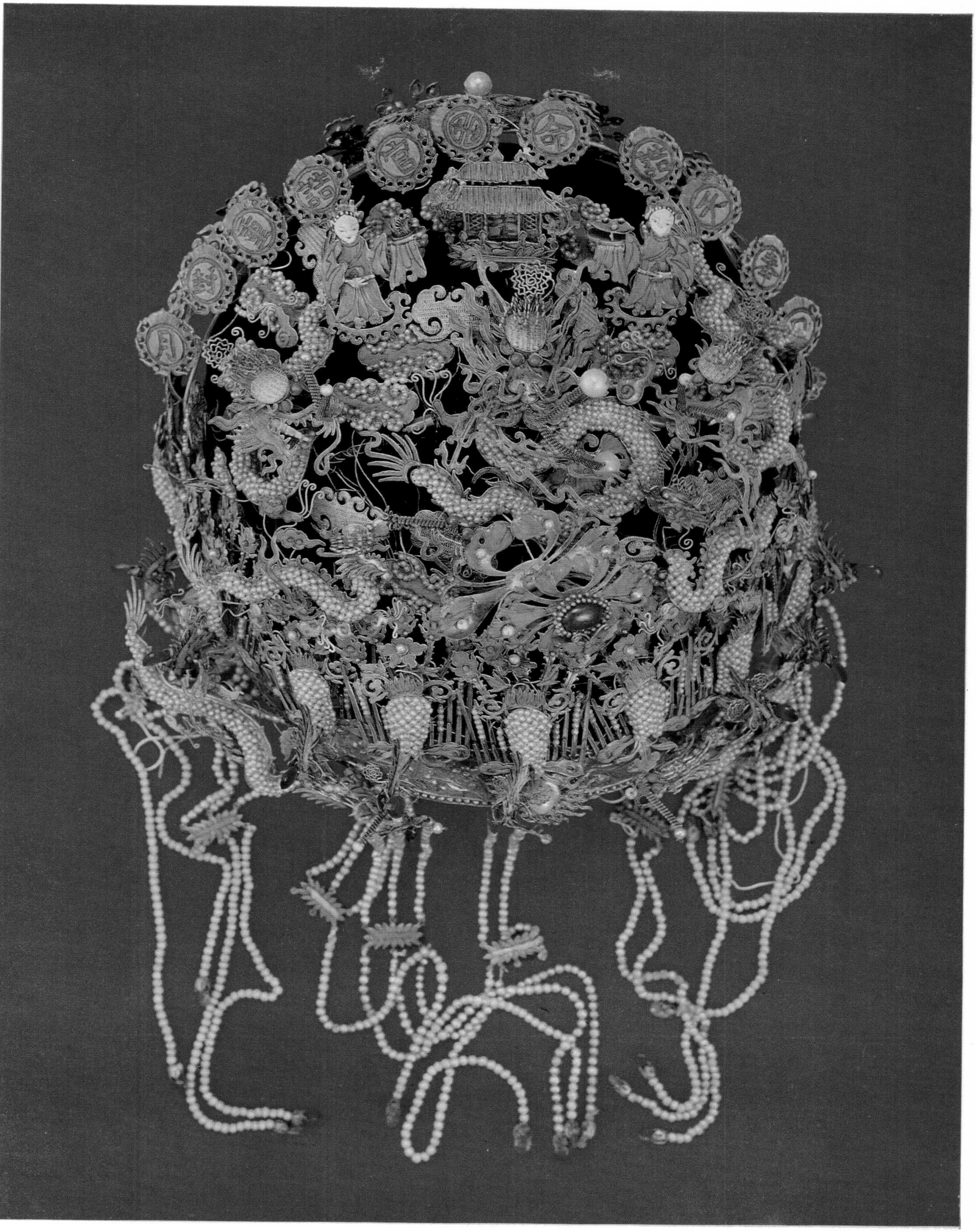

77　Empress Li, spouse of Ming Emperor Wang-Li, with rich hair-dress, on dragon's back. Chinese painting, *c.* 1600.

78　Two women, the elaborately styled hair decorated with comb, pins and flowers, Japanese women's most common adornment. Woodcut by Kitagawa Utamaro (1753–1806).

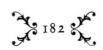

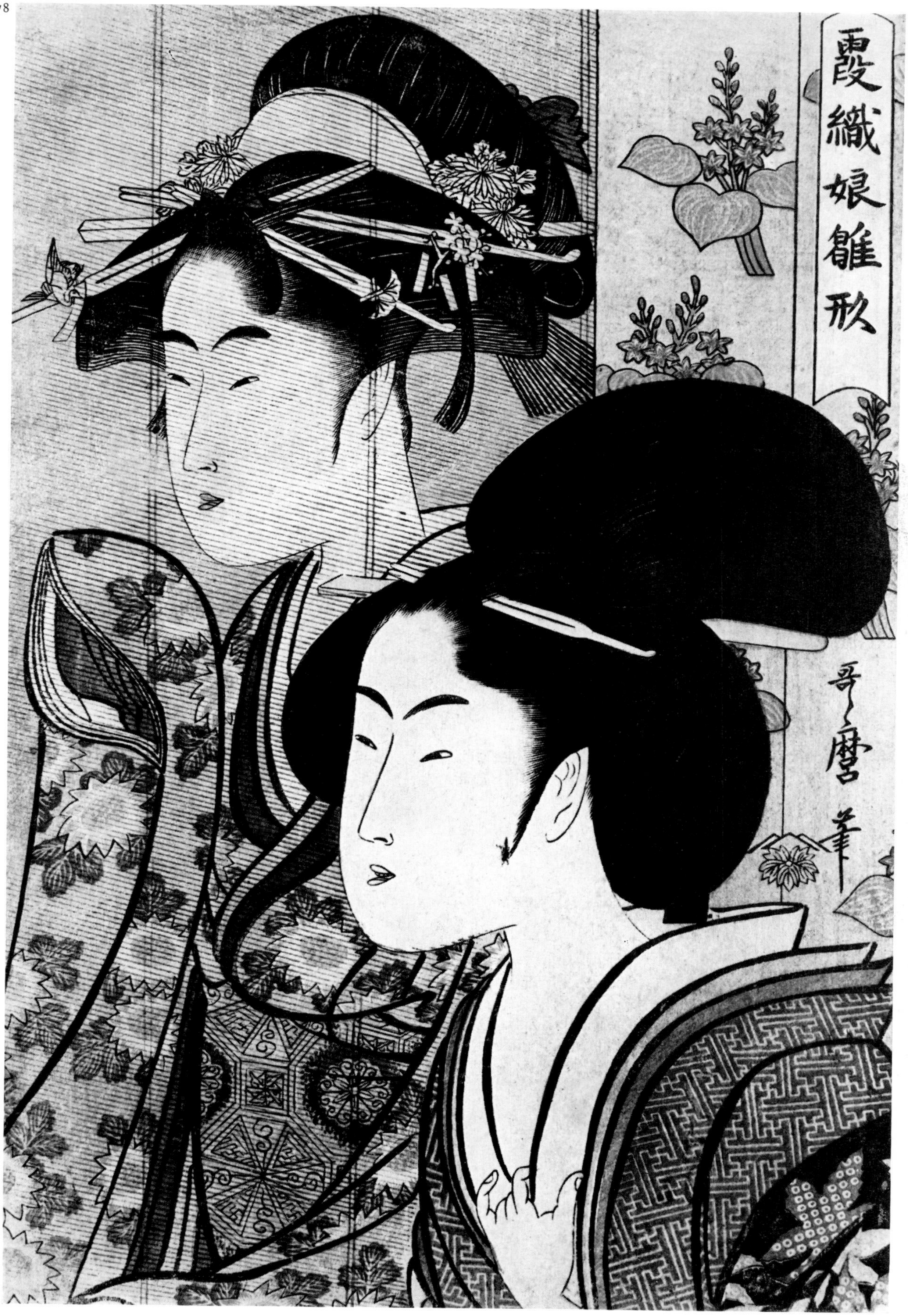
霞織娘雛形
哥麿筆

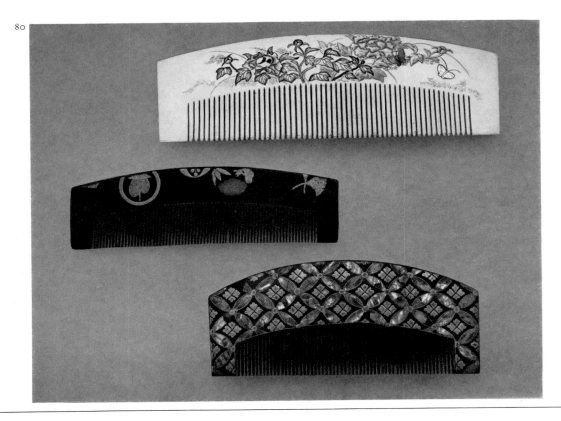

79 Decorative comb. Ivory, carved in openwork: a crane—symbol of longevity—among firs and clouds. Japan, 19th century.

80 Three decorative combs, from top to bottom: Wood and red lacquer finish, horn and lacquer, horn and mother-of-pearl inlay. Japan, 2nd half of 19th century (?).

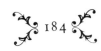

81 Imperial crown of Constantine Monomachos.
Gold and *cloisonné*. Made between 1042 and 1050 in
the imperial goldsmith workshop of the Byzantine
court at Constantinople.

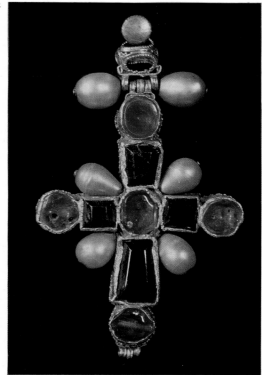

82, 83 Gold pendant in shape of cross, originally reliquary. Set with rubies, emeralds and pearls, niello inscription on the reverse. Georgia, 12th/13th centuries.

84 Enamel pendant in form of triptich. Relation to Byzantium is evident. Centre: Christ between Mary and John, wings: angels, cast and chiselled. Georgia, 8th/9th centuries.

85 Crown of Queen Constance of Aragon. Gold, enamel, pearls and precious stones, originated under Byzantine influence. 12th century.

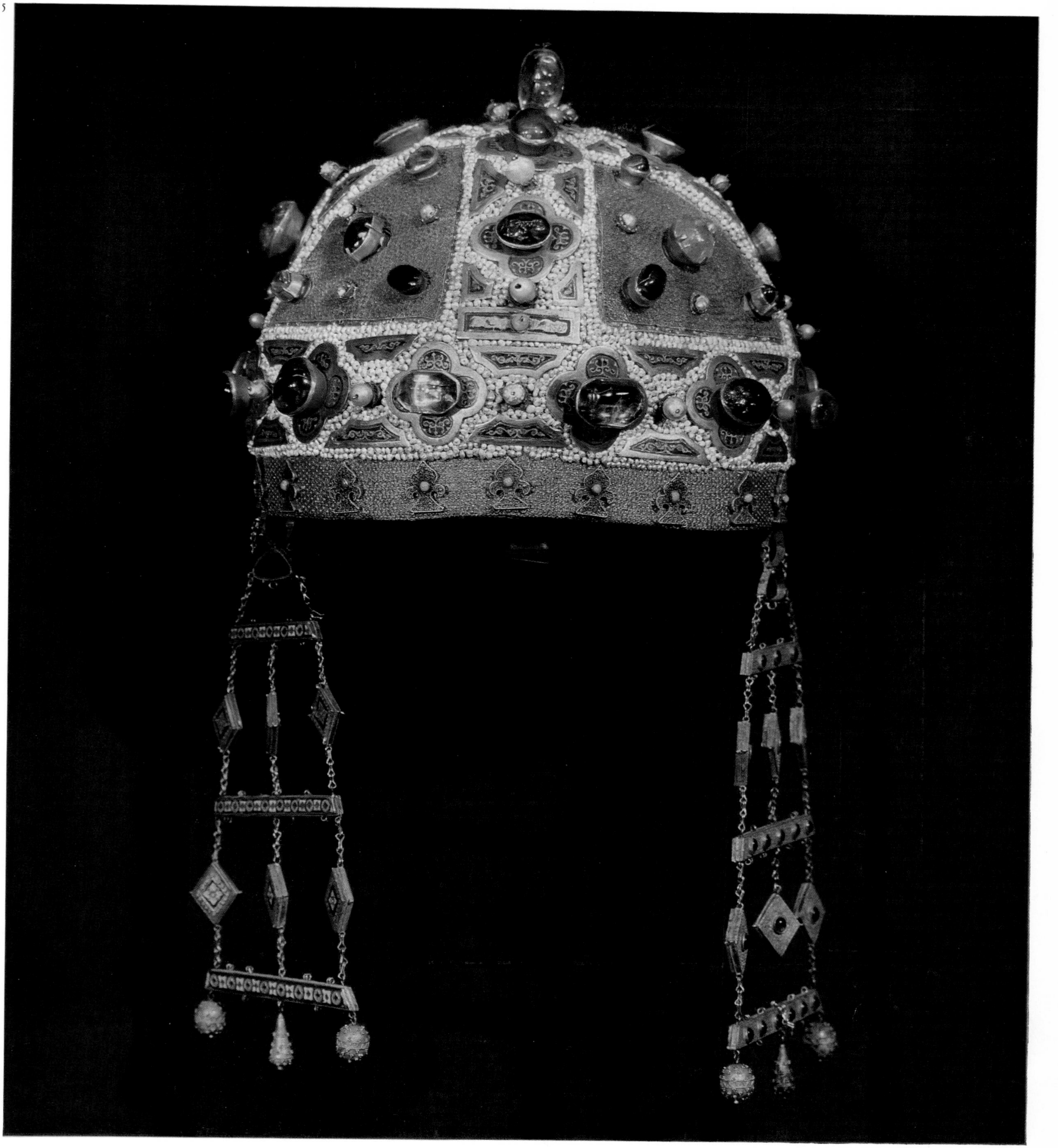

86

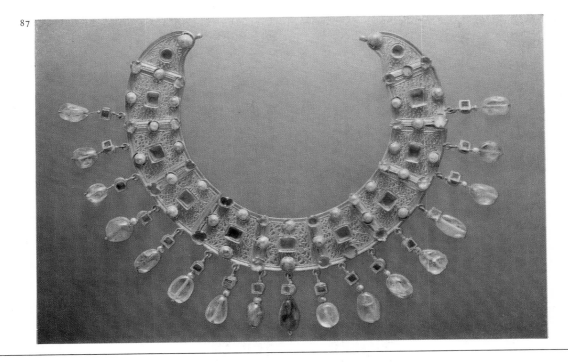

87

86 Byzantine gold neck and breast ornament with annunciation scene. Part of a find from Assitût, Upper Egypt, 6th century.

87 Crescent-shaped necklace. Gold, pearls and precious stones. Terminals in form of stylized sparrowhawks. Byzantine, part of a find from Assitût, Upper Egypt, 6th century.

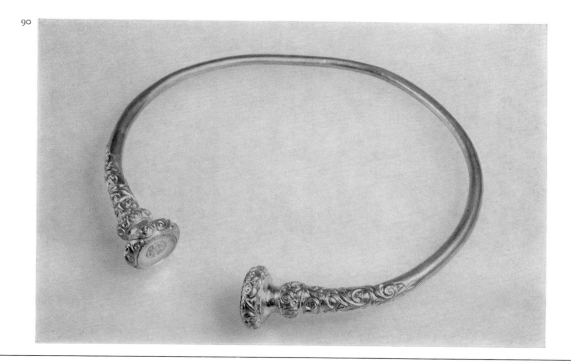

88 Celt torque. Solid gold. Richly ornamented neck-rings of this type were often found in graves of tribal 'princes'. 3rd–1st centuries B.C.

89 Gold neckring. Celtic, 3rd–2nd centuries B.C.

90 Gold torque of Waldalgesheim, Hunsrück, German Federal Republic. Celtic, late 4th century.

93

91 Gold finger-ring of Anglo-Saxon King Æthel-wulf of Wessex. The obverse bears the possessor's name, 9th century.

92 Gold finger-ring of Anglo-Saxon Queen Ethels with of Mercia, 9th century.

93 Collar of intersecting hollow and solid gold elements decorated with delicate rings and tiny representations of animals. North Teutons, Ålleberg, Sweden, c. 6th century.

94 Seven-button fibula. Silver gilt, niello decoration borders top plaque. Buttons and terminal of the fibula in shape of animal heads, the empty mounts were probably set with almandines. Laucha, Halle county, GDR, 6th century.

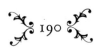

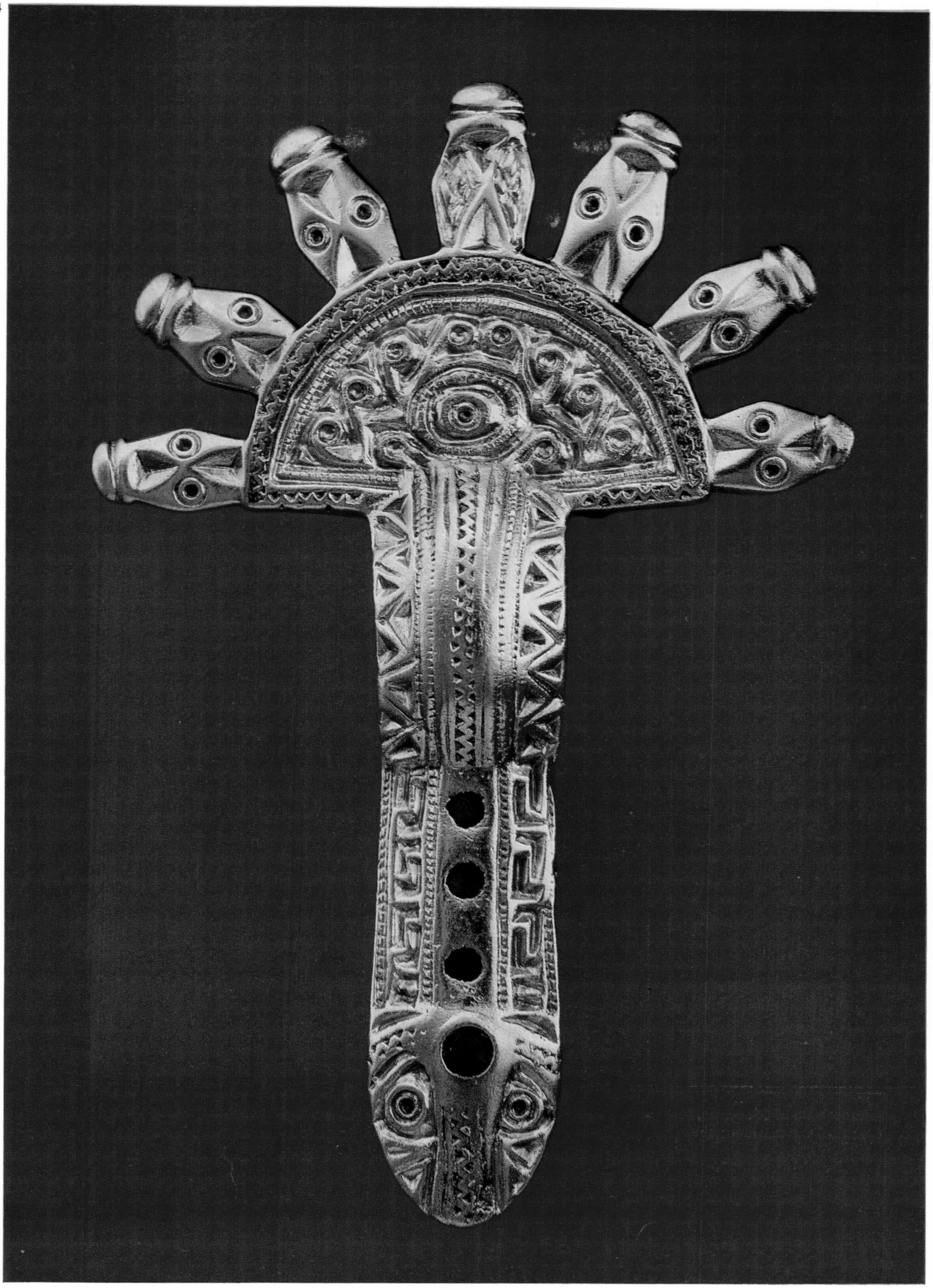

95–103 Parts of the Viking treasure of Hiddensee, found after the 1872 and '74 tidal waves, among them cross-shaped pendants with stylized animal heads (95–97), and reverse pieces (98–100). The disc fibula (101, 103) shows intertwined animal representations. The choker (102) was twisted from strong gold wire.

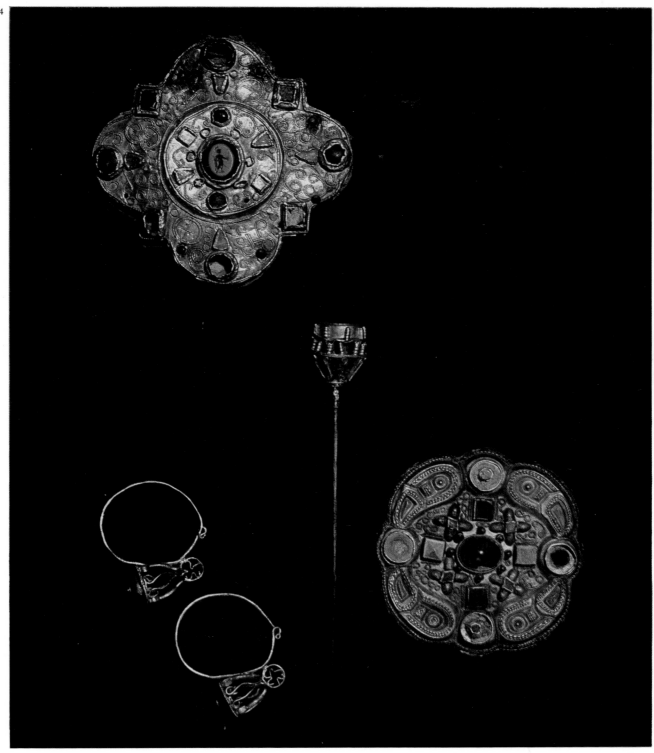

104   Gold pins, fibulae and earrings from Frankish
graves in the Rhineland, 7th century.

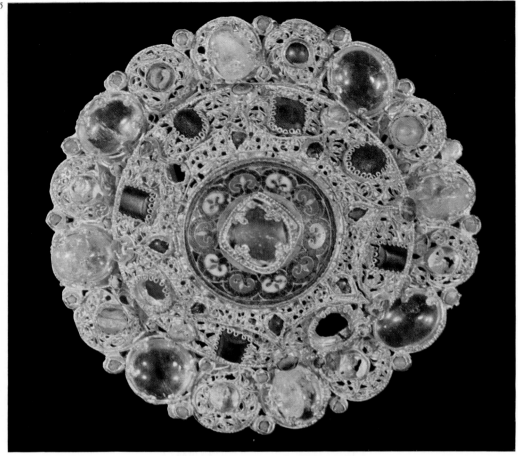

105

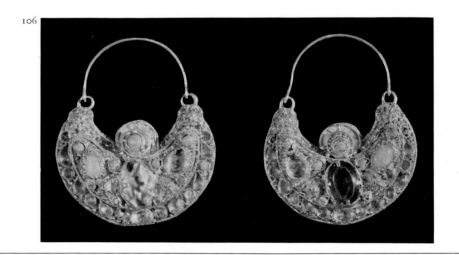

106

105 Large *Fürspan* of the so-called Gisela Jewellery. Gold filigree, precious stones and enamel, probably late 10th century.

106 Gold filigree earrings set with precious stones from the so-called Gisela Jewellery, probably late 10th century.

107 The imperial insignia of the Holy Roman Empire. The imperial crown consists of precious stones, pearls, gold filigree and enamel plaques. *C.* 960. Bow and cross were added later on.

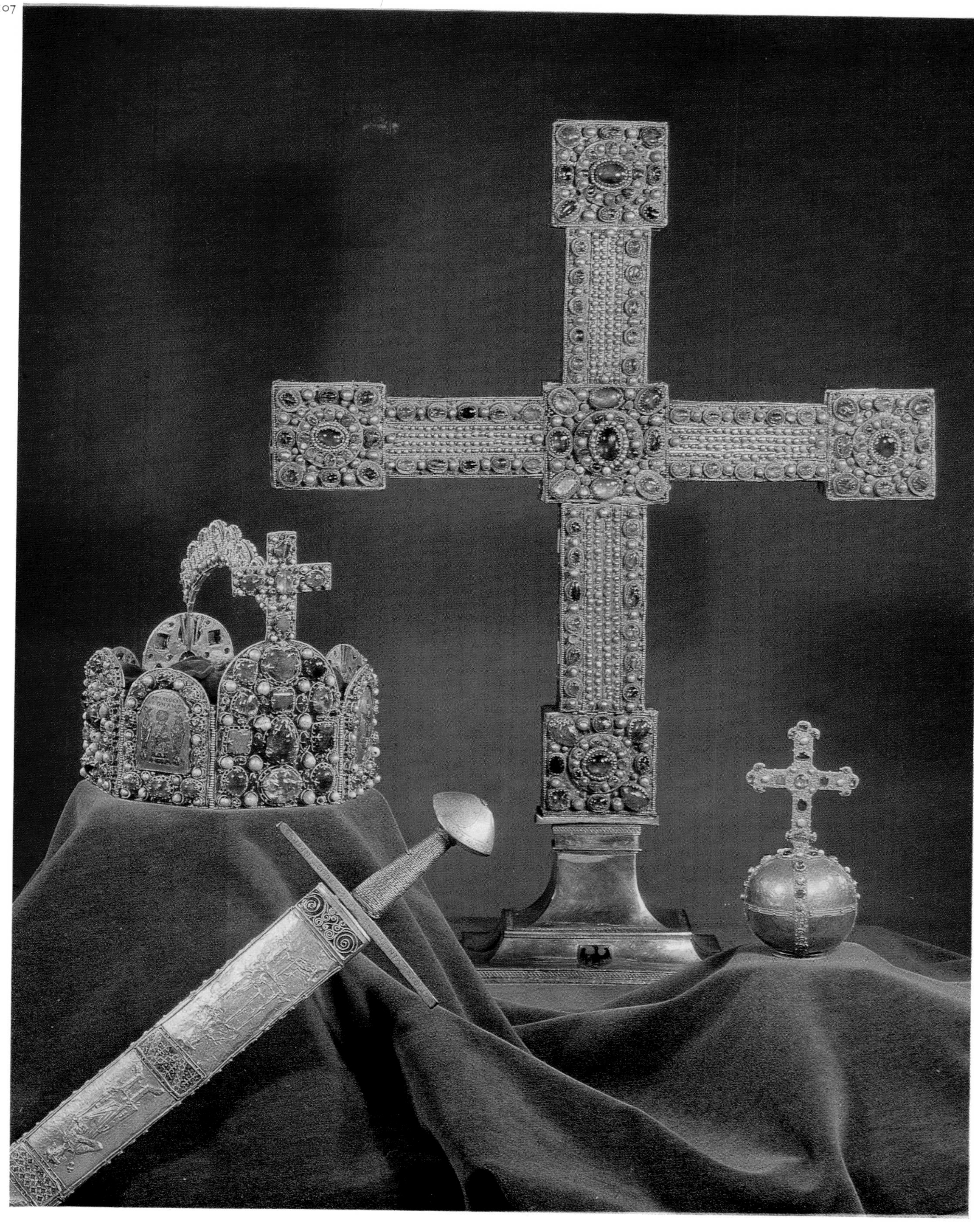

108   Openwork pendant. Bronze gilt. Found in
Magdeburg county, German Democratic Republic.
Originated in western Europe (?), early 11th century.

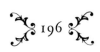

109
110
112
113
111
114

109   Necklace with hollow gold beads, 12 century.
110   Gold brooch, set with violet amethysts and blue sapphires, 12th/13th centuries.
111   Ear ornament, characteristic of Slavonic women's jewellery. Silver, was attached by loops to the head-ribbon. Russian (?), 12th century.

112   Silver-gilt brooch with representation of four peacocks amidst foliage and flowers. Hungarian, 13th century.

113   Decorative discs. Copper gilt, openwork, 12th/13th centuries.
114   Silver-gilt brooch. Hungarian (?), 14th century.

115

116

117

115   So-called knight's amulet. Pendant of enamelled silver, Mary and angels with scrolls. Upper Rhineland, 1340–50.

116   Engagement brooch, inscribed 'Ave Maria Gracia'. Silver and niello. From the Pritzwalk silver hoard, Potsdam county, German Democratic Republic.

117   Gold brooch, pearls and precious stones with the Virgin Mary's monogram 'M'. English or French, late 14th century.

118   Brooch. Gold with sapphires, rubies, emeralds, amethysts, originally also pearls. Motala, Sweden, 1st half of 14th century.

119   Crown of Princess Blanca. Gold, precious stones and pearls, late 14th century.

120 Cape brooch with annunciation scene. Silver gilt, mainly cast, engraved, decorated with pearls and enamel. Aachen, 1360–70.

121 Simonetta Vespucci, painting by Piero di Cosimo (1462–1521). Elaborated hair-dress with pearls and artificial plaits were typical of Italian early Renaissance. It was common to wear an agraffe over the shaved forehead.

121

SIMONETTA IANVENSIS VESPVCCIA

122

123

124

122   Finger-ring. Silver gilt, with two pairs of inter-twined hands. Inscription: 'Marie'. Central Europe, late 15th century.

123, 124   Pomander with hinges to open it. Inside figures of saints and a statuette of Mary. Rhineland (?), *c.* 1470.

125   Kunigunde of Austria (1465–1520) in contemporary garment, decorated with great head-dress and cross-pendant. Painting by Ludwig Kunraiter.

126 Battista Sforza, painting by Piero della Francesca (c. 1416–92), detail. Hair-ornament with ribbons and agraffes, and richly decorated necklace with pearl chain.

127 Gold finger-ring with malachite pyramid. The mount is decorated with knots of gold wire. Central Europe, c. 1500.

128 Gold pendant in shape of flower with an angel. Enamel, pearls, sapphires, rubies, amethysts and glazing. France or Burgundy, early 15th century.
129 Medallion, is associated with portrait of Count Philip the Good of Burgundy. Gold enamel and chalcedony. Burgundy, c. 1440.

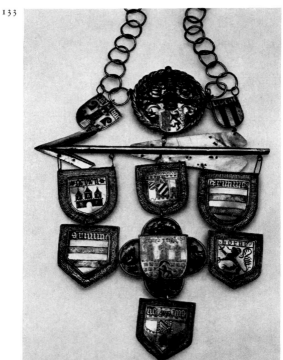

130   Brooch or pendant with allegoric representation
of Love. Silver gilt, cast and chiselled. South German,
c. 1580.

131   Design for pendant by Albrecht Dürer (1471–
1528). Two dolphins enclose foliage.

132   Silver pendant with figure of St. Anthony,
surrounded by flowers and foliage. German, c. 1500.

133   Silver 'marksman's chain' with cross-bow arrow
and pendant in form of coat of arms. German, 1461–
1501.

134, 136   Obverse and reverse of silver cross-pendant. Stag, pierced by an arrow, is enclosed by the letters H-I-A-T. Reverse with chiselled foliage and floral motifs. German, 1st half of 16th century.

135   Silver, originally gilt, adornment, obviously hat agraffe, representing Saint George slaying the dragon. German, 1st half of 16th century.

137, 138   Obverse and reverse of gold-enamelled *Gnadenpfennig* of Count Wilhelm of Bavaria by Antonio Abondio, with gold chain and grotesque decoration and hanging pearls. C. 1572.

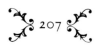

139 Cross-bow marksman, painting by Hieronymus Bosch (c. 1450–1516). The ordinary man, too, wore a medal on his beret. He piereced a cross-bow arrow through the cloth and decorated his chest with the marksman's badge.

140 Portrait of Henry VIII in contemporary, rich garment. Cap, chest, fingers and the whole garment are heavily laden with adornments. Painting by Hans Holbein the Younger (1539/40).

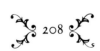

· ANNO · ÆTATIS ·   · SVÆ · XLIX ·

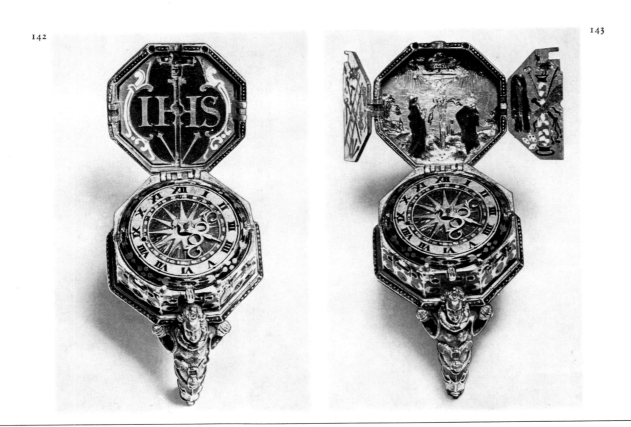

141, 142, 143   Gold finger-ring incorporating a striking watch, closed, half open and open. Inside lid with devotional picture. Augsburg, c. 1580.

144   Lucretia von Berlepsch, painting by Lucas Cranach the Younger, 1580. Lucretia bears the rich jewellery characteristic of a gentlewoman in late 16th-century Germany: gold enamel, pearls and precious stones.

CLEOPHAS · FRATER · CARNALIS · IO·
SEPHI · MARITI · DIVAE · VIRG · MARIAE

I
JACOBVS · MINOR · EPVS · MARIA · CLEOPHAE · SOROR
HIEROSOLIMITANVS · VIRG · MAR · PVTATIVA · MA·
TERTERA · D · N·

III   II
IOSEPH · IVSTVS · SIMON · ZELOTES · CONSO·
BRINVS · DNI · NRI ·

148

145   Family of Maximilian I in typical Renaissance garment and jewellery. Painting by Bernhard Strigel (1460/61–1528).

146   Gold pendant, colour-enamelled, dove on a flower-basket. 2nd half of 16th century.

147   Gold siren-pendant. Enamel, rubies, pearls. Upper body of figure is an irregular Baroque pearl. Probably French, 2nd half of 16th century.

148   Two gold pendants with gondola motifs. Enamel, precious stones and pearls. The body of the boat on the right is a Baroque pearl. 2nd half of 16th century.

149

149 *Gnadenpfennig* of Cardinal Andreas of Austria with medallion. Gold-enamelled frame with coat of arms and hanging pearls. German, *c.* 1600.

150 Portrait of Emperor Rudolf II (1552–1612), painting by Hans von Aachen. On the hat a ribbon of jewels and feathers. Under the collar a gold chain with precious buttons and the Order of the Golden Fleece.

151 Gold pendant or sleeve-decoration with representation of Cleopatra. Enamel, emeralds, rubies, diamonds. Head and hands cut from hyacinths. South German, late 16th century (?).

152 Pendant with Christ in sorrow. Cast gold, partly with grooving, enamel pearls. Austria, c. 1600.

153 Detail of portrait of Jacqueline de Caestre by Peter Paul Rubens (1577–1640). The hairstyle with the decorative ribbon at the back of the head is characteristic of early Baroque. There are also delicate ear ornaments, gold-and-pearl neck and breast ornaments, and a big agraffe at the décolleté.

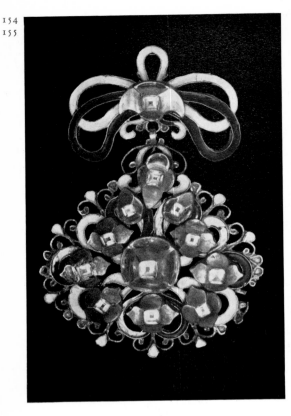

154   Pendant glass and gold with contemporary slip-knot ornaments on upper part. Italian and German, mid-17th century.

155   Part of a set of jewels. Silver, diamonds and rubies in slip-knot and floral design. Bohemia, late 17th century.

156   Gold-enamelled *panhagia* with rubies, sapphires, and emeralds. The medallion with a representation of the Virgin Mary used to be worn by spiritual dignitaries of the Orthodox Curch. Russian, 1650–1750.

157   Gold ring with *à jour* (pierced) cut and chiselled flowers and leaves. German, late 17th century.

158   Anton van Dyck painted Henriette of France, spouse of Charles I, in 1634. She wears several rows of pearls tied in a bow at the waist.

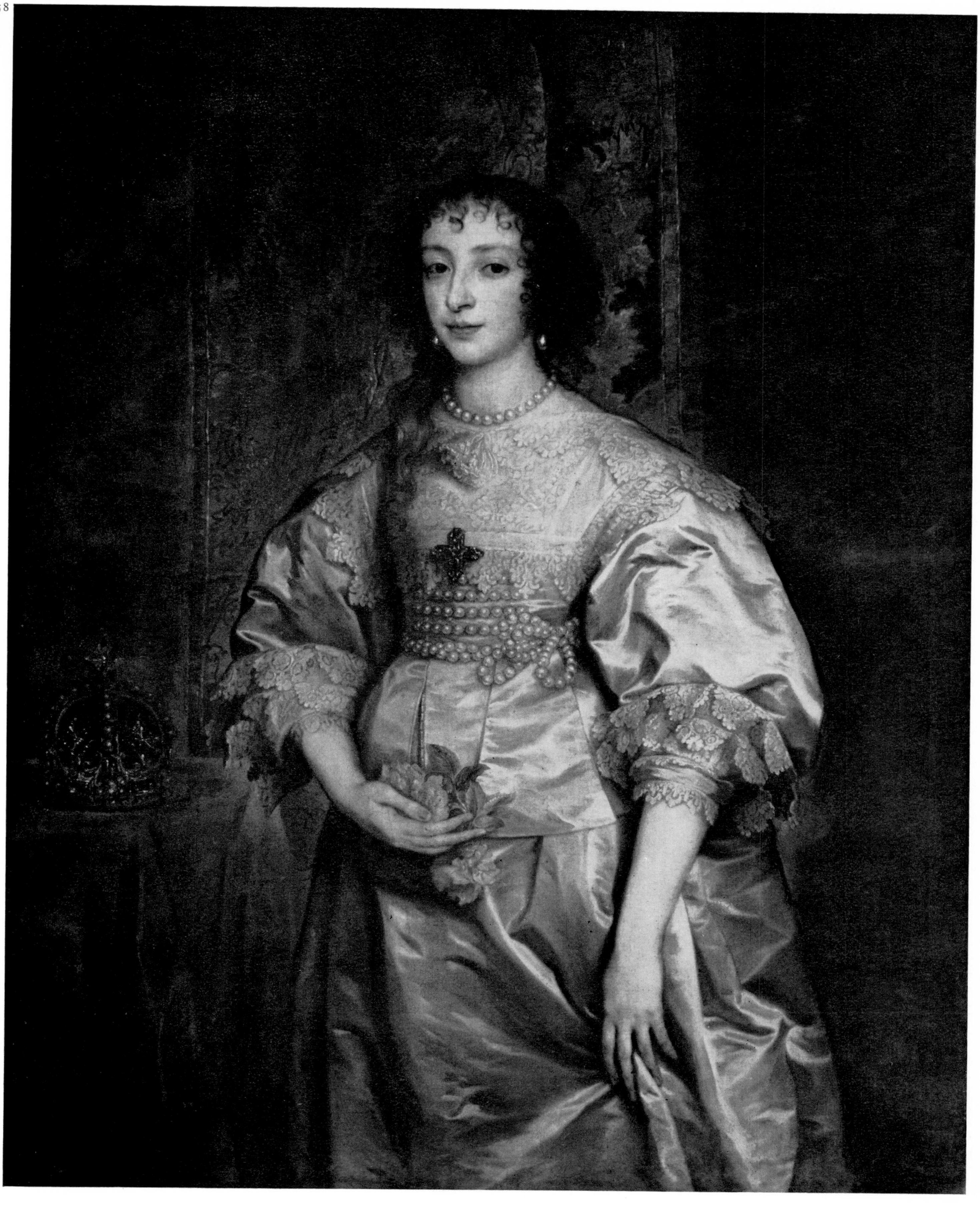

159

160

159 Brooch. Gold enamel, set with emeralds in foliage pattern. Mid-17th century.

160 Necklace. Gold, blue and white-enamelled, links in form of slip-knots. Pendant consists of drop-shaped rock crystal and pearl. Mid-17th century.

161 Hat agraffe. Gold with emerald, diamond, enamel in form of a bunch of flowers. German, *c.* 1620.

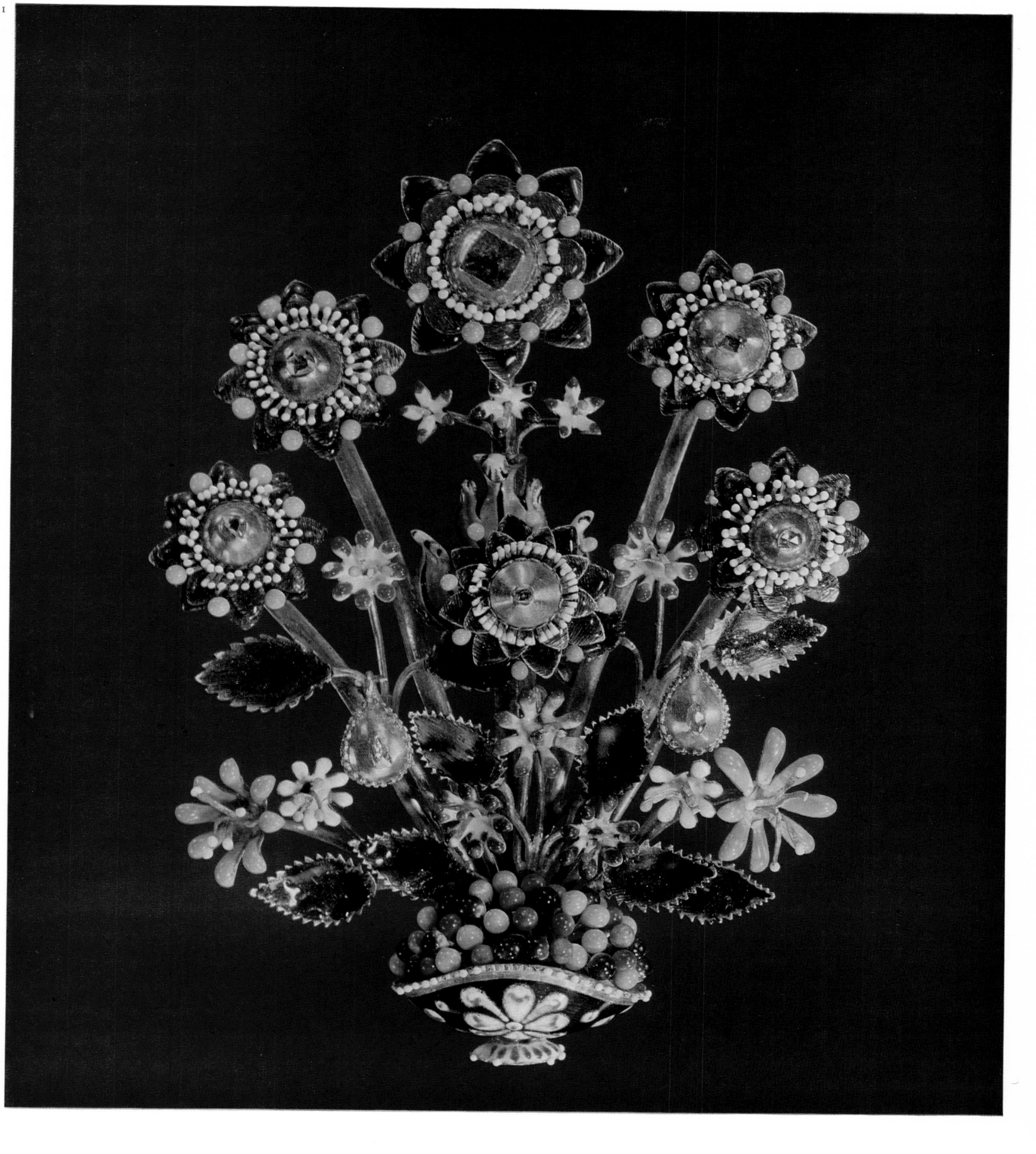

162 Chest ornament, so-called sticker. Silver with
diamonds and pear-shaped pearls, to be taken apart.
When mounted it emphasizes the tightly strapped waist
of court fashion. German, *c.* 1710–30.

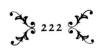

163 Portrait of Countess von Hohnstein, painted by
George de Marées (1697–1776), displaying a complete
set of Rococo-style jewellery: aigrettes in the hair,
girandoles, jewels to underline silk rosettes on breast
and sleeves.

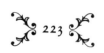

164

164   Part of carnelian set belonging to Augustus the Strong of Saxony. Gold, carnelians, and diamonds.

Hat aigrette (before 1719), tabatière (1917), and big and small hunting knives were made at Dinglinger's workshop. Hunting whip and elongated case are attributed to Dinglinger. Order of the Golden Fleece was made after 1719, hunting tabatière and watch in 1721, three buckles also from the first half of 18th century.

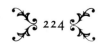

165

166

165   Jewellery set of Danish chamberlain Johann Frederik Lindencrone. Gold enamel and garnets. His protrait, a miniature by Andreas Thornberg, was formed as a brooch; two shoe-buckles, two trouser-buckles, two small brooches. *C. 1760.*

166   Necklace. Silver with diamonds, pink diamonds and topazes. Mid-18th century.

167

167 Folk-art: Colourful peasant's bridal crown. Glass beads, glass balls, cloth, gold-paper tinsels, mirrors, gold threads. Black Forest late 19th – early 20th centuries.

168 Hair-pin. Silver, partly gilt with filigree and glass beads. Upper Bavaria, 19th century.

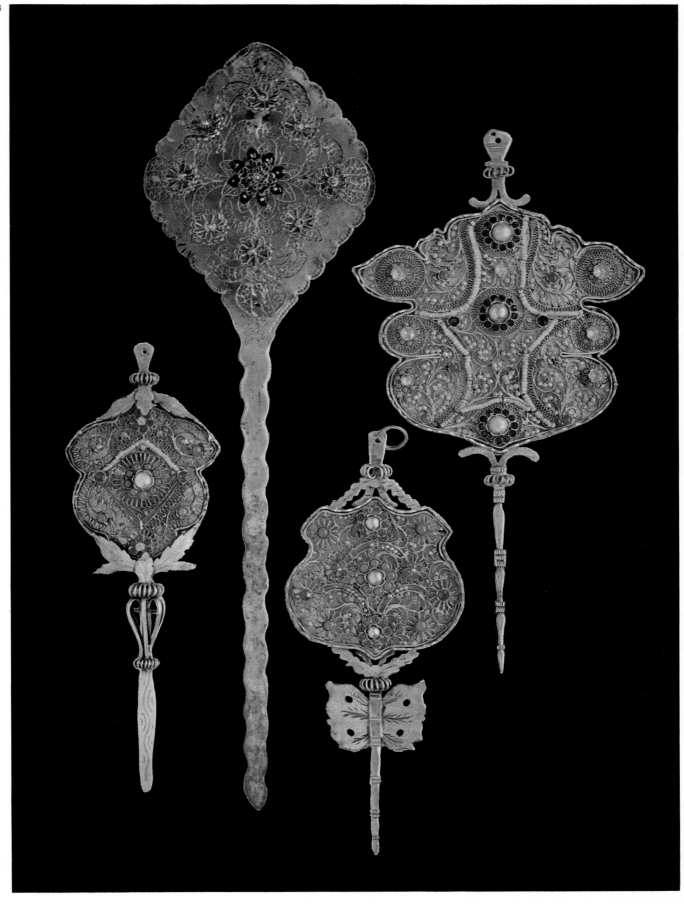

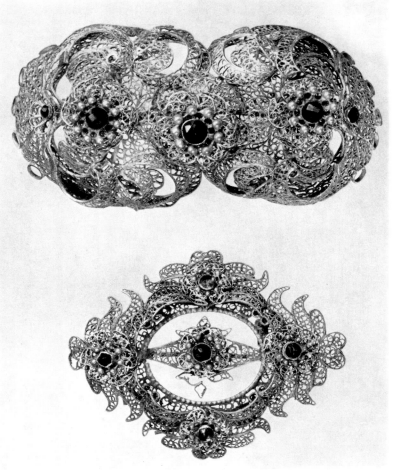

169   Jewellery of traditional costume. Silver filigree with crucifixes and representations of saints. Schwäbisch Gmünd, 18th or 19th century.

170   Two ornaments from national costume. Silver filigree and glass stones Schwäbisch Gmünd. 18th or 19th century.

171   Heart-shaped pendant. Gold-mounted with miniature portrait, signed 'Sauvage'. French, late 18th century.

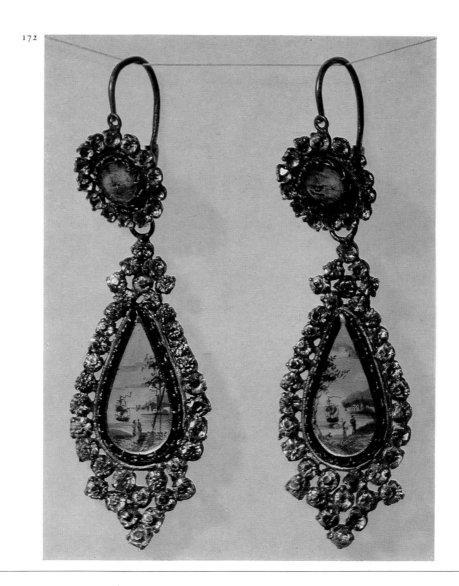

172 Gold ear ornament with landscape miniatures,
mounted in diamonds. Italy, late 18th century.

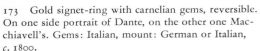

173   Gold signet-ring with carnelian gems, reversible. On one side portrait of Dante, on the other one Macchiavell's. Gems: Italian, mount: German or Italian, *c.* 1800.

174   Finger-ring with sardonyx cameo, cut into mask, by Giovanni Pichler. Italy, *c.* 1785–1790.

175   Finger-ring. Bezel holds three-layer agate cameo with representation of Germanicus. Italy, *c.* 1800.

176   Gold châtelaine with pendants. Blue- and white-enamelled medallion shows shepherdess with lamb. French, late 18th century.

177   Gold commemorative with miniature: widow by a grave under weeping willows. German, late 18th century.

178   Decorative comb. Tortoise-shell with three shell-cameo inlays representing mythical scenes from antiquity. Part of a set. Probably Dutch, *c.* 1790.

179

180

181

179 Earrings. Silver gilt with three pearls each. Late 18th century.

180 Necklace. Particularly delicate, classical style of the late 18th century.

181 Finger-ring. Silver gilt with chiselled decoration. The bezel was made of precious stones in form of a Jacobin cap on a dagger. Central Europe, c. 1800.

182 Brooch. Gold, silver, diamonds, blue glass. German or French, early 19th century.

183 Gold ear ornament with three big, irregular pearls each, mounted in diamonds. Lower edge with short twisted gold wires. German or French, c. 1820.

184 Paolina, painting by François Josèphe Konsoen (1771–1839), shows women's garment, and jewellery characteristic of Empire style: head-dress set with gems, pearls and gold tresses on the dress.

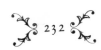

185, 186   Hair-dress, necklace and bracelet in Berlin
fine cast-iron. Large numbers of these were produced
between 1820 and 1840.

190

187   Armlet. Silver gilt with garnets, part of a set. Bohemian, *c*. 1840.

188   Gold bracelet. Wire links set with enamel flowers. In the centre a large carnelian with engraved Persian letters. Russian, mid-19th century.

189   Bracelet of hair. Clasp in form of a snake's head, chiselled and set with jewels. Bohemian, *c*. 1845.

190   Gold *parure*. Machine-made set in a jewel box. It consists of necklace, two pairs of ear ornaments, belt-buckle and two bracelets. French, 1830-40.

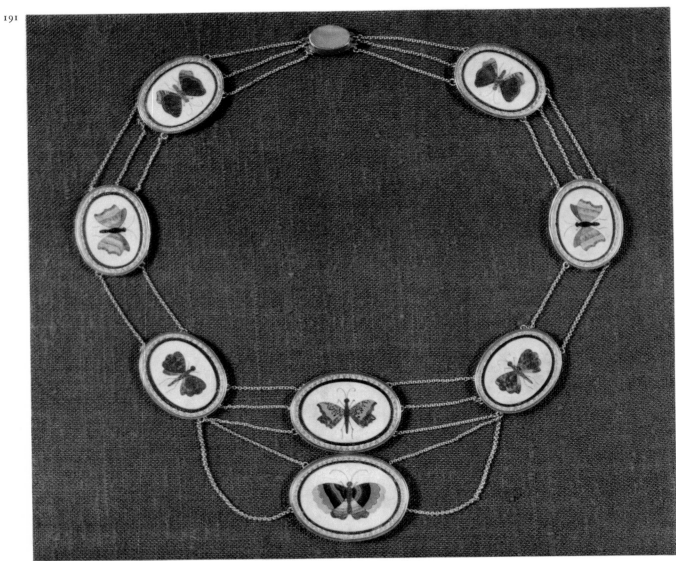

191

191   Gold necklace. Delicate small chains and oval
links with butterfly-motifs in mosaic of jewels. Italy,
c. 1830.

192   Set of jewels. Gold, pearls, rubies and emeralds. The big cartouche of the double-linked chain is the clasp. German, *c.* 1840.

193   Gold necklace. Delicate links with lyra and flower-basket motifs. In the centre a big ornament with foliage. German, *c.* 1830.

194   Gilt armlet with enamel décor. On the plaque, enamelled in black, a butterfly amidst flowers. Russian, mid-19th century.

195

196

197

198

195   Brooch. Cast silver, partly gilt, with red and green glass stones, in the style of Neo-Renaissance. German, 2nd half of 19th century.

196   Ear ornament. Silver gilt, set with garnets and pearls. Bohemain, 2nd half of 19th century.

197   Gold armlet with spiral-shaped centre piece and granulation-like décor. Late 19th century.

198   Silhouette brooch in gilt mount. Late 19th century.

199   Bracelet. Oval links with flower motifs of precious stones. Mount and connecting elements gold in neo-baroque style. Florence, c. 1870.

200   Brooch-pendant made from two shells of a Siberian snail, connected to diamond setting by a white-gold band, shaped as a slip-knot. In the centre a bigger diamond. Russian, late 19th century.

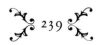

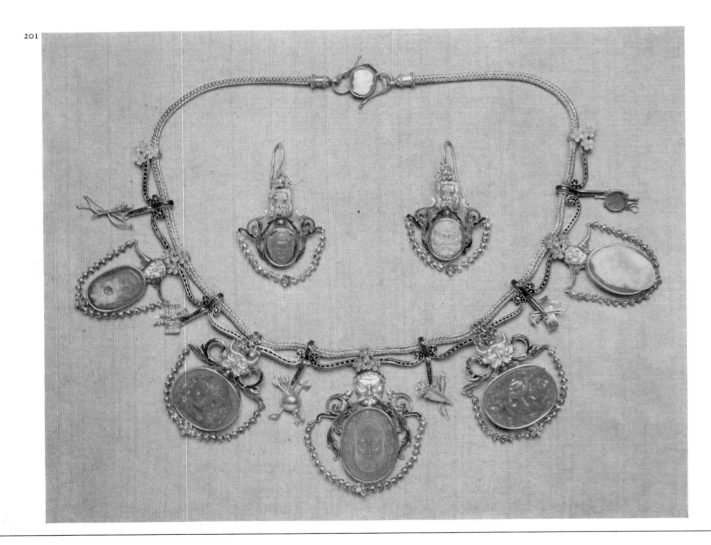

201 *Parure* consisting of neck and ear ornaments.
Interlaced gold chains with gold-enamelled flowers,
masks, cameos and small gold pendants. English,
1867.

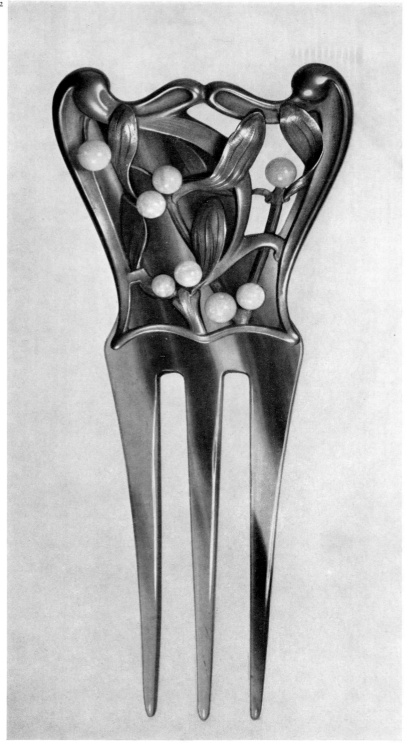

202 Decorative horn comb. The decorative part is a
mistle-toe of gold leaves and opals. Paris, 1900.

203 Gold pendant in form of a woman's head with
diadem. Cut shells, diamonds, pearls, emerald. Paris,
1900.

204

205

204 Brooch, so-called *gorgoneion*. Gold with opal glass green stones and pearls. Wilhelm Lucas von Cranach. Berlin, 1902.

205 Gold adornments, probably belt-buckle, in form of an anemone-twig. Enamel, cut stones. René Lalique Paris, 1901.

206 Brooch. Gold, enamel and chalcedony in form of a woman's head with loose floral motifs. René Lalique. Paris, 1900.

207 'Sylvia'-pendant. Gold agate, enamel, rubies, diamonds. Paul and Henri Vever. Paris, *c.* 1900.

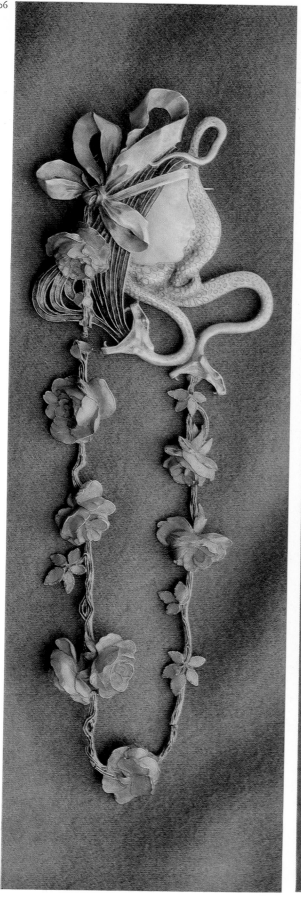

208   Brooch in the style of Cubism. Yellow gold
with black lacquer, onyx, rock crystal and diamonds.
Jean Fouquet. Paris, *c.* 1925

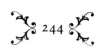

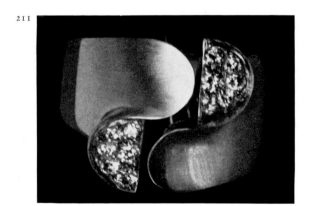

209　Gold chain with dagger-shaped green nephrit pendant. German, *c.* 1938.

210　Interwoven silver chain with cylinder elements and solid ball sin the Art Nouvea style of the late '20s. German 1930.

211　Diamond-set brooch of platinum. Raymond Templier. Paris 1920s.

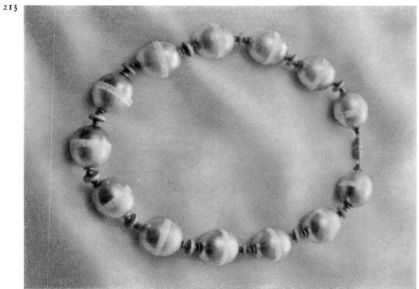

212   Three amber pendants, metal-mounted. Lucia Schulgaite, Vilnius, U.S.S.R., 1973.

213   Necklace of porcelain beads. One half of each bead is decorated with gold and silver painting between wooden discs. Berliner Manufaktur, *c.* 1930.

214   Set of jewels: key pendant, bracelet, brooch,
pendant, and two buttons. Metal, enamel and cord.
Edit Stefaniai. Budapest, 1973.

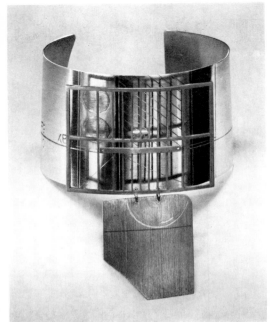

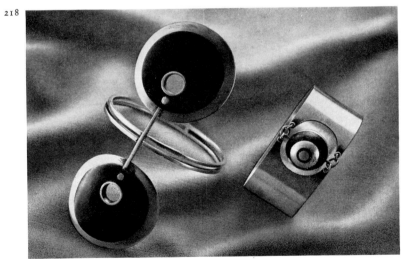

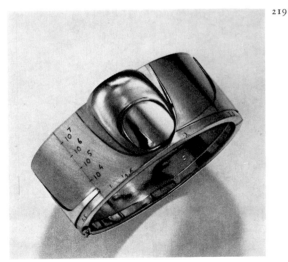

215   Collier. Silver and amber. Severyna Gugula-Stolarska. Warsaw, 1973.

216   Armlet. Partly silver, partly gold. Anton Cepka. Bratislava, 1969.

217   Two brooches. Silver. Teers Lundahl. Vaxjö, Sweden, 1967.

218   Two armlets. Left: silver and enamel, 1973; right: silver and steel. 1972. Monika Winkler. Leipzig.

219   Bangle of yellow and white gold. Bruno Martinazzi. Turin, 1972

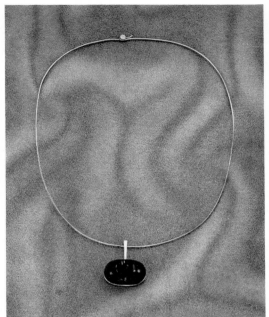

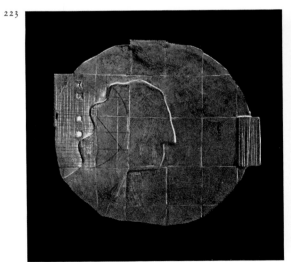
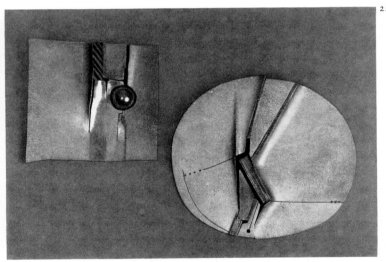

220 Brooch and finger-ring. Ring: white gold with an amethyst and chrysopras hemisphere; brooch: white gold set with diamonds, rubies, sapphires, and emeralds. Friedrich Becker. Düsseldorf, 1968.

221 Neck ornament. Thin gold ring with cut smoked topaz as pendant. Václav Plátek. Czechoslovakia, c. 1972.

222 Pendant. Carved slate. Alois Hubicka. Jablonec, Czechoslovakia, 1972.

223 Brooch. Gold with diamonds. Reinhold Reiling. Grumbach near Pforzheim, 1970.

224 Two brooches. Left: yellow gold with sphere of black Plexiglas. Right: yellow gold, Plexiglas, enamel. Othmar Zschaler. Berne, 1972.

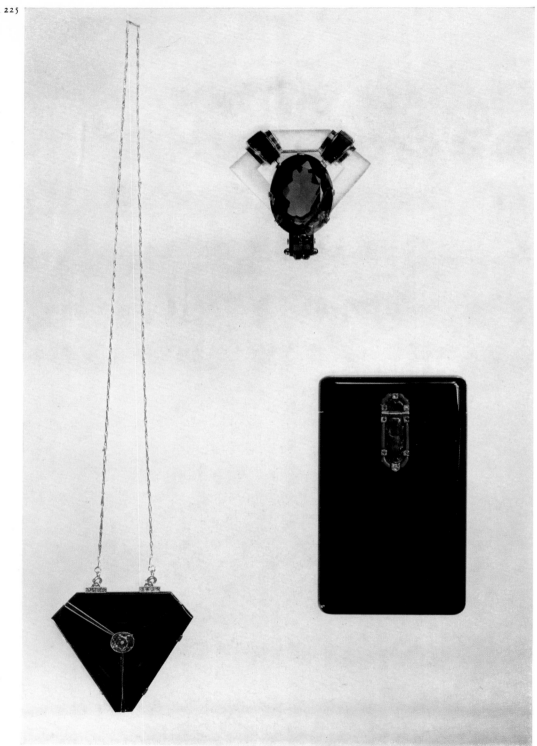

225 Cigarette case, pendant and brooch. Onyx case with platin-mounted diamonds, enamel and jade. Cartie.

London, c. 1925. Brooch made of platinum, amethyst and rock crystal. Georges Fouquet. Paris, c. 1925. Pendant. Onyx plaques, decorated with silver ribbons in shape of rays and *Zitrin* in the centre. Janesich Company. Paris, c. 1925.

226 Gold pendant with various structures. Arnoldo Pomodoro. Milan, 1968.

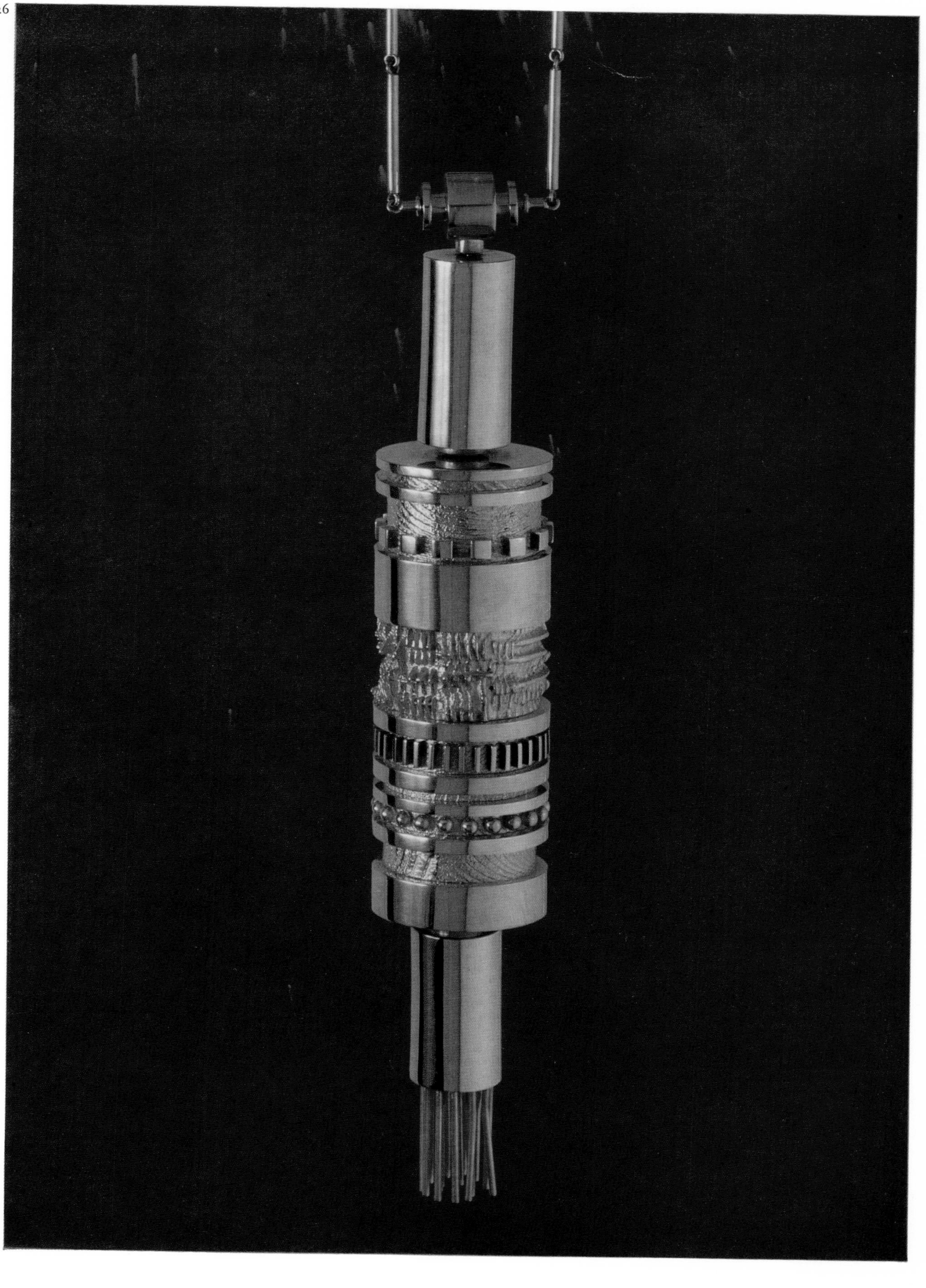

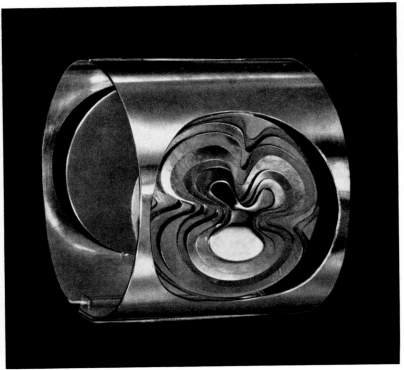

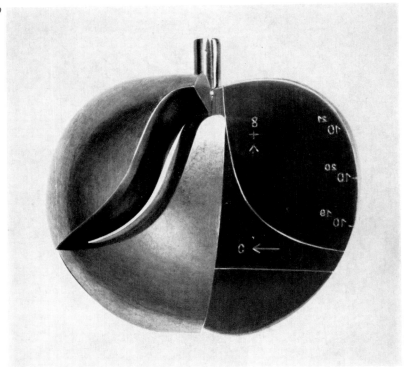

227 Kinetic brooch. White gold spessartite. Revolving spiral moves in front of a white-gold concave mirror. Friedrich Becker, Düsseldorf, 1968.

228 Bracelet. Silver, gold. Floral elements consisting of gold and silver discs were mounted into two large, cut-out holes. Josef Symon. Vienna, 1970.

229 Apple-shaped brooch. White and yellow gold. Bruno Martinazzi. Turin, 1972.

Appendix

LITERATURE

Amiranashvili, Shalva: *Kunstschätze Georgiens*. Prague 1971

Arnold, Ulli: *Schmuckanhänger aus dem Grünen Gewölbe. Schriftenreihe der Staatlichen Kunstsammlungen*, Dresden 1968

Artamonov, Michael & Werner Forman: *Goldschatz der Skythen in der Ermitage*. Prague/Leningrad 1970

Babelon, J.: *L'Orfèvrerie française*. Paris 1946

Baerwald, Marais & Tom Mohoney: *The story of Jewellery*. New York 1960

Barth, Hermann: *Das Geschmeide*. Berlin 1903

Bassermann-Jordan, Ernst: *Der Schmuck*. Leipzig 1919

Battke, Heinz: *Die Geschichte des Ringes*. Baden-Baden 1953

Bauer, M.: *Edelsteinkunde*. Leipzig 1909

Benda, Klement: *Mittelalterlicher Schmuck*. Prague 1966

Berndt, Jürgen: *Japanische Kunst*. 2 vols. Leipzig 1975

Bhusan, Brij Jamila: *Indian Jewellery*. Bombay 1964

Biehn, Heinz: *Juwelen und Preziosen*. Munich 1965

Black, Anderson: *Die Geschichte des Schmucks*. Munich 1976

Bock, Franz: *Die byzantinische Zellenschmelze*. Aachen 1896

Boehn, Max von: *Das Beiwerk der Mode*. Munich 1928

Bossaglia, Rossana: *Art Nouveau*. London 1973

Bossert, H. Theodor: *Geschichte des Kunstgewerbes aller Zeiten und Völker*. 6 vols. Berlin/Vienna/Zurich 1928–1932

Bott, Gerhard: *Ullstein Juwelenbuch*. Berlin (West)/Frankfurt (Main)/Vienna 1972

Bradford, E.D.S.: *English Victorian Jewellery*. London/New York 1968

Bradford, E.D.S.: *Four Centuries of European Jewellery*. London 1968

Brelier, L.: *La sculpture et les arts mineurs byzantins*. Paris 1936

Capelle, Torsten: *Der Metallschmuck von Haithabu*. Neumünster 1968

Carducci, Carlo: *Gold- und Silberschmuck aus dem antiken Italien*. Vienna/Munich 1962

Coarelli, F.: *Greek and Roman Jewellery*. London/New York 1972

Coche de la Ferté, E.: *Les bijoux antiques*. Paris 1956

Creutz, Max: *Kunstgeschichte der edlen Metalle*. Stuttgart 1909

Davenporz, C. J. H.: *Jewellery*. London 1905

Davis, Mary & Greta Pack: *Mexican Jewellery*. Austin 1963

De Ridder, A.: *Catalogue sommaire de bijoux antiques des Musées du Louvre*, Paris 1924

Dongerkery, Kamala: *Jewellery and Personal Adornment in India*. Delhi 1970

Dunâreanu-Vulpe, Ecaterina: *Der Schatz von Pietroasa*. Bucharest 1967

Egger, Gerhardt: *Gold- und Silberschätze in Kopien des Historismus. Ausstellung des österreichischen Museums für angewandte Kunst*. Vienna 1972

Emmerich, André: *Sweat of the sun and tears of moon. Gold and silver in the Pre-Columbian Art*. Seattle 1965

Evans, A. J.: *The Palace of Minos*. London/New York 1970

Evans, Joan: *A History of Jewellery 1100–1870*. London 1972

Fabri, Charles: *A History of Indian Dress*. Calcutta/Bombay/Madras/New Delhi 1961

Falke, Otto von: *Der Mainzer Goldschmuck der Kaiserin Gisela*. Berlin 1913

Falkiner, Richard: *Investing in Antique Jewellery*. London n. d.

Flower, M.: *Victorian Jewellery*. London 1951

Fouquet, Jean: *Bijoux et Orfèvrerie. L'art international d'aujourd'hui*, No 16. Paris 1928

Fraser, Douglas: *Primitive Art*. London/New York 1962

Frégnac, Claude: *Les Bijoux de la Renaissance à la Belle Epoque*. Paris 1966

Furtwängler, A.: *Die antiken Gemmen*. Leipzig/Berlin 1900

Galanina, Ludmila & a group of authors: *Yuvelirye izdeliya v Ērmitazhe* (Jewellery of the Ermitage). Leningrad 1967

Gerstner, Paul: *Die Entwicklung der Pforzheimer Bijouterie-Industrie von 1767–1907*. Tübingen 1908

Gierl, Irmgard: *Trachtenschmuck aus fünf Jahrhunderten*. Rosenheim 1972

Gregorietti, Guido: *Gold und Juwelen*. Gütersloh 1971

Greifenhagen, Adolf: *Schmuckarbeiten in Edelmetall*. 2 vols. Berlin (West) 1975

Gyllensvärd, Cf. Bo.: *Chinese Gold and Silver in the Carl Kempe Collection*. Stockholm 1953

Haberland, Wolfgang: *Gold in Alt-Amerika*. Hamburg 1960

Haevernick, The Elisabeth: *Die Glasarmringe und Ringperlen der Mittel- und Spätlatènezeit auf dem europäischen Festland*. Bonn 1960

Hawley, Henry: *Fabergé and his Contemporaries. The India Early Mushall Collection of the Cleveland Museum of Art*. Cleveland 1967

Héjj-Détári, Angéla: *Altungarischer Schmuck*. Budapest 1965

Higgins, R. A.: *Greek and Roman Jewellery*. London 1961

Himmelheber, Hans: *Negerkunst und Negerkünstler*. Braunschweig 1960

Hoffmann, Edith & Barbara Treide: *Schmuck früher Zeiten, ferner Völker*. Leipzig 1976

Hoffmann, Herbert & Patricia F. Davidson: *Greek Gold*. Mainz 1965

Holzhausen, Walter: *Prachtgefäße, Geschmeide, Kabinettstücke*. Tübingen 1966

Hughes, Graham: *Erlesener Schmuck (1890 bis zur Gegenwart)*. Ravensburg 1965

Jacobsthal, P.: *Early Celtic Art*. Oxford 1944

Jenny, Wilhelm Albert von & Wolfgang Fritz Volbach: *Germanischer Schmuck des frühen Mittelalters*. Berlin 1933

Jenny, Wilhelm Albert von: *Keltische Metallarbeiten*. Berlin 1935

Jenyns, R. Soame & William Watson: *Chinese Art (The minor Arts)*. London 1963

Jessup, R.: *Anglo-Saxon Jewellery*. London 1950

Kohlhausen, Heinrich: *Geschichte des deutschen Kunsthandwerks*. Munich 1955

Krickeberg, Walter: *Altmexikanische Kulturen*. Berlin (West) 1956

Kužel, Vladislav: *Das Buch vom Schmuck*. Prague 1962

Lanllier, Jean & Marie-Anne Pini: *Fünf Jahrtausende abendländischer Schmuckkunst*. Munich 1971

László, Gyula: *Steppenvölker und Germanen*. 1971

Leitermann, H.: *Deutsche Goldschmiedekunst*. Stuttgart 1953

Lessing, Julius: *Gold und Silber*. n. p. 1892

Leuzinger, Elsy: *Wesen und Form des Schmuckes afrikanischer Völker*. Zurich 1950

Luthmer, F.: *Goldschmuck der Renaissance*. Berlin 1881

Malinovski, Bronislav: *The Argonauts of the Western Pacific*. London 1922

Marshall, F. H.: *Catalogue of the jewellery in the British Museum*. London 1911

Mason, Anita: *An Illustrated Dictionary of Jewellery*. London 1973

Medding-Alp, Emma: *Rheinische Goldschmiedekunst in ottonischer Zeit*. n. p. 1952

Mehta, Rustam J.: *The Handicrafts and Industrial Arts of India*. Bombay/London 1960

Menzhausen, Joachim: *Das Grüne Gewölbe*. Leipzig 1968

Moderner Schmuck von Malern und Bildhauern. Catalogue of the Hessisches Landesmuseum Darmstadt, editor Renée Sabatello Neu) Darmstadt 1967

Morant, Henry de: *Histoire des arts décoratifs*. Paris 1970

Mujica Gallo, Miguel: *Gold in Peru*. Recklinghausen 1967

Mundt, Barbara: *Historismus. Kunsthandwerk und Industrie im Zeitalter der Weltausstellungen*. Berlin 1973

Oved, Sah: *The book of Necklaces*. London 1953

Pack, Greta & W.M. Flinders: *The Arts and Crafts of Ancient Egypt*. London 1909

Paulsen, P.: *Der Goldschatz von Hiddensee*. Leipzig 1936

Pazaurek, Emil: *Perlmutter*. Berlin 1937

Pohl, Helga: *Gold*. Stuttgart 1958

Popescu, Matin Matei: *Mittelalterlicher Schmuck in den rumänischen Landen*. Bucharest 1970

Rademacher, Franz: *Fränkische Goldscheibenfibeln*. Munich 1940

Reyerson, Eglizon: *The Netsuke of Japan*. Londox 1958

Rosenberg, Marc: *Geschichte der Goldschmiedekunst auf technischer Grundlage*. Frankfurt (Main) 1918

Schlossmacher, Karl: *Edelsteine und Perlen*. Stuttgart 1965

Schollmayer, Karl: *Neuer Schmuck*. Tübingen 1974

Schondorff, E.: *Schmuck und Edelsteine*. Munich 1955

Seidler, Ned: *Schmuck und Edelsteine (Knaurs bunte Welt)*. Munich/Zurich 1965

Steingräber, Erich: *Alter Schmuck*. Munich 1956

Stöver, Ulla: *Freude am Schmuck*. Gütersloh 1968

Sutherland, C. H. V.: *Gold*. London/New York 1969

Vever, Henri: *La Bijouterie française au XIXme siècle*. (3 vols.). Paris 1908

Vílímková, Milada: *Altägyptische Goldschmiedekunst*. Prague 1969

Wilkins, Manja: *Das Schmuckbrevier*. Hamburg 1960

Willcox, Donald: *Body Jewellery*. London 1973

Wolf, Richard: *Die Welt des Netsuke*. Wiesbaden 1970

Zahn, Robert von: *Ausstellung von Schmuckarbeiten in Edelmetall der Berliner Staatlichen Museen*. Berlin 1932

INDEX

SOURCES OF ILLUSTRATIONS

Acknowledgments are due to the following photographers and institutions for providing photographs:

Antiquarisk-Topografiska Arkivet, Stockholm 1
Ferdinand Anton, Munich 27
Arts and Crafts Museum, Prague 122, 127, 155, 157, 176, 181, 189
Bayerisches Nationalmuseum, Munich 123, 124
Klaus G. Beyer, Weimar 144
British Museum, London 17, 19, 53, 72, 91, 92
Corvina Publishers, Budapest 81
Danske Kunstindustriemuseum, Copenhagen 165
Walter Danz, Halle 134, 135, 136
Deutsche Fotothek, Dresden 58, 77, 78, 125, 131
Rolf Dvoracek, Bautzen 163
Germanisches Nationalmuseum, Nuremberg 167, 168
Sören Hallgren, Stockholm 93, 118
Hallwylska Samlingen, Stockholm 180, 199
Historisches Museum Stralsund 95, 96, 97, 98, 99, 100, 101, 102, 103
Irish National Museum, Dublin 4
Jürgen Karpinski, Dresden 9, 10, 11, 73, 74, 75, 76, 80, 132, 133, 171, 172, 177, 193, 194, 206, 209, 210, 212, 213, 214, 215, 218, 221, 222
Kunstgewerbemuseum Schloß Köpenick, Berlin 105, 106
Kunsthistorisches Museum, Vienna 150
Dietmar Kuntzsch, Berlin 195
Landesmuseum für Vorgeschichte, Halle (Saale) 6, 7, 108
Harald Lange, Leipzig 18
Magyar Nemzeti Muzeum, Budapest 109, 110, 111, 112, 113, 114
Foto Meyer, Vienna 107, 145
Günter Meyer, Pforzheim 40, 154, 156, 169, 170, 173, 174, 175, 178, 183, 187, 188, 200, 208, 216, 217, 219, 220, 223, 224, 226, 227, 228, 229

Musée des Arts Décoratifs, Paris 190, 207, 211
Museum für Ur- und Frühgeschichte, Weimar 2, 3, 94
Museum für Völkerkunde, Hamburg 30, 31
Museum of Far Eastern Antiquities, Stockholm 70, 71
Museum of Fine Arts, Boston 66, 67, 68, 69
National Archaeological Museum, Athens 37
National Museum Copenhagen 8
Prado, Madrid 139
Gerhard Reinhold, Mölkau 164
Rheinisches Landesmuseum, Bonn 104
SCALA, Florence 5, 20, 21, 22, 23, 24, 25, 44, 45, 52, 55, 56, 63, 64, 85, 90, 119, 120, 121, 126, 140, 146, 147, 148, 153, 166, 184
Schatzkammer der Residenz, Munich 129
Schmuckmuseum Pforzheim 50, 61, 161, 182
Rolf Schrade, Berlin 49, 82, 83, 84
Adolf Sickert, Vienna 57
Staatliche Antikensammlung und Glyptothek, Munich 47
Staatliche Kunstsammlungen, Dresden 158
Staatliche Museen Preußischer Kulturbesitz, Berlin (West) 12, 15, 16, 28, 29, 32, 33, 34, 35, 36, 38, 39, 41, 42, 43, 46, 51, 54, 59, 60, 79, 86, 87, 115, 116, 128, 130, 149, 151, 152, 192, 202, 203, 204, 205, 225
Staatliche Museen zu Berlin 26, 237, 138, 185, 186
Peter Thiele, Berlin (West) 13, 14
Town Museum Prague 179, 196, 197, 198
Verlagsarchiv Edition Leipzig 62
Verwaltung der Staatlichen Schlösser, Gärten und Seen, Munich 141, 142, 143, 162
Victoria and Albert Museum, London 65, 159, 160, 191, 201
Yan, Toulouse 88, 89

Acknowledgments are due to the following museums and collections for the per mission to publish their objects:

Archaeological National Museum, Cagliari 52

Arts and Crafts Museum, Prague 122, 127, 155, 157, 176, 181, 189
Bayerisches Nationalmuseum, Munich 123, 124
British Museum, London 17, 19, 53, 72, 91, 92
Cabinet des Medailles Louvre, Paris 64
Cathedral Treasure, Palermo 85
Collection Julius Böhler, Munich 125
Danske Kunstindustriemuseum, Copenhagen 165
Egyptian Museum, Cairo 21, 22, 23, 24, 25
Germanisches Nationalmuseum, Nuremberg 167, 168
Hallwylska Samlingen, Stockholm 180, 199
Historical Museum, Stockholm 1, 118
Historisches Museum Stralsund 95, 96, 97, 98, 99, 100, 101, 102, 103
Hungarian National Museum, Budapest 81
Irish National Museum, Dublin 4
Kleinurleben bei Langensalza, Village Church 144
Kunstgewerbemuseum Schloß Köpenick, Berlin 105, 106
Kunsthistorisches Museum, Vienna 107, 145, 150
Dietmar Kuntzsch, Berlin 195
Landesmuseum für Vorgeschichte, Halle (Saale) 6, 7, 108
Magyar Nemzeti Muzeum, Budapest 109, 110, 111, 112, 113, 114
Museé Condé, Chantilly 121
Musée des Arts Décoratifs, Paris 190, 207, 211
Musée Saint Raymond, Toulouse 88, 89
Museo Barbarini, Rome 140
Museo degli Argenti, Florence 147, 148
Museo Gregoriano Etrusco, Vatikan 55, 56
Museo Napoleonico, Rome 184
Museo Archeologico Nazionale, Taranto 44, 45
Museo Poldi Pezzoli, Milan 146, 166
Museum Bagdad 20
Museum of Fine Arts, Brussels 153
Museum für Kunsthandwerk, Leipzig 132,

The line-drawings are due to:

The following publications were used for further line-drawings.

Deutsche Kunst und Dekoration, No. XIII, 1903/04 56

L'Art Décoratif Aux Salons, 1906 57